A History of
The Library Association
1877–1977

J. Y. W. MacAlister (1856–1925)
Hon. Secretary 1887–1898
President 1915–1919

A Library Association Centenary Volume

A History of
The Library Association
1877-1977

W A Munford

Director-General, National Library for the Blind

The Library Association/London

First published by
The Library Association,
7 Ridgmount Street,
London WC1E 7AE.   1976

ISBN: 0 85365 488 3

© W A Munford, 1976

Munford, William Arthur
  A history of the Library Association,
  1877–1977.
  Bibl. – Index.
  ISBN 0-85365-488-3 ✓
  1. Title   2. Library Association
  020'.622'41 Z673.L7
  Library Association – History

Design: Graham Bishop
Index: F J Cornell
Set in 11 on 12 pt Garamond
On Fyneprint paper

Made and printed in Great Britain by
Unwin Brothers Limited
The Gresham Press,
Old Woking, Surrey

Dedication

To my own College, the London School of Economics and Political Science, where between 1902 and 1915 the first British School of Librarianship was established, and to the memory of Sidney Webb, Lord Passfield, founder of the LSE, who more than any other man of his time foresaw librarianship as a graduate profession.

'There was nothing which was more likely to be for good in the future than the union of librarians and their binding together in the desire to make themselves the efficient as well as the zealous custodians of what was committed to their charge, and dissemination of knowledge on all hands.' *Mandell Creighton, 1898*

'We have been accustomed to look on librarianship as under the special influence of the planet Saturn, who is said to preside over all occupations in which money is obtained with very great difficulty'. *Richard Garnett, 1899*

Contents

Illustrations		Acknowledgments

Foreword

We librarians respect the Library Association as our professional association; the text which follows may also be regarded as one token of one librarian's regard and affection. But over the century past our Association has been so much more, and so much less, than a professional association.

We began splendidly. It is impossible to read through the yellowing press reports of the 1877 Conference without a real sense of pride in the initial achievement of our ancestors. The conferences which followed, so to speak, recharged our batteries year by year, as gatherings of one hundred enthusiasts so easily can, and gatherings of one thousand cannot. The parallel activity of the monthly meetings in London was in sober contrast. But the Association then lacked administrative machinery and the London-based honorary officers were much influenced by the slow pace of their library life in the 1880s.

Writing with hindsight, it seems that, if our profession was to be fully integrated from the outset, then it was essential for municipal libraries to gain much greater hold in London and, contrariwise, for non-municipal libraries to increase provincially. Coincidentally, the status of the librarians and library staffs throughout the country needed to become much more similar and, in theory at least, more nearly interchangeable. Salaries and educational standards were, and are, the obvious touchstones by which to judge the reality of integration.

Following the flood-tide of municipal development from the 1880s onwards, and in London as well as throughout the country, it was, perhaps, inevitable that the Association should have been all but 'taken over' by their representatives. The period of their 'control', the period of Duff Brown, Jast, Pacy, Savage and McColvin, lasted for a full half of our century and with McColvin became so international in scope and influence that part, at least, of the initial promise of 1877 seemed at last to be nearing fulfilment. But only since World War Two has the full and adequate integration of all types of library and librarian become possible.

Throughout the present work I have sought objectivity above all else. But since I have, myself, practised professional librarianship for the whole of the second half of the Association's century – I obtained my first library post, and it was a public library post, in 1927 – this has not

always been easy of achievement. I have done my best.
Readers of *Tom Jones* will remember Fielding's habit of
punctuating his narrative with paragraphs – occasionally whole
chapters – of moralizing. Few things are better calculated to
irritate the well disposed reader wanting, above all else, to get
on with a splendid story. But, in present context, I gladly forgive
him since, in one of his prosy interludes, he distinguishes
between 'Alderman History' and 'Monsieur Romance'.
Alderman History, he reminds us, 'tells his tedious tale', while
Monsieur Romance 'performs his surprising tricks of dexterity'.
Although this book has been written by Alderman History, I
hope that it may do something more than 'sooth thy wearied
limbs in slumber', to continue the Fielding quotation. If there
are any 'surprising tricks of dexterity' here, I trust that they will
be found to relate only to the arrangement of some of the
material – my years as a contributor to *The year's work in
librarianship* taught me much – and not to the quality of my
imagination.

The present work is, however – when all is said and done – the
story of an association and not of a person or persons. I had
therefore to decide, with reluctance, that the biographical aspect
must be severely limited. Readers who hoped for more must
await the *Biographical dictionary of British librarians* which I hope to
publish during the early years of the Association's second
century. If I have one other regret it is that I have felt unable to
devote space to comparative study of the American and British
Library Associations, apart from the earliest years of their stories
when such attention seemed imperative. An historical sketch
comparison will be found however in Volume 7 of *Advances in
librarianship*.

Book writing tends to be a lonely task; friendly support
during the gestation period is always welcome. Many friends
have helped with the present book. Naturally enough, in view of
its subject, most help has been sought from, and has been most
willingly given by, the Association's own administrative and
library staff. I mention in particular the Deputy Secretary,
Mr D. D. Haslam, whose own historical article on the
Association (vol. 14 of the American *Encyclopaedia of library and
information science*; also in *Journal of librarianship*, 1974, vol. 6,
pp 137–164) is a most useful and succinct account. Among other

helpers I may mention Bodley's Librarian and his staff, and particularly Mr D. G. Vaisey; Mr K. A. Manley; Mr D. Clarke, Librarian of the British Library of Political and Economic Science; Mr K. C. Harrison, City Librarian of Westminster, and his staff; and by no means least, my daughter, Alison, who read the proofs.

W A Munford
Cambridge August 1976

Before World War One

Chapter One

Background to Beginnings: the 1870's

On 2 October 1877, the first International Conference of Librarians opened at the London Institution. Why during the 1870s? Why in 1877? Why at the London Institution?

The 1870s in Victorian Britain were the heyday of Gladstone/ Disraeli rivalry and also witnessed the early cooperation of Gilbert and Sullivan. Citizens with a liking for sterner conflicts could interest themselves, at the beginning of the period, in the first Blitzkrieg between Germany and France; the reading rooms of the pioneer municipal libraries were thronged with connoisseurs of war dispatches and telegrams. Britain herself was at war during these years only in distant places, notably Ashanti, Afghanistan and Zululand. She played a notable part, however, at the end of another war between Russia and Turkey; following the consequential Congress of the Great European Powers, her Prime Minister, on his return from Berlin in 1878, felt able to claim that he had brought back 'peace with honour'. Little enough of either was then clearly apparent in Ireland; during another decade of unrest a new and influential character appeared on the chronically troubled scene, Charles Stewart Parnell.

The 1870s witnessed some very necessary measures of reform in both Army and Navy, the former being assured of the minimum cooperation of the Commander-in-Chief, the Duke of Cambridge. Nevertheless both the purchase of commissions and the use of muzzle-loaders were discontinued and the first serious efforts made to formulate distinctions between service in the ranks and sentences in the prisons. The Navy, too, began to abandon sail.

Increased foreign competition was substantially responsible for depression in both agriculture and industry during the 1870s. Farming was beginning to feel the full effects of the repeal of the Corn Laws, and industry the loss of the tremendous lead gained during and after the war with Napoleon. Industrial and commercial changes were far-reaching. Firms which, in the past, had been mostly privately owned and capitalised, were beginning to take advantage of new legalised opportunities and were changing into companies with liability limited by share capital. As personal relationships between employers and employed also began, inevitably, to change, so new developments in Trade Unionism were equally inevitable, as were new Acts of Parliament to attempt to control them. The new opportunities for shareholders encouraged the growth of a new rentier class and of new and enlarged towns where they could live. But there was also new legislation to ease the burdens of life for ordinary working people, Acts to encourage rural housing and to reduce the everyday risks still endemic in the consumption of food, liquor, water and drugs. The establishment of local and not very effective boards of health helped to prepare the way for modern local government; more effective contributions were being made, during the 1870s, by the civic enterprise of some of the largest cities, Birmingham and Glasgow in particular. To ease the lot of the most unfortunate, both the Salvation Army and Dr Barnado's Homes were founded.

Current free thinking normally ascribes the modern system of gratuitous state education to the Act of 1870. In fact, this elementary education Act, logically enough, was concerned primarily with the indispensable preliminary provision of school buildings; where there was no local deficiency, as in a few towns such as Cambridge, the Act was almost irrelevant. The full implications of compulsory school attendance were not felt until the 1880s, and of free education until the 1890s.

Society, whether capitalised or not, was outwardly very respectable during the 1870s. A less formal Sunday was noticeable, as yet, only in the highest circles and only among the most advanced of these had the weekend habit yet struck root. There were, consequently, few signs as yet of informal clothes for men and fewer still for women. Divorce, although admittedly facilitated by the Act of 1857, was still difficult and expensive and a divorced person could have *his* career or *her* social standing damaged beyond repair. Most well-to-do men with a taste for simple or complicated vice thought it wiser to seek it in other countries. As for organised vice for the lower classes, the 1870s saw and heard much agitation for the repeal of the Contagious Diseases Acts of 1864–1866 which had placed roving ladies in seaports and military towns under police supervision and medical examination. It must have been difficult, sometimes, amid all the turmoil, to remember that these Acts had been ostensibly passed to protect the Armed Forces of the Crown. The Duke of Cambridge, at least, was in no doubt of their value to *his* Army.

For those who liked to read about other people's divorces, the case of Mordaunt v. Mordaunt and Johnstone had unexpected aspects. But the several cases involving heresy, church ritual and the refusal of Holy Communion possibly attracted more attention. These, in their turn, were completely dwarfed by the public appeal of the case of the Tichborne Claimant which ran from 1871 to 1874 and of which the most remarkable features were the amount of the total legal costs and the subsequent disbarring of counsel for the defendant and his removal from the list of Queen's Counsel. For newspaper readers with more mundane tastes – and the popular daily newspaper with significant mass appeal was still some years away – the 1870s provided a representative selection of murder trials and subsequent executions. But the opportunities for reasonably full participation, which had been so greatly appreciated in an earlier England, had been seriously diminished by the abolition of public executions in 1868. Fresh opportunities for crowd

5

participation would assuredly come with the development of professional sport but not in the 1870s, and it would be many years before the new sporting events attracted crowds comparable in size with those normal at public executions. As Dr Johnson had said, a hundred years earlier:

Sir, public executions are intended to draw spectators. If they do not draw spectators they don't answer their purpose.

1877 was not untouched by irony. The year came in like a lion with gales, storms and floods of unusual violence and went out like a lamb, following Queen Victoria's visit to her favourite Prime Minister at his Buckinghamshire residence. Between these events the Oxford and Cambridge boat race had ended in a quite unprecedented dead-heat; there were, later, equally unprecedented landings of herring at Great Yarmouth. Railway travel had become reasonably safe and acceptably fast. The safety was marred, in 1877, by a serious accident to the *Flying Scotsman*, and the speed set in perspective by a carrier pigeon which, in a race with the mail train from Dover, reached London twenty minutes before the express. The first really successful British experiments with the telephone, which also took place in 1877, suggested that the pigeon must, nevertheless, look to its own laurels. There were also ironic twists for trains; the first Tay Bridge was opened and the first Channel Tunnel begun in 1877.

1877 was only lightly distinguished by its new books. Anna Sewell's *Black Beauty* was certainly assured of immortality – of a sort – while Harriet Martineau's *Autobiography*, readable as it still is, was not. Aspects of the burgeoning American scene were glimpsed by one ageing novelist, Anthony Trollope, in *The American Senator*, and by one much younger one, Henry James, in *The American*. Yet it is pleasing to remember that an ironic year also witnessed publication of one of the classics of English irony, *The New Republic*.

Henry James' novel, at least, was a harbinger of future achievement. There were other foretastes of bibliographical promise. On 2 October 1877, the first International Conference of Librarians opened at the London Institution. Why during the 1870s? Why in 1877? Why at the London Institution?

Readings

This short chapter owes most to R. C. K. Ensor *England 1870–1914*, 1936, and to the volumes of the *Annual Register*, 1870–1877.

Chapter Two

Beginnings:

1853-1877

In January 1859 two thick quarto volumes, containing a total of two thousand pages and entitled *Memoirs of libraries*, had been published in London by Trübner and Company. Those volumes were the work of Edward Edwards who, until the previous October, had been Principal Librarian of the pioneer municipal public library in Manchester. The book was substantially a world history but the second half of the second volume was the first modern textbook of library administration and management. Edwards included there:

The question is a professional organization of Librarians practicable and likely to be useful? is one of much interest. But at present the materials scarcely exist for any definite answer to it. If such an organization could be created upon a solid basis without ostentation, and without attempting to achieve too much, some, at all events, of the difficulties which beset appointments, under circumstances such as have been glanced at, would be put in a way of removal. In proportion as the number of Public Libraries shall increase and as the public concern in them shall be broadened, both the means and the desirableness of creating a Librarians Association will, in all probability, evince themselves. . . . But unless an Association bring with it increased means of systematic study, and of public evidence of the fruits of study, no result of much worth can be looked for. . . . ,[1]

Such a comment, like many another from Edwards' fertile brain and laborious pen, might have seemed advanced or far-seeing at the time. *Memoirs of libraries*, however, had been in the making for at least ten years, probably even before the author had been the most important witness to testify before the House of Commons Select Committee on Public Libraries in 1849.

Edwards' answers at the Select Committee had been designed to show how deficient was the public library service of the country, the term 'public library' according to him:

embracing first of all libraries deriving their support from public funds either wholly or in part; and I would further extend it to such libraries as are made accessible to the public to a greater or less degree....

The Select Committee, following Edwards' lead, had argued that

our present inferior position is unworthy of the power, the liberality and the literature of the country

and had recommended:

a power be given by Parliament enabling Town Councils to levy a small rate for the creation and support of Public Libraries.

The power sought had been provided by the Public Libraries Acts of 1850 and 1855 which William Ewart, MP, Chairman of the Select Committee, had piloted through the House of Commons.[2] But the Town Councils were not quick to take advantage of their new opportunities and when *Memoirs of libraries* was published in 1859 Edwards was able to include accounts of no more than ten libraries established under the new legislation. It may be fairly argued that Edwards' Commons' evidence, together with that of some of the witnesses who followed him, paid far too little attention to existing libraries provided other than from public funds.[3] But as far as services for the poorer members of the community were concerned it was clear enough that most of the libraries of the working men's clubs, mechanics' institutes, self-improvement societies and the rest had failed to live up to the expectations of their founders. And since it surely remained as true as in 1345 when Richard De

9

Bury had insisted 'No dearness ought to hinder a man from buying books, if he has that which is asked for them',[4] many working class readers still lacked that essential wherewithal. The situation, too, had changed but little when, ten years later, he published in *Free Town Libraries* one of his several sequels to *Memoirs*. But, nevertheless, the local organisers of the new libraries and the larger number of enthusiasts whose local campaigns for the adoption of the Acts were unsuccessful, needed advice and guidance and there was no association to help them. Some of them wrote, not unnaturally, to Ewart and he passed on their enquiries to Edwards who also received many direct applications himself. But after 1858 Edwards did not hold a public library post. His place was taken to some extent by J. D. Mullins, Librarian of the Birmingham Public Library which first opened its doors in 1861. But Mullins found the burden excessive and it was partly at his suggestion that Edwards produced *Free Town Libraries* as a *printed* guide.[5]

Developments in the United States had been broadly similar. Up to 1854 most of the libraries freely open to the public had been small service points provided by local societies, working men's clubs and the YMCA's. The so-called Mercantile libraries which initially resembled those of the mechanics' institutes in Britain, frequently changed, like them, into general subscription libraries. University and college libraries were still small, indeed, as 'Bookhunter' Burton wrote in 1863,

There is probably no country so well stocked as the States with libraries of from 10,000 to 20,000 volumes.[6]

The Library of Congress itself only began its fantastic transformation from the library of Congress into the National Library of the United States following the appointment of Ainsworth Spofford as Librarian in 1867.[7] Local tax support for US libraries began *via* the district school system in the State of New York in 1835. During the next thirty years Connecticut, Rhode Island, Iowa, Indiana, Maine, Ohio, Wisconsin, Missouri, California, Oregon and Illinois followed suit, but the results were diffused and disappointing and cannot be said to have laid satisfactory foundations for future development.[8]

The turning point in the United States came in 1854. But the
first major event of that year, the opening on 1 February of the
New York Public Library, provided under the will of John
Jacob Astor, of fur and real estate fame, is ironically comparable
with the initiation of the great reference library in Glasgow in
1877 under the will of Stephen Mitchell, the tobacco magnate:
both cities had, perhaps consequentially, to wait until the end of
the nineteenth century for their fully municipally financed
public library services. The opening of the locally tax-supported
Boston Public Library later in 1854, and the subsequent
appointment of Librarian C. C. Jewett, marked the real
transition in America just as the opening of the Manchester
Public Library in 1852, under Librarian Edward Edwards, had
marked it in Britain.

If a library association was needed, it was assuredly needed at
least as much in the United States as in Britain. In fact the first
attempt to create one had been made in 1853. Edwards must
have known of the attempt since two of the organizers, Daniel
Gilman and Seth Grant, visited him in Manchester in 1854 and
1855[9] but he nevertheless makes no reference to it in *Memoirs of
libraries*.

Hindsight suggests that two of the essential requirements for
library association formation are the initiative of a young
secretary of outstanding energy and enthusiasm and the support
of some of the best-known and older librarians of the period.
The first conference, held in New York in September 1853, had
been urged on librarians by Charles B. Norton (1825–1891),
publisher of *Norton's literary and educational register*, later *Norton's
literary gazette*, with the aid of his two young editors, Seth
Hastings Grant (1828–1910) who acted as secretary, and Daniel
Coit Gilman (1831–1908). Grant was then Librarian of the New
York Mercantile Library and Gilman newly graduated from
Yale.

Two well-known librarians supported them – Charles Coffin
Jewett (1816–1868), Librarian and Assistant Secretary of the
Smithsonian Institution in Washington, and Reuben A. Guild

(1822–1899), Jewett's successor as Librarian of Brown
University at Providence, Rhode Island.

Eighty-two librarians from forty-seven libraries in thirteen of
the thirty-one States of the Union, including one from the then
extreme far distance of San Francisco, came to New York for
the conference of 1853. No women were there and no visitors
from overseas. The chief subjects discussed were classification
and cataloguing; the need for a national reference library – the
Smithsonian then seemed a much more natural candidate than
the Library of Congress, particularly as Charles Jewett
dominated the conference; the need for public libraries on the
new Boston model; and wide distribution of and easy access to
government publications. The delegates commended Poole's
Index to periodical literature, of which the first edition had been
published in 1848 and an advance copy of the second shown.[10]
They called for a manual of library economy, more than five
years before Edwards published *Memoirs*. On the second day of
the conference Reuben Guild successfully moved for a
permanent library organisation with annual meetings, the first
to be held in Washington one year later.[11]

Both Washington conference and permanent library
organisation came to nothing. Of the 1853 convenors, only
Reuben Guild, Librarian at Brown University from 1848 to
1893, was unaffected by changing professional circumstances.
Norton subsequently experienced severe financial problems;
Charles Jewett, at odds with Dr Joseph Henry, the
Smithsonian secretary, lost his post there in 1854; Grant moved
from librarianship into business; and Gilman travelled abroad
before taking up the academic career which was to lead to the
Presidency of the University of California in 1872 and of Johns
Hopkins in 1875. Then came the Civil War and the long period
of reconstruction and Jewett, who had soon found another post
as Superintendent of the Boston Public Library, died in 1868.

1776, the year of the Declaration of Independence, was and will
obviously remain the seminal year of American history and
Philadelphia, where it was signed, the unique city. In the early
1870s eyes began to focus on centenary celebrations and a great

international exhibition was planned. The idea of another
library conference, loosely associated with it, and of another
attempt at a permanent library organisation, came more slowly
than might have been expected. The first tentative suggestions
were made in 1875 but curiously enough it was a letter,
published anonymously but from Max Muller (1823–1900), the
Anglo-German orientalist and philologist, in the well-known
London literary weekly *The Academy* in its issue of 18 March
1876, which acted as catalyst. Frederick Leypoldt (1835–1884),
editor and publisher of the then recently founded American
Publishers weekly, reprinted the letter there on 22 April, and the
campaign began:

In these days of International Congresses, it is strange that no attempt
should have been made to convene a Congress of Librarians. Very
great improvements have of late years been made in the arrangement
and management of public and private libraries. In some the
machinery for placing and shifting books, in others the binding, in
others again the classifying and cataloguing of books have been
brought to great perfection; but though there are journals in which
these improvements, and what may in some cases be added, these new
discoveries, are discussed, there has seldom been, what is so useful, an
exchange of ideas by word of mouth between those who know the
real difficulties that have to be met, and the success that has attended
recent experiments. Let me mention one point only.
When I was a librarian myself, I always wondered at the extraordinary
waste of power in cataloguing new books. While I was writing my
slip, according to the rules followed in most English libraries, I felt
that there were probably a hundred people doing exactly the same
work which I was doing, not only in England, but in every civilised
country of the world. Yet what would have been easier than to have
my slip printed, and any number of copies sent round by book-post
to every library in Europe. With a little arrangement, every English
book might be catalogued at the British Museum, every French book
at the Bibliothèque Nationale, every German book at the Royal
Library at Berlin, every Russian book at St Petersburg etc. At a
trifling expense these printed slips might be sent to every small or
large library, and each of them might have three or four kinds of
catalogues – an alphabetical catalogue of the authors, a chronological
catalogue, a local catalogue, a catalogue classified according to
subjects etc. Even when a library is too poor to buy a book, the slip
might be useful in its catalogue. The saving that might thus be

effected would be very considerable. The staff of librarians might be greatly reduced, and the enormous expense now incurred for catalogues, and mostly imperfect catalogues, would dwindle down to a mere nothing.

There are, of course, other ways in which the same object might be obtained, if only the principal libraries would agree on a common line of action. Each author might be requested to write a proper slip of his own book, and the publisher might forward copies of these slips with the book itself.

All this and much more could be done, if a general understanding was once arrived at between the librarians of the principal libraries of Europe. If we look at the balance-sheets of these libraries, the differences are very great. The expenses are, of course, much greater where books are lent out, than where they are not. But even where the expenses are lowest, the chief item of expenditure is always the catalogue. A few resolutions, carried at an International Congress of Librarians, might cause a saving of many thousands of pounds annually, and would certainly give us better catalogues than we find at present even in best administered libraries. . . .[12]

The indispensable secretary then appeared, a young man of twenty-four, Melvil Dewey. Dewey (1851–1931) was then Assistant Librarian of Amherst College Massachusetts, his exceptional mind already teeming not only with the first version of his decimal classification but also with spelling reform, metric reform and library reform as well. By May 1876 Leypoldt and Dewey envisaged a library magazine of regular issue and, with Leypoldt as publisher, his partner R. R. Bowker as General Editor, and Dewey as Managing Editor, were planning the first number. On 20 May the editorial of *Publishers weekly* referred to the proposed *American library journal* and concluded:

We submit that such a congress of the leading librarians, and as many of the less experienced ones as have a thirst for bibliographical knowledge, and could come, would at least be of decided usefulness; and as it is the fashion to organise Centennial congresses, it is certainly proper to take advantage of the fashion and have a conference at Philadelphia this year. We are glad to state that a preliminary call is being signed by several gentlemen connected with the library interest, for such a congress, and we have no doubt that good will come of it. It is proposed to combine all promising suggestions that come in reply to this preliminary call in a further address to the library interest, definitely naming the date, and setting forth the points which may usefully be brought up. Such a conference was held in 1853, but since then our libraries have grown tenfold, and there is twenty times the need for co-operation. We are sure that the conference will prove an effective meeting.[13]

There were, however, some initial difficulties due mostly to the fact that Dewey's name was unknown to senior librarians in May 1876 and Leypoldt was not a librarian but a publisher. William Poole (1821–1894), of *Index* fame, and Librarian of Chicago Public Library from 1874 to 1887, was particularly suspicious of publisher interest; he suggested to his friend since the 1853 conference, Justin Winsor (1831–1897), Superintendent of the Boston Public Library from 1868 to 1877, that 'It won't pay for you and me to attend that barbecue'.[14] Ainsworth Spofford (1825–1908), Librarian of Congress from 1864 to 1897, told Leypoldt that:

I confess that I look with perhaps undue distrust upon mixing the methods of the bibliographer, which are those of patient and accurate research, with the methods of the stump, which are conspicuously the reverse.[15]

But conversions *were* made and when the first printed 'calls' were circulated, some at least of them with *Publishers weekly*, the document

inviting librarians and all interested in library and bibliographical work to meet at Philadelphia on the 15th of August next, or otherwise as may be found more generally acceptable[16]

bore twenty-eight signatures. Poole and Winsor were included together with Charles Ammi Cutter (1837–1903), Librarian of the Boston Athenaeum from 1868 to 1893; H. A. Homes (1812–1887), Librarian of the New York State Library from 1862 to 1887; Lloyd P. Smith (1812–1886), Librarian of the Philadelphia Public Library from 1851 to 1886; and Reuben Guild. Spofford was still missing but, from many points of view, including that of Federal support, the most important name included was that of John Eaton (1829–1906), United States Commissioner of Education from 1870 to 1886. His rapidly expanding statistical office had in preparation the monumental report on American public libraries, the first copies of which were to reach Philadelphia before the end of the conference, and which printed Cutter's epoch-making *Rules for a dictionary catalogue*, as appendix. Eaton agreed to mail the definitive 'call' and sent out more than 1000 copies of it at the end of July 1876, by which time the conference date had been finally agreed for early October. Meantime the programme was being planned by the organising committee of Winsor, Poole, Lloyd P. Smith and Dewey.

A total of 103 delegates assembled in the pleasant library of the Pennsylvania Historical Society, with its attractive garden view, on Wednesday 4 October 1876. More than twenty of them came from Philadelphia itself and fewer than a dozen from States west of New England and the Eastern Seaboard. Twelve women were of the number – one or two even dared later to contribute to discussions although their modest remarks were naturally voiced for them by friendly male librarians sitting near them. There was one foreign delegate, James Yates (1843–1913), Librarian of Leeds Public Library from 1870 to 1897.

The introductory address by James Wallace, President of the Historical Society of Pennsylvania, was inacceptable general terms appropriate for a new conference of librarians. It was followed by the election of conference officers. Winsor became President, Spofford, Yates, Poole and Smith Vice-Presidents; and Dewey, Guild and Charles Evans (1850–1935), Librarian of Indianapolis from 1872 to 1884 and 1889 to 1892, Secretaries. The organisers had wisely planned a blend of general papers on books and readers with more technical ones on cooperative indexing and cataloguing, the preservation of pamphlets, book sizes and copyright. The conference went off to an animated start with Poole's paper on 'Some popular objections to public libraries'. He himself ended his vigorous treatment of the evergreen fiction problem with an apposite quotation from Edward Edwards:

It may be truthfully said that at no previous period in the history of English literature has prose fiction been made, in so great a degree as of late years, the vehicle of the best thoughts of some of the best thinkers. Nor, taking it as a whole, was it ever before characterised by so much general purity of tone or loftiness of purpose.

But it was already clear that, by 1876, the *discouragement* of American readers with good appetites for fiction had many strong advocates; there was a vigorous exchange of opinions. Later there was a comparably animated discussion, also initiated by Poole, on library relationships with publishers and booksellers, with special reference to discounts. A modern reader of the conference proceedings may note with interest that the marketing techniques of encyclopaedia publishers have long, deep and convoluted roots.

Other general papers were presented by, *inter alia*, Winsor and Smith while Cutter, Evans, Guild and others read more technical ones on pamphlet preservation, book sizes, and bibliography as a science. Spofford, who *did* come for the last day of the conference, addressed it on 'Copyright in its relations to libraries and literature'. Yates, as the only foreign delegate, was made much of and was frequently asked for his own expressions of opinion; these, it must be fairly admitted, were seldom of the calibre of the better American ones.

As Poole's *Index* was discussed at length – the compiler gave a moving account of his publishing problems in 1848 and 1853 – and its possible continuation as a cooperative venture was referred to a special committee, it may be considered that the Librarian of Chicago was the 'lion' of the conference. In fact, however, Melvil Dewey's outstanding professional career really began there. His obvious secretarial prowess, his contributions to discussions, his editorship of the *American library journal*, of which the first number had appeared in September, and his own account of his new *Decimal classification* earned him much respect and brought him many admirers.

On the last day of the congress, Friday 6 October 1876, those present were invited to append their signatures to the following:

For the purpose of promoting the library interests of the country and of increasing reciprocity of intelligence and good-will among librarians and all interested in library economy and bibliographical studies, the undersigned form themselves into a body to be known as the AMERICAN LIBRARY ASSOCIATION.

A permanent organisation was proclaimed, a draft constitution proposed and the *American library journal* adopted as the official organ. Winsor became President, Spofford, Poole and Homes Vice-Presidents, and Dewey Secretary.[17] Meantime in London another young librarian was waiting for *his* opportunity. His name was Edward Nicholson.

Edward (later Williams) Byron Nicholson (1849–1912) had graduated at Oxford in 1872 and, after a short period as a schoolmaster, had been appointed resident Librarian and Superintendent of the London Institution in 1873 at a salary of £200 per annum, plus residential emoluments and 'free of income tax'. The London Institution had been established as a proprietary body by Royal Charter in 1807 'for the advancement of literature, science and art'. After using temporary accommodation nearby, it had moved into its new purpose-built brick and Portland stone premises on the north side of Finsbury Circus where its massive size and impressive Corinthian portico dominated the neighbouring dwelling houses from 1819 until its demolition in 1936. But its library, once-splendid laboratory and lecture theatre holding 700 had all seen much better days when Nicholson had arrived in February 1873. He had gone through the dusty old place like a whirlwind, cleaned it up, rearranged and re-classified the library of reference books, built up a small but very popular and successful circulating library, and still found time to write and publish a volume of undistinguished verse. He had made a splendid impression on the Institution's members and upon their governing body; they had soon symbolised that impression by increasing his salary to £300 per annum.[18]

On 27 January 1877 Nicholson published in *The Academy* a commentary on the report of the American conference in the second, double, number of the *American library journal,* which concluded:

The unequivocal success of the Conference and its permanent results suggest the advisability of English librarians holding a similar meeting and establishing a similar organisation for mutual interchange of ideas.

His famous letter, printed in *The Times* of 16 February, showed that he had begun to seek the support of some of the leading librarians of the time:

Reviewing in a recent number of the *Academy* the proceedings of the Philadelphia Conference of Librarians, I suggested a similar meeting in England for the interchange of ideas upon all points of library management. As you reproduced most of the review in question, I trust you consider the subject important enough to allow my appealing in your columns for co-operation in realizing the suggestion.

I have written to the Principal Librarian of the British Museum, Mr J. Winter Jones, asking whether, on receipt of a reasonable number of requisitions, he would consent to preside over such a Conference. In his reply he says:- 'Strenuous efforts are now being made and made successfully, for the establishment of libraries in large centres and I think that such a Conference as you suggest might produce good practical results. Whether my presidency would be beneficial is a question upon which I cannot presume to offer an opinion; but should others think that my services in such a position might be useful, I shall be prepared to give them to the best of my ability.

I have also written to the Librarians of the Bodleian Library, Oxford, the Cambridge University Library, the Advocates Library, Edinburgh – the largest in Scotland – and the Library of Trinity College, Dublin – the largest in Ireland – asking whether they would be willing to act as Vice-Presidents. I give extracts from their answers.

The Rev H. O. Coxe, of the Bodleian, writes, 'I am in your hands to use me as you list in forwarding the Conference you suggest. Only good can come of it'.

Mr Bradshaw, of Cambridge, writes – 'I shall be very glad to take part in your Conference, and do what I can, and learn what I can, but I had very much rather not be a Vice-President, or anything of that kind'.

Mr Clark, of Edinburgh, writes – 'I say at once that I concur very heartily with your suggestion as to a Conference of English Librarians – a subject that I have thought and spoken strongly about for some time past. I believe that we have already lost a good deal from the want of united work. Use my name in any way you think best'.

The Rev Dr Malet, of Dublin, writes – 'I am sure the proposed Conference will prove to be a matter of great importance. I shall have much pleasure in co-operating in any way I can'.

I now ask the rest of our profession whether they will join in promoting a Conference to be held under the auspices of these gentlemen. I would willingly call on all librarians in London and write to those of the largest provincial libraries, but official duties would prevent me doing this very quickly. If a sufficient number will do me the favour of writing to acquaint me with their assent, I propose to ask the London Librarians to meet and elect a committee, which, corresponding with the provincial librarians and the officers-designate, should arrange all details.

I hope the Conference might be held in London, where the members would have the opportunity of inspecting, not only the largest library in the Kingdom, but many others of very considerable size. Were such meetings to be of at all frequent occurrence, they might be held at other towns in turn.

The time should not be so near as to prevent the perfect organization of the Conference. Many of its members would, moreover, wish to master, beforehand, such works as Edwards' 'Memoirs of libraries', and the great 'Library Report' just published by the Government of the United States. Some would have papers to prepare for the Conference. The summer or early autumn would interfere with our holidays. Altogether, the end of autumn or beginning of winter seems the most fitting time. But these are points to be settled by the future committee. I only offer the above remarks to elicit the views of others. I shall not occupy your space with the reasons why such a Conference would be most useful until I know that a single librarian disputes its utility. I fail to see how there can be two opinions on this head among those of us who have had any experience. Those who have not will, I trust, grant some weight to the judgment of men in the position of Mr Winter Jones, Mr Coxe, Mr Bradshaw, Mr Clark and Dr Malet.[19]

Progress was, however, not quite unimpeded. On 24 February *The Athenaeum* published a latter from James Yates:

As the only English librarian who attended the American Conference held in Philadelphia last autumn, perhaps I may be permitted to offer a few remarks on the proposal made in the *Times* last week for a Conference of Librarians in England. . . . My only fear is that some of the preliminary steps suggested in the *Times* by Mr Edward B. Nicholson will, if carried out, do much to weaken the movement. At the American Conference the first business transacted was the election of the President and Vice-Presidents. It appears, however, that Mr Nicholson is desirous to take all this trouble out of the hands of the Conference by electing the officials in advance. . . . If we are to have a Conference . . . and if it is necessary that a President should be nominated beforehand there is one man whose claims for such an office are far above those possessed by any other in this country. I refer, of course, to Mr Edwards, the author of 'Memoirs of Libraries. . . . At the American Conference Mr Edwards was quoted as an authority in every branch of library management, and I was assured over and over again that if the author of the 'Memoirs of Libraries' had visited America, he would have been welcomed as the one man in England to whom they were most indebted for his valuable suggestions on library work.

Nicholson replied, a week later:

It seemed, therefore, important that the Conference should, if possible, be held under a presidency which would attract all who, having had least occasion to know the want of such a meeting, most need attend to it. For this reason as much as any I asked the chief of our national library – far the largest in this kingdom, and one of the largest in the world – whether he would be willing to accept that position . . . the head of the British Museum for the time being is the man whose presidency will do most to attract to a first gathering those who, as I said, most need attraction, and, let me add, to draw public attention to the Conference. . . . There are, probably, hundreds at least of small librarians who – more's the pity – know nothing of Mr Edwards and 'Memoirs of Libraries' and to whom his name would be no charm. The rest of us would have his labours so frequently on our lips that the addition of the title of President could do him no greater honour. . . . No one would be more ready to join in some special recognition of our indebtedness to him – such as the Presidency of any permanent organization which might result from the Conference. . . .

The reply was persuasive and, while it did not completely silence Yates, it made him the less convincing. It may be doubted whether Nicholson knew that the young Edwards – at the beginning of a not very successful professional and literary life – had shown little affection for Winter Jones.[20] It may be doubted

whether he knew that the elderly Edwards, then labouring
through an immense cataloguing task at the Bodleian Library,
had become deaf, peppery and impossible. But so it was.

Encouraged by the letters of support received following his
letter in *The Times*, Nicholson invited librarians in the London
area to meet on 9 April for preliminary consultations, not
however at his own Institution, but at the London Library
whose chief officer, Robert Harrison, had become a strong
supporter. Nineteen were present and following a favourable
report from Nicholson a conference was decided upon, with
Nicholson as secretary, and an organising committee consisting
of Harrison, George Bullen, Richard Garnett and two other
members of the British Museum staff; W. H. Overall, Librarian
to the Corporation of London; H. R. Tedder, Librarian of the
Athenaeum Club; B. R. Wheatley, Resident Librarian of the
Royal Medical and Chirurgical Society; and thirteen others. The
committee met frequently, invited correspondence with
provincial librarians, and circulated a 'Rough list of some
leading subjects connected with library formation and
management' with the object of providing a planned coverage
for speakers. A summary of the 'Rough list', compiled by
Nicholson, and based on Edwards' two works, *Memoirs of
libraries* and *Free town libraries,* the United States Government
Report and the issues to that date of *American library journal,*
follows:

i   Extension of libraries
     a Libraries for general readers
          Free and public
          Subscription
     b Libraries for special classes
ii   Formation of libraries
iii Library buildings
iv   Selection of contents
v   Acquisition of contents
vi   Cataloguing
vii Shelf arrangement
viii Arrangement and preservation of pamphlets
ix   Binding

Edwards was invited to become a Vice-President of the conference; he courteously declined, on health grounds.

Conference arrangements were completed and, Nicholson's own governing body having given their hearty consent and approval, the Conference was announced for October at the London Institution.[25]

Before the London conference opened, however, the first Annual Conference of the American Library Association had been held, from 4 to 6 September 1877, in the lecture room of the Young Men's Christian Association in New York. The attendance there of sixty, including six women, was disappointingly smaller than in 1876; hardly any of the delegates had travelled long distances and there were no foreign visitors. Few papers were read on this occasion but there were lengthy discussions on a wide range of topics as varied as planning, iron bookstacks, the renovation of books damaged by fire and water, the problem of infected books, cataloguing and accession methods and procedures, the distribution of public documents, and the value of three new inventions – buckram, the telephone and the typewriter.[26] Perhaps the most important business of the meeting was to adopt the new Association's constitution, its object being:

to promote the library interests of the country by exchanging views, reaching conclusions, and inducing cooperation in all departments of bibliothecal science and economy; by disposing the public mind to the founding and improving of libraries and by cultivating good-will among its own members.[27]

A promisingly large number of American librarians were planning to attend the forthcoming conference in London; they carried with them the cordial good wishes of their own colleagues, and proposals for Anglo-American cooperation in the preparation of a new edition of Poole's *Index*.[28]

The London conference of 1877 began in the lecture theatre of the London Institution at 10 a.m. on the morning of Tuesday 2 October. Some of the delegates, it must be admitted, had experienced difficulty in finding hotels conveniently placed near to Finsbury Circus; as one of them, W. H. K. Wright, Librarian of Plymouth Public Library, subsequently wrote:

Well do I remember the Finsbury Circus Meeting, the difficulty of finding hotel accommodation in the immediate neighbourhood and how after many delays and disappointments I was allotted an extemporised bed in the sitting room of the hotel which was our headquarters ... shared this too with J. D. Mullins. ...

He remembered also, however, the warm enthusiasm of the delegates and the pleasant breakfast parties with the American visitors.[29]

Of the 218 delegates assembled for the Conference, only four were female and two of these American. The two English ladies were Mrs Sarah Cooper, from the Wolverhampton library; and Miss Isabella Stamp from Mr James Heywood's voluntary free public library in Kensington. The overseas representation was impressive; this conference, unlike its American predecessors, was international in reality as well as in name. Three foreign Governments – the French, German and Greek – were represented and librarians had come also from Belgium, Denmark, France, Italy, Australia and the United States. No fewer than fifteen Americans were present; twelve of them had been at Philadelphia, nine at New York and two – Guild and Poole – at the 1853 gathering. The two American ladies present were Mrs Cornelia Olmsted, from New York State, and Miss Annie Godfrey, from Wellesley College, Massachusetts, who was to marry Melvil Dewey, also a delegate, in the following year.[30]

By the time of the London conference seventy British towns had opened municipal libraries and twenty-eight of them had sent representatives. But up to this date municipal library development had made least progress in the London area. Joseph Radford, once one of Edwards' staff at Manchester and now Librarian of the only municipal library in London –that provided in Great Smith Street, Westminster, since 1857 by the parishes of St Margaret and St John – who had been a member of Nicholson's organising committee – was present; his nearest neighbour, municipal-library-wise, came from Brighton. The municipal libraries of the provinces were well-represented, the most notable absentees being Cambridge, Norwich, Salford, Sheffield and Warrington and, in Wales, Cardiff. All of Nicholson's organising committee were loyally present; of the librarians of the national libraries originally approached Malet, of Trinity College, Dublin, and Bradshaw, of Cambridge University, had failed him. Eirikr Magnusson, of Bradshaw's staff, had come instead; his ponderous and exhausting dogmatics were to punctuate the conference proceedings as alternatives to the unfailing good humour of the British Museum representatives, the unforced vivacity of the Americans and the unplumbed national pride of the Baron de Watteville. La France! Plus ça change, plus c'est la même chose! There was also a distinguished company of laymen and other professionals including James Crossley, Stanley Jevons, Leone Levi, Mark Pattison, Bernard Quaritch, Henry Stevens, Nicolas Trübner and J. Vernon Whitaker.

The Conference began with the election of officers and committee and the long list submitted by the organising committee was approved; Winter Jones becoming President and Nicholson and Tedder secretaries. Winter Jones then delivered his 'Inaugural Address' which was received with 'long continued applause'.[31] His lengthy but always carefully considered and carefully ordered remarks were much more relevant to the papers to follow than had been the introductory address at Philadelphia, and his conclusion provided its own effective summary:

I have touched very slightly on some of the principal topics which have been proposed for discussion, and have merely ventured to indicate some of my own experiences, and to lay down a few principles which I believe to be sound. I do not expect nor, indeed, is it desirable, that my opinions should pass unchallenged by the Conference. But I do earnestly desire to promote discussion, to promote that ventilation of thoughts and opinions on the subject of library science which may tend to further the objects of this Conference of librarians of all Nations.[32]

It seemed a pity that he felt unable to attend further meetings but he was not in the best of health and had a meeting of his Trustees immediately ahead. Chairmen were subsequently elected each morning and evening. Justin Winsor, who was to be President of the American Library Association for its first ten years, and Poole were outstanding among them.

For the rest of the week the delegates settled down to morning and evening sessions with afternoons of conducted tours and more informal visits to London libraries. Many of those present had already taken the opportunity of visiting the British Museum before the conference began, and parties – in total more than a hundred people – were conducted over it on the afternoon of Wednesday 3 October, some even penetrating into

the many subterranean passages made visible by dim lamplight, by which the lower part of the Museum is honeycombed.[33]

They then

repaired to the official residence of Mr Winter Jones, where they were hospitably received and entertained by him and his daughter, Miss Jones, who had invited a large party, including the principal officers of the Museum, to meet them.[34]

On the evening of Thursday 4 October the delegates were entertained to dinner by the Lord Mayor of London at the Mansion House. At least one of the American guests was enormously impressed by the Lord Mayor's costume and retinue, the elaborate ceremonial and dinner and the circulation of the loving cup.[35] But then, l'Angleterre, plus ça change, plus c'est la même chose!

The first group of papers dealt with the main types of library. W. H. K. Wright, who had experienced the hotel problem

already referred to, looked forward to a time when 'ere another
generation shall have passed away, the Free Library movement
will have spread like a great tidal wave.' W. E. A. Axon was
critical of the British Museum and called for the printed
catalogue which was still some years in the future, this proving a
subject on which there were illuminating differences of opinion,
even among senior members of the Museum's own staff. Charles
Robarts, whose 'University libraries as national institutions' was
statesmanlike and far-reaching in the best Oxford manner,
proposed an integration of the Bodleian Library with All Souls
which has not yet taken place. Full discussions on buildings
followed. W. H. Overall, Librarian of the London Guildhall,
opened by asserting that 'the two great enemies to libraries are
architects and gas' and many of those present seemed to agree
with him. Gas-lighting is, of course, no longer a problem for
librarians.

The most controversial of the next group of papers, on book
stocks, was read by Peter Cowell, Librarian of Liverpool Public
Libraries, whose remarks

when summarized, are intended to show and maintain that the theory
of a regular upward progress of reading from lower-class novels to
the higher departments of literature is rather of the nature of a fiction
itself,

were, assuredly, just as inflammatory in 1877 as at any later date.
The Baron de Watteville was most critical:

La question de l'introduction des romans (moraux, bien entendu) et
des fictions dans les bibliothèques populaires et scolaires s'est posée
depuis longtemps à l'attention du gouvernement français. Depuis dix
ans nous avons fondé en France plus de 1,000 bibliothèques
populaires, plus de 17,000 bibliothèques scolaires. Ces dernières
possèdent plus de 1,500,000 volumes, et prêtent près de 2,000,000
volumes par an. Vous le voyez, messieurs, je parle en m'appuyant sur
les faits. Or, la règle constante, la voici. Quand une bibliothèque est
crée dans un village, on lit d'abord les romans, puis les voyages, puis
les ouvrages d'histoire; et quand les ouvrages sont lus on peut dire
que le goût de la lecture a été inculqué aux habitants. Je m'étonne,
messieurs, de voir cette question soulevée dans cette assemblée.

L'Europe entière rend homage au talent et à la moralité de vos écrivains, et partout on est heureux de pouvoir introduire les romans anglais dans les bibliothèques populaires – ce sont les hameçons avec lesquels on attire les lecteurs. J'ajouterai que ces bibliothèques sont assez frequentées qu'il ait été nécessaire pour quelques-unes de renouveler absolument leur stock de livres usés par le nombre des lecteurs.[36]

Poole, too, was in strong disagreement. Had not his own Philadelphia paper pointed in a direction quite different to Cowell's? But Poole's contribution, together with those of other Transatlantic delegates at earlier sessions, made it clear that American public libraries in 1877 were concerned, understandably enough, more with the *education* of readers in a new country; British ones, at least as much, were concerned with the social and moral *welfare* of those in an old one.

In the group of papers covering classification and cataloguing, Henry Stevens' plea for a bibliographical clearing house included the following:

We trust, however, that at no distant date the letters FLA (Fellow of the Library Association) may carry as much weight as FSA or even FRS.[37]

This was indeed looking forward. Cornelius Walford's demand for, in effect, a *Cambridge bibliography of English literature* and J. A. Cross's for a universal bibliography of bibliographies both struck timeless notes. Richard Garnett's 'On the system of classifying books on the shelves followed at the British Museum' was an informative yet modest introduction worthy of this great Victorian librarian, of whom more later. It would be a pity to forget that when, in the discussion, George Bullen revealed that selected readers at the Museum were allowed special access to the shelves containing the literature of their specialisms, he was taken up by one of the Americans, C. A. Cutter:

Let me bring forward one instance in support of Mr Bullen's advocacy of shelf-classification. I have for a dozen years had in hand a bibliography of works relating to the devil. I am encouraged by what Mr Bullen has said, to hope that he will allow me to visit, under the supervision of an attendant, that portion of the British Museum which is devoted to Demonology. There, in an hour or two, I can make valuable notes of many works hitherto unseen; whereas, if there were no shelf-arrangement, I should not even attempt to look through the million and a half volumes. And even a classified catalogue would not answer the purpose so well, for then I should be obliged to write two or three hundred slips, and send two or three hundred attendants running all about the library, instead of sitting down quietly with all the desired works almost within reach of my table.

MR. BULLEN said that, if Mr Cutter wished to extend his acquaintance with the devil, he should be happy to hand him over to Mr Garnett, who would doubtless assist him to the utmost in his diabolical researches.[38]

On the last morning of the Conference, Friday 5 October, there were free discussions on a wide range of topics – minimum age qualifications for readers, particularly at the British Museum, initiated by a rather indignant Nicholson; hours of admission, including the vexed question of Sunday opening; reader-access to shelves and staff; and salaries, on which Nicholson again

must express his indignation at the low salaries which he believed many heads of large public libraries in the provinces were receiving. To be a good librarian a man ought to have most of the qualities of a gentleman, a scholar and a man of business, whereas the salary generally offered for this combination of qualities was an insult to the liberality and intelligence of our great towns.[39]

The Americans spoke highly of the women members of their staffs – women were to be a rarity on British library staffs for many years to come – and Justin Winsor, at least, was just as enthusiastic about the potentialities of that promising new invention, the telephone.

On the Friday evening the Conference moved on to its most important business. At 7 p.m., James Clark of the Advocates Library being elected to the Chair in place of the still absent Winter Jones, Robert Harrison moved, Henry Stevens seconded and it was unanimously agreed: 'That a Library Association of the United Kingdom be founded'. The constitution proposed by the organising committee was then considered, lightly amended and approved.

Its main object shall be to unite all persons engaged or interested in library work, for the purpose of promoting the best possible administration of existing libraries and the formation of new ones where desirable. It shall also aim at the encouragement of bibliographical research.

The annual subscription was to be half a guinea and there was to be an annual meeting, and monthly meetings in London. The first Officers and Committee were next elected:

President   J. Winter Jones.
Vice-Presidents   James Clark, H. O. Coxe and J. A. Malet.
Committee   W. E. A. Axon (Manchester), F. T. Barrett (Mitchell Library, Glasgow), George Bullen, Peter Cowell, Andrea Crestadoro (Manchester Public Library), Richard Garnett, J. D. Mullins, W. H. Overall, J. Small (Edinburgh University Library), W. S. Vaux (Royal Asiatic Society), B. R. Wheatley and James Yates.
Secretaries   E. B. Nicholson and H. R. Tedder
Treasurer   Robert Harrison

It was then agreed that:

i   The first annual meeting be held at Oxford
ii   The *American library journal* drop the first word of its title and become also the official journal of the new Association
iii An English committee cooperate with the Americans in preparing a new edition of Poole's *Index*
iv   The Council take steps to prepare a 'General catalogue of English literature'
v   A committee be appointed to promote the adoption of the Public Libraries Acts in London

Nicholson presented his entirely satisfactory accounts, the votes of thanks were expressed and the Library Association's inaugural conference ended. The British representatives dispersed to their homes or libraries; the majority of the

Americans moved on to Paris to investigate French librarianship before returning to the United States.[40]

For Nicholson the completed conference represented a substantial achievement. It may be doubted, however, whether he had made such a wholly favourable impression as Dewey at Philadelphia. His energy, enthusiasm and organising powers demonstrated not only in the arrangements for the conference itself, but also in those for the quite ambitious exhibition of photographs, shelf fittings, catalogues, printed guides, bindings and books on librarianship, mounted in his own library, were fully appreciated and admired. But some of his contributions to discussions had displayed more than a little arrogance, impatience and tetchiness which boded ill for long-continued success as a secretary. Nevertheless he and the delegates had little reason to complain of the press publicity which the conference had obtained. *The Times* had provided lengthy, day-by-day, reports and a full column of supporting leader, in total amount more than one whole page of the newspaper. Other newspapers had given shorter accounts and the weeklies, including *The Academy, Illustrated London News, Spectator* and *The Athenaeum* had been generous. In fact, as the latter rightly remarked:

It is not to be denied that the début of the Librarians has been so far successful as to make an impression on the outer world, and draw attention to them and their important work. . . . We have only to hope that the Library Association of the United Kingdom will flourish and that it will justify itself in public estimation by assisting libraries to become what they ought to be, efficient instruments of national education.

Twelve years later, in R. L. Stevenson's and Lloyd Osbourne's *Wrong box*, John Finsbury was to express profound dissatisfaction with *The Athenaeum*. To him

It was all full of the most awful swipes about poetry and the use of the globes. It was the kind of thing that nobody could read out of a lunatic asylum . . . Golly, what a paper.

John Finsbury had, admittedly, been sorely tried by

circumstances. The newly-founded Association and Nicholson himself had assuredly much less reason for displeasure. As Barrett of the Mitchell Library had told him in a letter dated 8 May 1877:

No slight credit is due to you for having *done* what so many of us have been content with talking about and wishing for. I am sure you will have the thanks of the whole body of British Librarians . . .[41]

References

1. E. Edwards, *Memoirs of libraries.* 1859, 2 vols, vol 2, pp 937–8.
2. W. A. Munford, *Penny rate.* 1951, Ch 4; T. Kelly. *History of public libraries.* 1973, Ch 1.
3. A. E. Dobbs, *Education and social movements.* 1919, pp 186–7.
4. *Philobiblon,* ed Archer Taylor. 1948, p 17.
5. W. A. Munford, *Edward Edwards.* 1963, pp 169–171.
6. *The Book hunter.* 1862; p 176 in 1863 edition.
7. A. Esdaile and F. J. Hill, *National libraries of the world.* 2nd ed. 1957, pp 291–2.
8. E. Edwards, *Free town libraries.* 1869, Book 3, Ch 5 and particularly pp 327–338.
9. Munford, *Edwards,* p 116.
10. W. L. Williamson, *William Frederick Poole.* 1963, p 18.
11. G. B. Utley, *The Librarians conference of 1853.* 1951; and J. Frost, 'The Library conference of 1853' in *Journal of library history,* 7; pp 154–160.
12. Reprinted in E. G. Holley, *Raking the historic coals.* 1967, pp 23–4.
13. *Ibid,* p 40.
14. *Ibid,* p 49.
15. *Ibid,* p 43.
16. *Ibid,* pp 54–5.
17. *LJ,* 1; p 95.
18. W. A. Munford, 'Nicholson of the Bodleian', *LR,* 18; pp 507–512; and K. A. Manley, 'E. B. Nicholson and the London Institution', *JL,* 5; pp 52–77.
19. Conveniently reprinted in J. L. Thornton, *Selected readings in the history of librarianship.* 1966, pp 199–201.
20. Munford, *Edwards,* pp 44–5.
21. *Ibid,* pp 187–195.
22. *LJ,* 1; pp 304–5.
23. Full list in *Transactions and proceedings of the Conference of librarians held in London, October, 1877.* 1878.
24. Munford, *Edwards,* p 187.
25. *Minute book of organising committee* (in Bodleian Library, Department of western mss Eng misc d55).
26. *LJ,* 2; pp 16–40.
27. *LJ,* 1; p 253.
28. *Transactions, 1877.* 1878, pp 199–206.
29. 'The Library Association 1877–1897'. *L,* 10, p 197.
30. *Transactions,* pp 253–260.
31. *Ibid,* pp 1–21.
32. *Ibid,* p 21.
33. *Ibid,* p 230.
34. *Ibid,* p 231.
35. S. S. Green, *The Public library movement in the United States, 1853–1893.* 1913, pp 70–1.
36. *Transactions,* p 152.
37. *Ibid,* p 71.
38. *Ibid,* p 167.
39. *Ibid,* p 177.
40. B. Gambee, 'The Great junket: American participation in the Conference of librarians, London 1877', *JLH,* 2, pp 9–43.
41. Bodley mss. Misc d4; letter no 25.

Chapter Three

1877-1898

The *Notes and queries* reporter of the 1877 Conference wrote of it enthusiastically:

Circumstances and place could scarcely have been more fortunate for an event which is to give an impetus to libraries and librarians such as they have never yet experienced. At least I confidently believe this will be the result to England of this important meeting of the librarians of so many nations.[1]

The successor conferences did more than a little to maintain the high standard. At Oxford (1878), Manchester (1879), Edinburgh (1880), London (1881), Cambridge (1882) and Liverpool (1883), the Conferences were attended by an average of about ninety delegates and this at a time when the Association's total membership was less than 400.[2] Delegates insisted on annual conferences although the original council had less ambitious ideas.[3] The papers and discussions were of relatively high standard and on a wide variety of subjects ranging from local/county collections and the evergreen distribution of government publications to libraries, to the employment of women assistants of which Manchester Public Library had, exceptionally, gained useful experience by 1879.[4] The London conference of 1881 approved the *Cataloguing rules of the LAUK* which owed much to the first American code and which would provide the basis for the Anglo-American rules of a later date. The Edinburgh conference of 1880, less fortunately, endorsed

the use of indicators in municipal lending libraries: the
Cotgreave versions, certainly, were not yet available although
their formidable inventor was already attending conferences.
The conferences were, overall, representative and forward-
looking events, partly at least because the provincial municipal
libraries as well as the older types of service were well
represented. The monthly meetings at the London Institution,
by contrast – partly at least because London still lacked
municipal libraries – were concerned much more with
antiquarian topics and were usually poorly attended. It could be
argued, of course, that the two kinds of meeting provided
opportunities for the study of librarianship *and* bibliography,
both of them included in the 1877 constitution. But the officers
were all London-based and although the early councils included
provincial and municipal representatives, few could spare time
and money to attend meetings. At the first twenty meetings of
the council, held during 1878 and 1879, for example, attendances
by non-London members were made at only three of them, one
of these being held during the Oxford conference. The average
attendance at these first twenty meetings was five, including the
two secretaries.[5] The constitution revision approved at
Liverpool in 1883 provided, *inter alia*, for a council of ten
London and ten country members and this was soon to be
adjusted further to eight London and twelve country. These
adjustments were symptomatic of a London *v.* country
controversy which began early; it was obviously very much
easier to amend constitutions than to facilitate or encourage
attendance at meetings. But it may be remembered that the
appointment of local secretaries, to represent the Association in
twenty towns and districts did something to integrate the
membership between annual meetings; it also did something to
recruit new members.[6]

Writing, again with hindsight, the new Association needed
above all else a President or Chairman of stature and experience
as leader, and a dynamic young secretary who could cope with
business quickly and efficiently and could provide a supply of
new ideas. The Americans envied the LAUK's compact and
seemingly convenient area but they were much more fortunate
in their chief officers. For the first ten years of the ALA's life

Justin Winsor and Melvil Dewey did most, if not all, that could reasonably have been expected of them; British experience was less fortunate.

John Winter Jones was prevented by illness from occupying the Presidential chair at the Oxford conference of 1878 and, although Bodley's Librarian, H. O. Coxe, took his place, he himself was similarly indisposed during 1879 – his own Presidential year; both men died in 1881. Jones was as diligent and methodical as legal training and immense experience as Panizzi's right hand man could make him but he had little of his great chief's energy and drive. As Richard Garnett wrote of him:

He was not the man to innovate or originate, but was admirably qualified for the work which actually fell to his lot – first to be the right hand of a great architect, then to consolidate the structure he had helped to erect, and prepare it for still vaster extension and more commanding proportions in the times to come.[7]

Coxe, too, 'the large hearted librarian', as his friend Dean Burgon classically described him,[8] was certainly one of the most popular men in the Oxford of his day but a very gentle leader. Jones and Coxe each served, at least nominally for two years each; for the remaining years of the nineteenth century, and later, it became the practice to have one year Presidencies and to appoint 'friends' considered influential and local dignitaries more frequently than practising librarians.

Nicholson resigned within a few months his joint honorary secretaryship of the new association which he had done so much to create:

London Institution   May 23, 1878
To the Council of the Library Association of the United Kingdom
Gentlemen,
I have to signify to you, very unwillingly, my resignation . . . and in so doing I beg leave to state the reasons which impel me to take this step.
My duties at the London Institution, which are not confined to the direction of its two libraries, not only limit very narrowly the time which I can give to other just claims upon me, but put a considerable

strain upon my unfortunately nervous temperament. Besides these
duties I have undertaken the joint-secretaryship of the Library
Association and the secretaryship of the Metropolitan Free Libraries
Committee, and I am now forced against my will to see that I have
undertaken too much. For more than a year past, long-slighted
symptoms have refused to be slighted any longer, and I have been
seriously warned that unless I moderate my habitual hurry and worry,
permanent ruin to health will surely and speedily result. I have
trifled with these warnings for some time, on the chance that the
pressure of work and anxiety at the London Institution might
become less constant; but this is now so far from being likely that the
Institution is about to enter on an entirely new phase of development.
I therefore at last feel compelled to resign my official connection both
with the JOURNAL and the Association.
I know well that any service of mine was in no way necessary to the
welfare of either. But I regret to abandon connections which gave me
so much pleasure and pride, and I fear to risk your good opinion as a
seemingly capricious deserter from duty. It is only this fear which has
prompted me to trouble you with a statement which I fear you may
have thought, in the reading of it, egotistical and unnecessary.[9]

It may be suspected that Nicholson also quickly became
impatient with his *joint* secretaryship in the Association which he
tended to regard as his own creation. But his subsequent career,
as Bodley's Librarian from 1882 until his death in harness in
1912, is, seen from one angle, an exceptionally unhappy record
of one man's inability to cooperate on even tolerably amicable
terms with his governing body. His continued reluctance, too,
to have the LA's Annual Meeting at Oxford until the Bodleian
was much nearer to his own heart's desire is another aspect of
the tragedy of a lone 'perfectionist'.[10]

Nicholson's colleague, Henry Richard Tedder (1850–1924), was
Librarian of the great Athenaeum Club, founded in 1823–4,
which had, and has, occupied its splendid building in Waterloo
Crescent, on part of the site of the Prince Regent's Carlton
House, since 1830. In common with other, if less influential,
London Clubs the service provided by the Athenaeum Library
and the status of its Librarian were much more important, prior
to World War One, than is now readily understandable. 'He
(Tedder) really is a devil for work' wrote Robert Harrison to

Nicholson in 1893;[11] his talent for tenacious management did
not pass unnoticed by his own governing body and in 1889 he
was to be appointed to the new post of Secretary and Librarian
to the Athenaeum. Then he quickly revolutionised the Club's
ailing financial condition, cleared off the burden of debt which
had plagued it since 1855 and began a period of real financial
prosperity.*[12]

Tedder's reluctance to resign LA responsibilities, to which much
critical reference was to be made, after his death, by E. A. Savage
in particular, will be mentioned later. It is nevertheless a fact
that he was to resign the secretaryship in 1880 but not before he
had shown many evidences of his usual competent business
management and a good deal of sensible forward thinking, in the
field of professional education in particular. His reputation as a
librarian was sufficiently high by 1880 to encourage the Syndics
of the Cambridge University Library to invite him to inspect
their library and to report on its methods and problems.[13]

The outstanding member of the LAUK's first council was
Richard Garnett (1835–1906), Superintendent of the British
Museum Reading Room from 1875 until 1890 when he became
Keeper of Printed Books. Librarians can still enjoy his *Essays in
librarianship and bibliography* (1899), consisting as it does of
collected articles, talks, lectures, biographical sketches,
obituaries and papers read at LA meetings from 1877 onwards; it
is still one of the most attractively written and, in many ways,
one of the most far-sighted books published by an English
librarian.[14] English satire, too, since Garnett's time, has not been
sufficiently successful or prolific to enable the modern reader –
without great loss of pleasure – to overlook his *Twilight of the
gods* (1888, enlarged with added stories 1903).[15] This collection of
stories of east and west, introduced by the title story of
Prometheus and the maiden Elenko, is set in the period when
the gods of old were being sent packing, 'bag and baggage', by

---

* Tedder was to hold his Athenaeum
post until 1922 when he retired, very
reluctantly, on pension. The
complimentary speeches made by
members on the coincidental
presentation of his portrait made such
an impression on him that he withdrew
his resignation. He was subsequently
persuaded to reconsider his new
decision.

the newly victorious Christian Church. Garnett was to have his
Presidential year in 1893. It still seems a pity that this friendly,
self-educated, near-omniscient scholar, humanist, cat-lover, and
amateur astrologer could not have served the Association as its
senior officer for a much larger number of its formative years.
His astonishingly successful self-education had left him without
a trace of the arrogance which so marred the character of, say,
Edward Edwards; it gave him, instead, a wide and genuine
sympathy with the municipal library movement which was not
widely shared by the librarian-scholars of his own and later
times.[16]

Other London based librarians joining the council during its
early years were George Bullen (1816–1894), Garnett's senior
officer who had, like Winter Jones, been Edwards' contemporary
at the British Museum in the later 1830s and 1840s; he was a
jovial and popular Irishman who had been made Keeper of
Printed Books in 1875. William Overall (1829–1888) was
Librarian of the City of London from 1865 to 1884 and
B. R. Wheatley Resident Librarian of the Royal Medical and
Chirurgical Society. The provincial members, in addition to
James Yates, included J. D. Mullins (1832–1900), the
formidable martinet who was Librarian of Birmingham Public
Libraries from 1865 to 1898 and, understandably, a man always
more popular with his committees and council than with his
staff; Peter Cowell (1838–1909), Librarian of Liverpool Public
Libraries since 1875; two men from Manchester – Andrea
Crestadoro (1808–1879), the municipal librarian, and
W. E. A. Axon (1846–1913) who had spent his adolescent years
as a member of the municipal libraries staff, but had then left to
take up a career in business and journalism; and Francis
Thornton Barrett (1838–1919), Mullins' ex-deputy at
Birmingham, who had been the quiet and knowledgeable
English librarian of Glasgow's Mitchell Library since shortly
before the 1877 conference. A little later came Charles Sutton
(1848–1920), Crestadoro's successor at Manchester; Alfred
Cotgreave (1849–1911), of Indicator fame; John Potter Briscoe
(1848–1926), Librarian of Nottingham Public Libraries from
1869 to 1916 and the eminent historian of his county;
W. J. Haggerston (1848–1894), Librarian of

Newcastle-upon-Tyne from 1879 to 1894 which, during his period of office, gained the reputation of being an outstanding 'nursery' of other librarians; W. H. K. Wright (1844–1915), Librarian of Plymouth Public Libraries; and John Pink (1833–1906), Librarian of the pioneer municipal library at Cambridge from 1855 until his death.

The special responsibilities allocated to the Association and to its council by the 1877 conference were unsatisfactorily disposed of. The third edition of Poole's *Index*, which was published in December, 1882[17], owed much to its editor and to other American librarians and little enough to British ones. The grandiose project for a 'General catalogue of English literature' lapsed because of understandably inadequate cooperation by the British Museum; the indexers, too, quickly formed their own, shortlived, society.[18] The Metropolitan Free Libraries Committee, set up at Nicholson's instigation to 'promote the adoption of the Acts', was equally unsuccessful. Despite an impressive co-opted membership including the Bishop of London, Thomas Hughes and several well-known Members of Parliament, attendances at meetings were very small and did not significantly improve as the impressive membership increased. Funds available were pathetically inadequate, the income for 1877–8 being less than £30. The committee was reconstituted as the Metropolitan Free Libraries Association and Anthony Trollope became interested.

The Free Libraries Committee and Association wrote to Local Authorities and to local newspapers, and attempted what publicity was financially possible, all to no practical effect. They then prepared a Parliamentary Bill to consolidate the English Acts and to amend the provisions for polls of ratepayers, believing, with some justification, that this might facilitate local adoptions. Sir John Lubbock introduced the Bill as a Private Member's measure, after consultations with the LA and following the Government's refusal to act. It made no progress. The situation was complicated in 1882 when another Private Bill, sponsored by provincial library authorities, led by Manchester, and who had declined to cooperate with the LA,[19] was introduced by another Member. The provincial Bill sought to raise the permissible rate from one penny to twopence, a reform which the metropolitan Association considered fatal to their cause since local ratepayers – assuming its success – might be persuaded that their potential financial burdens could be *twice* as heavy as before. The provincial Bill also failed. Nicholson, whose personal enthusiasm for the municipal library cause had sustained both Committee and Association, resigned his secretaryship in December 1882, following his appointment as Bodley's Librarian: the Association held its last recorded meeting in the following month. During its last complete year it had enjoyed a total income of less than £10 of which Nicholson himself had provided a guinea, Tedder – who had acted as honorary treasurer – ten shillings, and Mary, daughter of William Ewart, the Parliamentary pioneer of municipal libraries, £2.[20] Ewart himself had died in 1869. Of the towns *near* London, Richmond, Kingston and Twickenham had adopted the Acts since 1877; within the administrative area soon to be that of the London County Council, there had been to date complete and utter failure. The Free Library cause in general was, however, soon to be taken up by Thomas Greenwood, a successful publisher who devoted much of his leisure time to it. The first edition of his propagandist, and not always accurate handbook, *Free public libraries,* was published in 1886.

The adoption of an existing periodical, the *American library journal,* as the official organ of the LA had obvious advantages; its publication in the United States, even when *American* had been dropped from its title, had equally obvious drawbacks. It was difficult to make it seem a real Anglo-American magazine, notably during 1880 when the tireless Melvil Dewey, become Dui, began to introduce 'simplified' spelling. It certainly gave quite full and speedy reports of British meetings. Original British contributions were also welcomed but few came. Cutter's assertion of 1882 – 'we are more practical and the English more antiquarian . . .'[21] – may be regarded as applicable more to the non-municipal London librarianship of the period than to the predominantly municipal librarianship of the provinces but it was certainly true that the established bibliographers were more likely than the aspiring librarians to be ready with their pens. The practical Americans were already busying themselves, not only with their own cataloguing rules, but also with such matters as a new supplies department for standardised stationery, printed forms, etc, which British libraries would accept only reluctantly.

By 1879 the inconvenience of relying *solely* on the *Library journal* was causing frustration. It remained the official journal until July 1882, after having itself survived a severe financial crisis in 1880 and consequently having appeared, from 1881 onwards, in more economical format. In January 1880 the first number of *Monthly notes of the Library Assocation of the United Kingdom* was published for the Association by the then well-known house of Trübner, ostensibly at threepence a copy but in reality free and post free to members; each issue of eight pages in 1880 and 1881 and of up to sixteen pages in 1882, carried also Trübner's monthly list of old, new and forthcoming publications. *Monthly notes* endeavoured to provide accounts of all proceedings, printed papers or resumés read at the monthly meetings; printed rather scanty 'Notes and news' and aspired also to other articles, space for which was usually lacking.[22] As from January 1883, the arrangement with Trübner was discontinued and the magazine appeared in green covers, quickly criticised by one 'fair and candid reader', as

so ugly and vulgar . . . as the LA is connected, through friendly intercourse with Cambridge and Oxford, could not one of the "blues" be substituted.[23]

William Brace was the first editor but the responsibility was taken over by E. C. Thomas in 1882.

Ernest Chester Thomas (1850–1892) was one of the more interesting LA personalities between Nicholson and MacAlister; his short life and poor health during its later years may well have robbed him, unfairly, of greater achievements. He was an Oxford graduate and barrister who built up a small practice but who also played many other, perhaps too many, parts. He was active as a teacher, law-coach, business man, journalist, miscellaneous writer, bibliographer and librarian-manqué; he liked friends and acquaintances to remember that he had once

been librarian of the Oxford Union! A slight man with a quick
walk, he was a witty conversationalist who brought distinction
to the office of Honorary Secretary which he had assumed
following Nicholson's resignation in 1878. When Tedder also
resigned in 1880 *he* was succeeded by Charles Welch of the
London Guildhall; following Welch's own resignation two
years later, Thomas reigned alone until 1887.

Thomas really came into his own, however, not as Honorary
Secretary, but as editor and proprietor of *The Library chronicle*
which succeeded *Monthly notes* in January 1884. He had suggested
a magazine of the sort as early as 1880[24] but had laboured on as
editor of *Monthly notes* during the later part of its unspectacular
career. His chance came when it became generally accepted that
the annual volumes of *Proceedings* and *Transactions,* which from
1878 to 1884 recorded the conferences in exceptionally
distinguished fashion, ought to be amalgamated for economy's
sake with *Monthly notes*: the Liverpool conference of 1883
officially endorsed the new approach.

The *Library chronicle* ran from 1884 until 1888. Thomas managed
and edited it

at his own risk, entirely as a labour of love. The literary side of the
undertaking was no trouble to him; but the commercial details and
the worries of the advertising columns brought neither intellectual
nor pecuniary profit.[25]

Its early numbers, understandably, seemed little different from
those of the later *Monthly notes* but space was soon found for
more library notes and news, details of new appointments and
movements of members; for a continuing 'record of
bibliographical and library literature' and for 'notes and queries'.
Thomas had hoped to pay more attention to bibliography and
published occasional articles of relevance, distinguished
examples being extracts from the abortive revised edition of
Memoirs of libraries which the pioneer veteran of municipal
libraries was working on, busily and fruitlessly, during his
chequered and impecunious retirement in the Isle of Wight.[26]
Letters from members also materialised, including the first

recorded suggestion that the Association's money be saved by avoiding the use of the services of the Post Office for distributing the official journal.[27]

Thomas was also one of the Association's pioneers of professional education. Tedder had successfully moved at the Edinburgh conference in 1880:

That it is desirable that the Council of this Association should consider how library assistants may be aided in their training in the general principles of their profession.[28]

but it was Thomas who produced the first draft syllabus.[29]

Following some controversy between the London and provincial members of the Association and of the Council – understandable enough in view of the obviously limited potentialities of the young and frequently poorly educated entrants attracted by the low staff salaries offered by the municipal libraries – the first examinations for 1st and 2nd class certificates in English and European literature, classification, cataloguing and bibliography and library administration were held in July 1885. Two 2nd class certificates were awarded on this first occasion, one of them to J. J. Ogle then of Nottingham Public Libraries. But the examinations then, and for many years to come, attracted very few candidates; for the still smaller number of successful entrants the tests were much more of memory than of creative thought. The questions set, for example, in September 1887, included the following memory test: 'Who have written lives of Nelson, Cromwell, Garrick, Hume, Wellington, Queen Elizabeth, John Hampden?' But also included was a subject assuredly more appropriate even then for a full scale thesis: 'What is the best method of lighting, warming and cleaning a Library? State also what protection against fire you would suggest'.[30] Raymond Irwin wrote nearly a century later, 'As always the essential basis is a liberal education'.[31] For the representative Board School boy of the 1880s who found his way on to the staff of a provincial public library in England that essential basis was normally lacking.

The delegates attending the Birmingham conference in
September, 1887 were members of what was still – at the
beginning of its second decade – a small and not very effective
society. Its total membership was still short of 500 and its
annual income – derived almost entirely from their half-guinea
subscriptions – provided little more than the money required to
cover its own housekeeping, including the always expensive
collection of overdue subscriptions. The LA had already been
much more successful, in 1881, 1883, 1884 and 1885, in
amending its own constitution than in raising its subscriptions.
It had certainly introduced an entrance fee of 10*s* 6*d* and
increased substantially the commutation for life membership but
these changes could obviously have little immediate effect. But
there were other signs of change. The London parishes – the
metropolitan boroughs were still more than a decade away –
were at last beginning to provide their citizens with the
municipal libraries which had already become commonplace in
the provinces. Wandsworth had adopted the Acts in 1883 and
Fulham and Lambeth in 1886, while during 1887 itself
St Martin-in-the-Fields (Westminster), Battersea, Putney,
Chelsea, Kensington, Clapham, Bermondsey, Rotherhithe,
Clerkenwell and Hammersmith had all fallen into line.[32] Queen
Victoria's Jubilee was not without influence: the new trend was
marked. Nevertheless the 1887 conference was notable above all
for the emergence of a new and very influential leader –
J. Y. W. MacAlister.

John Young Walker MacAlister (1856–1925) had begun a
medical training at Edinburgh which had been terminated,
ironically, by illness. He had taken a post as Sub-Librarian of
the Liverpool Library and in 1880 had been appointed Librarian
of the Leeds Library. He began to attend LA conferences and to
make himself known. He came to London early in 1887 on being
appointed the first Librarian of the new National Liberal Club
but abandoned this for the post of Resident Librarian and
Secretary of the Royal Medical and Chirurgical Society. At
Birmingham, his first conference since his London appointment,
two important things happened to him: he read his first paper
and was appointed Joint Honorary Secretary to succeed
E. C. Thomas. His paper, 'Wanted a librarian'[33] proclaimed that,

if librarianship was not yet a profession, it was certainly a skilled craft; vacancies for librarians should be filled only by skilled craftsmen. He made good use of the apocryphal story of a new library authority which had appointed as its first librarian, not a skilled craftsman but a man with exceptional qualifications in Andamanese.* Edinburgh, exceptionally fortified by a grant of £50,000 from Andrew Carnegie, had adopted the Acts and had shortly before the Conference appointed as its first Librarian Hew Morrison, a small-town schoolmaster known to have the Gaelic. The reference was not lost on the delegates and it may be doubted whether Morrison ever forgot it.† E. A. Savage, his successor at Edinburgh, was of the opinion that it proved an expensive joke for the Association as Morrison was influential with Andrew Carnegie and was indeed his own choice for the new post.[34]

It may nevertheless be asserted with confidence that, while Richard Garnett had claimed that John Dury, author of the classic *Reformed library keeper* (1650), was 'the first who discovered that a librarian had a soul to be saved',[35] MacAlister proclaimed it anew in 1887.

The LA's second decade was to be unmistakeably MacAlister's. Admittedly the years were auspicious. The Association's financial problem was solved – at least temporarily – by its decision in 1889 to abandon its entrance fee and double its subscription; within a year of the fateful decision the Honorary Treasurer, H. R. Tedder, who had just succeeded Robert Harrison, was reporting a satisfactory surplus and inviting the members in conference at Reading to suggest ways of spending it![36] 'New blood' from the public libraries came on to the Council, including J. J. Ogle (1858–1909) from Bootle; John Ballinger (1860–1932) from Cardiff and R. K. Dent (1851–1925)

* MacAlister may of course have underestimated the value of Andamanese in the context. Lavengro's use of Armenian as an effective protection against feminine wiles may seem, on reflection, scarcely less eccentric and not necessarily more plausible.

† The Council's Minutes for 9.9.1887 include the following: 'A letter was read from Mr Credland (Manchester) suggesting the boycotting of the non-librarian recently elected at Edinburgh, but the Council did not see its way to take any action'.

from Aston Manor, Birmingham. From the new municipal
libraries of London came Frank Burgoyne (1859–1913) from
Lambeth; Cecil Davis (1854–1922) from Wandsworth;
Lawrence Inkster (1854–1939) who had moved from South
Shields to Battersea in 1887; J. H. Quinn (1860–1941) appointed
to Chelsea in 1887 and, most important of all, James Duff Brown
(1862–1914) who had left the Mitchell Library, Glasgow, in 1888
to become the first Librarian of Clerkenwell. All of these men,
and Brown in particular, were to exercise much influence but
MacAlister proved the unmistakeable leader.

MacAlister's achievements as Honorary Secretary (jointly with
Thomas Mason until 1892 and then alone, on Mason's own
suggestion, until 1898)[37] may be discussed a little later. He made
his first and, in some respects, his most lasting impact as editor
of the Association's new 'organ', *The Library*. He had had
editorial ambitions for some years and had unsuccessfully
offered his services as editor of *Monthly notes* in 1882.[38] Then,
when Thomas decided that he could not continue the *Library
chronicle*, MacAlister's opportunity arrived.

The LA's problem, as always during the nineteenth century, was
to provide members with a regular journal at an acceptably low,
preferably nominal, cost. So *The Library* was launched as the
property, not of the Association, but of MacAlister personally.
The memorandum approved by the Council in December, 1888
is of interest:

MEMORANDUM OF AGREEMENT made this first day of
December, 1888 between John Young Walker MacAlister of
53 Berners Street, Marylebone, London, Honorary Secretary of the
Library Association of the United Kingdom of the one part, and
Elliot Stock, of 62 Paternoster Row in the City of London, Publisher
of the other part, for the publication of a monthly magazine to be
entitled "The Library" the property of the said J. Y. W. MacAlister;
the first number to be issued on December 20th 1888 and to be dated
January, 1889. The said Elliot Stock hereby agrees to produce the
said magazine at his own expense, taking all proceeds of sales and
advertisements, and to pay to the said J. Y. W. MacAlister the sum of
fourteen pounds for each number and a royalty of nineteen shillings
per hundred copies sold after the sale has reached One Thousand

copies, except on the first number which shall be free from such royalty. These payments to be made within one week after the date of publication each month.

The published price of the said magazine to be eightpence per copy, but copies required for the Library Association aforesaid to be charged sixpence per copy, provided that not less than four hundred copies are taken by them of each monthly issue. It is also agreed that the Editor of the said magazine shall supply all literary matter, correct all proofs and pass the sheets for press, the copy to be in the hands of the printer sufficiently early to allow the proofs to be passed for press by the 20th of each month so that the magazine shall be issued to the public by the 25th day of each month. This agreement to continue in force for two years from the first day of January 1889 and shall be continued after that time from year to year, six months notice being given on either side of a desire to terminate it. It is further agreed that all advertisements shall be subject to the approval of the said J. Y. W. MacAlister. It is further and hereby provided that on the termination of this Agreement, whether by fluxion of time or notice as aforesaid all copyrights and property in the said magazine shall be vested solely in the said J. Y. W. MacAlister and that after such termination he shall be entirely free to make such other arrangements for the publication of the magazine as he may think fit.[39]

The prospectus described *The Library* as:

A magazine of bibliography and literature: the organ of the Library Association of the United Kingdom. . . . As their organ the magazine will endeavour to advance the objects of the Association; will advocate the Free Library movements, and deal with the many important questions affecting the management and administration of public and private libraries. But The Library will have another, and to the reader of literary tastes, a more attractive side; every number will contain original literary articles . . . curious questions of bibliographical learning . . . justice to forgotten or little-known bookmen . . . every true book-lover dearly loves the gossip of his own *Fach* and to this amiable taste The Library will endeavour to cater . . . descriptive reviews of Books about books will be a leading feature . . . a useful feature will be a carefully selected list of the best books published during each month. . . .

while, among the contributors were to be 'some of the best known literary men and librarians of the period'.

If any Library Association publications can be said to have had
the morning dew on them, the quality belongs to the successive
issues of *The Library* from 1889 until 1898, when it was 'the
organ of the LAUK'. There is a charm and grace about them
which was not captured by its successor, *The Library
Association Record*, until Arundell Esdaile took over the
editorship of the latter in 1923. *The Library* was, of course, the
'organ' at a time when bibliography seemed at least as relevant
as librarianship to a substantial part of the membership.*[40]
The titles of many of the articles contributed to the early
numbers reflect this interest: 'The Brothers Foulis and early
Glasgow printing'; 'The monastic scriptorium'; 'The great
"She" Bible'; and, bestriding the two crafts, 'The bibliography
and classification of French literature'. During the course of his
initial planning, MacAlister had asked Richard Garnett to
suggest a bibliographer as his assistant and regular contributor,
and had been fortunate to secure the services of Alfred William
Pollard (1859–1944) of Garnett's own British Museum staff.
Pollard was of inestimable help to MacAlister and, indeed,
maintained his own connection with the magazine long after it
had ceased to be the 'organ of the LAUK'.[41]

From the point of view of the library side of the new magazine,
it is not without interest that the regular monthly feature which
began as 'the library chronicle' had split into 'library notes and
news' and 'the Library Association record' by the middle of
1890. Wise editors assuredly look forward as well as back. For
his chief adviser and contributor on subjects likely to appeal to
the librarians of the growing numbers of municipal libraries,
MacAlister turned in 1890 to one who seemed to him to be not
only a reliably practical man but who also promised to become a
writer of much better than average ability, James Duff Brown of
Clerkenwell.[42]

The Library and the Association gained much, and lost
something, as a result of MacAlister's personal responsibility
and personal approach. The Association gained a journal in

* In 1891 the total membership of 454
included only 187 librarians of whom
about half were from public libraries.

which comment was freer and less official than might otherwise have been the case. It lost because MacAlister's periodic illnesses caused numerous delays in publication although not during *The Library*'s early years. It may also be doubted whether it were better for the not infrequent problems inherent in balancing the magazine's budget to be shouldered by the editor personally, with Council aid when requested, than for the Association to have more direct responsibility. The publishing situation, too, proved even more difficult after 1891 when Stock withdrew and MacAlister became publisher as well as editor: appeals were made to members to find new subscribers.[43] The *quality* of the journal was never in doubt.

MacAlister was very well aware that the Association badly needed a Headquarters. During 1888 he suggested a London office which would provide a members' room, an office for *The Library* and a library bureau, based on Dewey's in America, for book-exchanges (not inter-library loans), with a bibliographical library and space for the display of publishers' catalogues, plans, drawings etc.[44] He was able, in March 1890, to provide the London headquarters by making available, at a low rent, a basement room in his own Society's new offices at 20 Hanover Square; the room could also be used for the monthly meetings.[45] 20 Hanover Square then became the Association's normal rendezvous, although meetings were also held from time to time in the new municipal libraries of Greater London, as these were opened. The Minutes of the meeting held on 17 June 1889, at Wandsworth Public Library, proclaim it as 'the first visit of the Association to a metropolitan rate-supported library'. The monthly meetings took on a new lease of life. Their Minute Books show that, whereas in 1887, the average attendance was less than seven, by 1892 it had risen to nearly thirty, a figure which was maintained until the turn of the century.[46] These were the meetings of which E. A. Savage subsequently wrote:

At a monthly in Hanover Square, after a talk over coffee, a paper was read and discussed by about twelve of the twenty or thirty present, all of whom listened; Oh they listened. A trivial affair, you will say; hole and corner. Not so. Each speaker, House of Commons fashion, amended the proof of his speech, and *The Library* took the paper and debate to all the members, most of whom, oddly enough, read them, as later talk at the Conferences proved. Critics alleged that the printed reports had more sense and finish. They had. . . . [47]

The Library Bureau, on rather less ambitious lines than envisaged by MacAlister, came in 1894 when it was provided in Bloomsbury by Cedric Chivers, who had not yet begun to concentrate his business activities in Bath. [48]

At the 1889 Conference MacAlister successfully moved resolutions to amend the Association's constitution and to prepare a manual 'on the establishment and organisation of libraries'. The constitutional changes call for some attention and may be returned to when the manual has been considered. But the manual's history was unfortunate. As finally planned it was to have had thirteen chapters but of these only Part 1 on 'Library legislation (1855–1890)' appeared. It was written by J. J. Ogle of Bootle Public Library, in collaboration with his one-time municipal colleague there, Henry Fovargue: the two had won a prize, given by MacAlister in 1890, for the best 'Draft of a Free Public Libraries Bill which shall include what is most worth keeping in the existing Acts and contain the best suggestions for new legislation'. Fovargue was now the Town Clerk of Eastbourne and was first appointed the Association's highly valued and long serving Honorary Solicitor at the Annual Meeting of 1893, on the motion of MacAlister. Ogle, Fovargue and the Association were unfortunate because the publication of Part 1 of the Manual in 1892 was quickly overtaken by the passing of the Public Libraries consolidating Act of the same year. MacAlister and the Association were unfortunate because other chapters hoped for from such notables as F. T. Barrett, J. P. Briscoe, W. H. K. Wright, F. J. Burgoyne, Thomas Mason, Cedric Chivers, W. May and C. Madeley did not materialise. The Council decided in July 1892 that in view of

the difficulty if not impossibility of getting the remaining contributions to the Manual within any reasonable time . . . each section should be published as ready.

Editors of later compilations calling for the time-observing cooperation of many librarians may breathe sighs of sympathy!

But at all events James Duff Brown's already busy pen had produced the manuscript of his *Handbook of library appliances* and this was issued as the first of the 'Library Association Series' in 1892 at one shilling. The substantially revised edition of Ogle and Fovargue's contribution appeared as Number 2 – *Public library legislation* in the following year. These were the only satisfactory results of MacAlister's original plan. Peter Cowell's skimpy *Public library staffs* also appeared in 1893 and was poor value even at its published price of sixpence. The five later pamphlets in the series, published between 1893 and 1904, did not derive directly from MacAlister's original plan and were notable chiefly as including Brown's important and influential *Guide to the formation of a music library* and for a useful printing of the British Museum, Bodley and LA cataloguing rules in one handy volume.

To return to constitutional matters, the objects of the LAUK, as now redrafted by MacAlister's successful resolution, read as follows:

i   To encourage and aid by every means in its power the establishment of new libraries.
ii To endeavour to secure better legislation for free libraries.
iii To unite all persons engaged or interested in library work for the purpose of promoting the best possible administration of libraries.
iv To encourage bibliographical research.

It may perhaps be remarked of (iii) that experience with the Manual was not encouraging. Item (iv) also fell on increasingly deaf ears. In 1891 the bibliographers, encouraged by W. A. Copinger and Pollard, and with strong support from *The Library*, decided to form their own Society. This development may be viewed as unfortunate although it may be argued, alternatively, that bibliography provides plenty of scope for a separate association and the bibliographers soon found it. It was also perhaps inevitable. As the years passed the increasingly influential municipal librarians of London, Brown in particular, were attracted much more by the idea of the library as workshop rather than as museum of historical bibliography. The librarians of the municipal libraries in the provinces, who were much farther away from the British Museum and the other great non-municipal libraries of London, were much less likely to be seduced by the 'either .. or' approach. See, for example, Ballinger's review of the first edition of Brown's *Manual of library economy* of 1903 in *The Library World*:

> In the Provinces the Public Library, instead of being the least of many libraries, either stands alone or is the greatest of the libraries available. The "workshop plan of library" which Mr Brown advocates so much and the hostility to the acquisition of rare books . . . imply a limitation upon the aims of the Public Library which will not command the general assent of librarians.[49]

One less serious criticism of the new 'workshop' idea came from Richard Garnett who, in the chair for an 1895 paper by Charles Welch on 'The Public Library movement in London', criticised the speaker's proposals for inter-library cooperation which

> if carried into operation would encourage what I consider one of the most serious nuisances of London – bicycles in the public streets.[50]

The LA objectives (i) and (ii), ie to encourage and aid by every means in its power the establishment of new libraries and to endeavour to secure better legislation for free libraries, may be considered together since they are relevant in particular to the immense development in the numbers and in the effectiveness of municipal libraries during the 1890s[51]. The qualitative contribution – especially in terms of the introduction of open access at Brown's Clerkenwell Library in 1894 – enthusiastically supported by MacAlister in *The Library* – is something with which the Association itself can hardly be credited but the apostle of public libraries, Thomas Greenwood, was generous:

> There is no association for the promotion of the Public Library movement. That excellent body, the Library Association, is doing much to create a spirit of emulation among librarians. Quite a new life has of late been infused into it, and its work is destined to permeate every section of library operations. Many members of the Association have rendered valuable help to the movement.[53]

The Council, at least, was closely concerned with the new Public Library legislation of the 1890s, with the consolidating Act of 1892 and the amending Act of 1893 which, in effect, legalised joint services by two or more authorities. MacAlister worked in close cooperation with Sir John Lubbock (1834–1913), later the first Baron Avebury, who as a Private Member piloted the 1892 Act through the House of Commons. Lubbock's achievement as a private legislator ranked with that of the Parliamentary pioneer of municipal libraries, William Ewart. His friendship for the Association has been nearly forgotten; he remains better known as the Member responsible for the Bank Holidays Act (1871), the Act for the preservation of ancient monuments (1882), and the Early Closing Act (1904). Librarians may also remember his *Hundred best books* of 1891.[54] MacAlister had in fact tried to persuade the Annual Meeting at Reading in 1890 to strive for legislation to make municipal library provision *compulsory* but his resolution was defeated by thirty-three votes to twenty-nine. On this occasion Tedder

thought they would be liable to be laughed at if they passed such a resolution . . . they had better adjourn any decision by a vote on this point for at least ten years, until people became a little more educated on the subject.[55]

In view of the state of library provision in Greater London in 1890, MacAlister's ambitions and Tedder's caution are equally understandable.

MacAlister's reputation underwent some eclipse when *The Library*'s publication dates became more irregular. After 1895 he and the Association also came under heavy criticism from a group of municipal librarians in London and the Home Counties forming the new Society of Public Librarians, of which Charles Goss, of Lewisham and later of Bishopsgate Institute, was Secretary and John Frowde of Bermondsey, Chairman. Some quotation from Frowde's Inaugural Address in December 1895 may be illuminating:

We are not in antagonism with the Library Association but that, on the contrary, we desire to work in harmony with it. . . . We shall

endeavour to remove some of the very unjust and improper
conditions and restrictions under which the Library Association is
carried on, and to introduce instead some more reasonable methods
of dealing with questions affecting our professional interests. . . . Our
only object is to exalt the profession we are engaged in, and as we
know best our own wants, so we are best fitted to make those wants
known to others. . . . It is evident that from the beginning the
Association was one not so much for the librarians of public rate
supported institutions as for gentlemen of literary tastes and librarians
of private or proprietary libraries. . . . Subscriptions had been
doubled and for it members receive a magazine appearing
intermittently and sometimes not for months together. . . . The
Council had become equal to the secret middle ages societies of Italy
or Spain. You never know what they do or what part of your liberty
they are engaged in stealing . . . a substantial subscription is paid
annually for benefits not received; but on the contrary our business
interests are controlled by persons who are not public librarians, and
whose policy is often injurious to our cause . . . These reasons seem
to me sufficient justification for forming a new society on broader and
more liberal principles, and as if to urge us forward we have the
splendid example of the societies formed in several parts of the
provinces. . . . These societies being so very popular and useful it is a
matter for congratulation that one on similar lines has been formed
for London and the adjacent counties . . . we are rather differently
situated and our membership somewhat different. The provincial
societies welcome those engaged in private and proprietary libraries.
The new Society is to be one for public librarians only, as we consider
the interests of private librarians are already more than sufficiently
represented by the Library Association. . . .[56]

There may be those who feel that the logic, consistency, balance
and broadmindedness displayed by Mr Frowde can best be
judged, not by modern standards, but by those of local London
politicians of his period. It is far from easy, nearly a century later,
to distinguish between those members of the Society who
remained primarily concerned with the reform of the
Association and the others who were more consistently eager to
damn open access and all its works – and all its supporters,
notably Brown and MacAlister.[57] In fairness to the LAUK
Council of the period, it must be admitted that MacAlister's
personal administration found critics outside the membership of
the Society of Public Librarians. His approach to his duties as

Honorary Secretary are neatly summed up in a letter which he
wrote to Nicholson in 1894:

> I find the best plan in working with a Council is to do things, and tell
> them about them afterwards as it is quite hopeless to get a large
> Council to work steadily on any given line. Of course if I come a
> cropper I shall be pitched into; but as long as things go well and they
> get the credit all is well. . . .[58]

At all events the Society of Public Librarians acquired limited
nuisance value and retained some of it, at least until the outbreak
of War in 1914. The other societies 'formed in several parts of
the provinces', to which Frowde had referred, were the
Librarians of the Mersey District, founded in 1887; the North
Midland LA of 1890; and the then very new Birmingham and
District LA of 1895. The Library Assistants' Association was also
founded in 1895. Further reference to the activities of these
societies will be made later.

Despite his many other achievements, MacAlister's fame, among
later generations of librarians, has been associated mostly with
the Royal Charter for which he persuaded the Association and
its Council to apply. Librarians and other readers of this book
who have ever been connected with unincorporated voluntary
societies which have found themselves in financial or legal
difficulties will assuredly testify to the advantages of having
their societies provided with legal identities and capable,
themselves, of suing or being sued in the Courts. The LAUK had
pursued its way, unincorporated, since 1877 until MacAlister
persuaded the Council to take an interest in the possibility of
obtaining a Charter – still, perhaps, for a voluntary society, the
most attractive and satisfactory method of incorporation. The
decision to apply was taken at the Council meeting of 29 March
1895. Voluntary contributions from members – to meet the
estimated total cost of £100 – were solicited and the councillors
themselves set good early examples.[59] The proposal was carried
by a large majority at the Cardiff conference in the following
September.[60] The petition and draft Charter with byelaws,
based on the extensive rules revision undertaken at a Special
General Meeting in London in January 1896, was submitted in

the following August. During 1897 further information was
sought by the Privy Council Office; questions were raised; there
was correspondence; legal points and queries were dealt with by
Fovargue. The approved Fair Copy was remitted to the Privy
Council Office and the Charter was granted on 17 February 1898.

MacAlister proudly presented to the first General Meeting of
the incorporated Association – no longer the LAUK but now the
LA – the Letters Patent under the Great Seal setting forth the
Royal Charter. He himself asserted that:

They owed more to Sir John Lubbock for having obtained their
Charter than to anyone else[61]

but, without his own initiative, steady encouragement and
determination, the Charter might have been indefinitely delayed.
Nevertheless a resolution to strike a commemorative medal was
rejected.[62]

The Council had also started to prepare the way for
twentieth-century activities by beginning, from 1894 onwards,
to work through standing committees. Prior to this date only
ad hoc committees had been appointed although it must be
admitted that the peculiar constitutional arrangements
originating in 1877 sometimes encouraged the monthly
meetings – responsible for most membership matters – to take
on the rôle of standing committees, that is when the Council
itself did not appear to be acting as a committee of the monthly
meetings! But as for many years the Council had normally met
one hour before each monthly meeting, and at the same place,
some confusion and perhaps overlapping were all but inevitable.
At all events, having rejected the idea of an executive committee
in 1893, the Council obtained the authority of the Annual
Meeting at Belfast in 1894 for its first standing committees.
Those appointed almost immediately were for summer schools,
examinations, legislation, publications, and museum. Their
activities and personnel during the period immediately prior to
the Charter of 1898 now call for some consideration.

Up to 1892 the Association's efforts to raise the educational and professional standards of its members, and particularly of its younger members, had been limited almost entirely to the setting of examinations; few sat them and fewer still passed. But at the 1892 conference – held wholly exceptionally, abroad, in Paris – two important papers were read; these helped to prepare the way for the Association to begin to act also as a teaching body. Miss Minnie S. R. James (1845–1903), who was then librarian of the free – but not rate-supported – East London People's Palace, and one of the first women to take an active part in LAUK affairs, presented one paper on 'A Plan for improving technical instruction for library assistants',[63] and J. J. Ogle another on 'A Summer school of library science', the latter envisaged to last for perhaps one week.[64] Both papers were read again at Liverpool in the following December. Interest was aroused and the first Summer School, providing lectures and demonstrations together with visits to libraries, printers and bookbinders etc was held in London during three days in July 1893. The announcements in *The Library* and *The Athenaeum* attracted forty-five students. Sixty-seven attended the next, four-day, School in June 1894.

When the first meeting of the new Summer School Committee was held in October 1894, it could already look back on promising beginnings. Charles Welch, of the Guildhall Library, was made first chairman and, almost automatically, J. J. Ogle, honorary secretary. Welch continued to occupy the chair for some years but Ogle, whose place of employment was 200 miles from London and who was shortly to leave librarianship for full-time technical education administration, gave place to W. E. Doubleday (1865–1959), Librarian of Hampstead since 1894, and he, in turn, to Henry D. Roberts (1870–1951), then Librarian of St Saviours, Southwark. The future of the summer schools was to owe more to Roberts than to any other man. Miss James also continued to be keenly interested – even after she had joined the Library Bureau and moved to the United States – as also did Miss M. Petherbridge, another pioneer woman member of the Association. The latter, however, was not a professional librarian; she ran one of the new typing bureaux in the Strand. MacAlister gave an annual prize for the best report on the summer school. Ambitions were tempted. The third summer school, of June 1895, was planned, too ambitiously, for five days and attendance dropped back to forty.

The Association's examination syllabus had also been over-ambitiously re-planned – for the needs of the period – in 1891. The new revision of 1894 provided for examinations only in what were regarded as professional subjects:

i   Bibliography and literary history
ii   Cataloguing, classification and shelf arrangement
iii Library management

Entrance fees were introduced although these were sometimes returned to candidates attending examinations: 10s was charged for the three 'sections' but each could be taken separately and in any order.[65] This new emphasis on the 'practical' encouraged the Association, late in 1895, to begin to try to link the work of the summer schools with preparation for the revised examinations. Some progress was made in this direction with the 1896, four-day, school. At a voluntary examination held at the end of the week, prizes of three, two and one guinea were awarded, to those judged the best three of the eleven sitting. As E. A. Savage was an unsuccessful entrant, being placed 6th, and as a visit had been paid to the pioneer open access library at Clerkenwell, it was probably this gathering to which he subsequently referred:*

One day in the mid-nineties I called at the Clerkenwell Library and asked to look around. With a few jeering students I had seen it before, but this second visit proved to be my first approach to friendship with Duff Brown.[66]

The 1897 Summer School was the last of what had proved to be a successful London experiment. Lecturers of the calibre of Cyril Davenport, C. T. Jacobi and Richard Garnett had

* In fairness to the memory of a great librarian it must be recorded that Savage won the second prize at the 1897 School. There was some controversy over the prizes on this occasion as the committee required winners to agree to sit the unpopular formal examinations within two years. They had subsequently to withdraw this stipulation as it had not been previously announced!

lectured, the organised visits had been instructive and useful, the committee had welcomed and entertained the students, had tried hard to make economically priced accommodation easily available and had encouraged the public libraries of Greater London to stock the recommended textbooks.* After this School the committee at the request of the council, began to consider arranging regular winter classes. Following unsuccessful approaches to the then quite new London County Council and London School of Economics, it was decided that, at least for the time being, it would be better to go it alone.[68]

The first LAUK classes were inaugurated at a well-attended meeting of prominent librarians and other notables at the Museum of Practical Geology in Jermyn Street on 25 February 1898, when a commencement address was delivered by the Bishop of London, Mandell Creighton. The address, which still merits careful reading, may be viewed as the reaction of one highly intelligent man to the librarian's world and the librarian's problems. It was full of sound advice and ended with an always well-merited tribute to the life and work of Richard Garnett.[69] The subsequent classes, held at Hanover Square, the St Bride Institute and the Central School of Arts and Crafts, were arranged by the Association's Education Committee, as the old and now inappropriate title of Summer Schools Committee had been changed at the beginning of the year. John MacFarlane gave ten lectures on cataloguing, Douglas Cockerell on bookbinding, Henry Guppy seven on elementary bibliography and John Southward ten on historical printing. A promising beginning at least had been made.

———

The members of the Publications Committee, which met for the first time on 6 October 1894, included Briscoe, Brown, Dent, Garnett, Mason, Tedder and MacAlister. Tedder became chairman and Mason honorary secretary. They began by proposing a new edition of the *Year Book*, for 1895, to contain, like its predecessors, current information, current list of

* But some librarians are never satisfied. Goss, of Society of Public Librarians fame, complained that the Summer Schools Committee had addressed circulars direct to the Chairmen of Library Commissioners instead of to the Librarians; and stated that, as he had been thus ignored, he would not permit his assistants to attend the School![67]

members (then 474 individual members and libraries plus
twenty-four honorary members), examination syllabus with
specimen questions and, as a new feature, a list of public
libraries in the United Kingdom, to be compiled by Brown.
The first *Year Book* had appeared in 1891 but it was not a regular
annual. The Committee was also responsible, a little later, for
the Library Bureau taking over, from Simpkins, the sale of the
Association's publications.[70]

The appointment of the Publications committee meant,
however, that sooner or later, and probably sooner, the question
of the 'organ', *The Library*, would be examined. Some members
of the LAUK felt, and with some justice, that under MacAlister's
very personal editorship, insufficient space was being devoted to
practical librarianship and official news and too much to
bibliography. There was also the corollary that too much of the
practical librarianship was being supplied by Brown, if largely
anonymously, although this criticism was always likely to be
voiced mostly by members of the Society of Public Librarians.[71]
But above all else – and there could be no possible doubt about
this – *The Library* was not appearing punctually. So, in January
1895, the Committee took a bold step *backwards* and resolved to
recommend the Council:

That the Association take steps to publish its own Journal and
further that this Committee are of opinion that such a Journal should
take the form of Monthly Notes.

The subject dragged on in desultory fashion. Occasional notes of
supporting criticism were heard at Council and Annual
Meetings: many more librarians felt that the limit had been
reached when no issues appeared between May and November
1897. It was true that MacAlister's health had deteriorated and
the missing numbers were later published in one issue.
Nevertheless, at a meeting of the Council on 18 May 1898,
Herbert Jones (1852–1928), Librarian of Kensington public
library, moved:

That in the opinion of this Council, on the conclusion of the present
arrangement as to *The Library*, any Official Journal of the Library

Association should be henceforth the property of the Association
alone, and under the control of the Council.

The whole subject of the Association's publications was then
referred, not to the Publications Committee, but to a new Special
Committee on Publications, of which the members were Welch,
Mason, Brown, Frank Pacy (1862–1928) – Librarian then of the
public library nearest to MacAlister's own office, St George's,
Hanover Square – Quinn, Doubleday, Jones, Frank Campbell
(1863–1906) of the British Museum, Tedder and MacAlister.

The new committee, with Tedder, whose Presidential year it
was, as chairman and Frank Campbell – who had voiced some of
the criticism of *The Library* already heard – as honorary secretary,
held four meetings between May and August 1898. The average
attendance of four was decidedly unpromising and the task
proved an uphill one as MacAlister chose to regard the
committee's activities as a continuation of Campbell's own
criticisms and resigned at its first meeting. But investigations
were made and numerous printing estimates – generally regarded
as too high – were obtained, and others called for. The
committee's report went to the Council at the beginning of
August 1898, and on to the membership at the 'three towns
Conference' (ie Southport, Preston and Wigan) at the end of the
same month. It recommended, *inter alia*, a journal of regular
publication, to be called *The Library Association Record,* which
was to be the official organ and property of the Association and
under the control of the Council. Tribute was tactfully paid to
MacAlister and *The Library*:

The arduous nature of the work is not generally realised by those who
have not had the actual experience.

The members assembled at the Annual Meeting of 1898 were,
however, more favourably disposed toward continuing the
now well established association with *The Library*. They were
perhaps not uninfluenced by the fact that MacAlister was
resigning the Honorary Secretaryship now that the Charter had
been granted – he had long since advised the Council of his
intention so to do – and were reluctant to run the risk of losing

completely the services of a man to whom the Association owed
so much; MacAlister was unanimously elected an Honorary
Fellow at the same meeting. So the Annual Meeting asked the
Council to 'endeavour to come to an arrangement with Mr
MacAlister for the transfer by him to the Association of the
copyright of *The Library*'.[72] MacAlister had previously stated his
willingness to transfer the copyright to a syndicate of 'leading
members' and now suggested an alternative:

i   That he should continue as Editor-in-Chief for two years
     certain (subsequently reduced to one year)
ii   That existing arrangements for certain main contributions
     should continue and that fees paid which 'average from five
     to six guineas per month should continue'
iii That, instead of payment, MacAlister himself should receive
     fifty free copies of the magazine.

There was inevitable quibbling over details but agreement
seemed possible until it was discovered, probably by Herbert
Jones, that there was outstanding:

a heavy liability for past printing and other expenses, which will
seriously cripple its finances, to the extent of a financial deficit at the
close of the year of over £200.[73]

So MacAlister, who was again threatening to resign and this
time from the Association, was 'offered the sum of £50 for the
unconditional sale of the copyright in the title of *The Library*'.
The Council decided to rub salt into the open wound by
amending the offer to read 'to be paid as soon as the Funds of
the Association allow'. MacAlister refused to accept the offer
and the Council, whose Special Committee had been, wisely,
conducting parallel enquiries with printers, advertising agents
and with Mr Henry Guppy, of Sion College Library, as possible
editor – 'helped' by a new advisory committee – bravely decided
to launch *The Library Association Record*.

The short history of the LAUK's museum does not provide one of
its greater success stories. Inspired by his successful planning of
an exhibition of library appliances, to be mounted at the Annual

Meeting at Nottingham in September 1891, James Duff Brown, earlier that month, offered to 'form and catalogue a permanent collection of appliances',[74] at his Clerkenwell Library. The offer was accepted and the collection stayed there until 1894 when it was moved to Chivers' Library Bureau. The situation then was as described in the *Year Book* for 1895:

The object of the Museum is to furnish a ready means of affording information in every detail of library management, and should be helpful to librarians, architects, library committees or anyone interested in the subject. Plans of library buildings, catalogues, books of record, charging systems, indicators, shelving arrangements, binding, forms, stationery etc, are shown in their different kinds. . . . A large contribution of American library appliances, forms and catalogues has been sent by the American Library Association. . . . The Museum is open from 10 to 5 except on Saturday, when it closes at 1, and during these hours the Honorary Curator, Miss M. S. R. James will gladly show the museum to visitors. Any further information concerning the Museum may be obtained from the Honorary Secretary of the Museum Committee, Mr J. D. Brown, Public Library, Clerkenwell, London, EC.[75]

But in January 1896, the Museum Committee felt bound to advise the Council:

That in view of the little use that has been made of the Museum and the difficulty experienced in securing models of apparatus, etc, the Council be recommended to close it as from December 31st 1895 and that the plans and forms be kept at 20 Hanover Square in future and the models etc stored for the present.[76]

This chapter would be incomplete were reference not made to the Second International Library Conference held in the Council Chamber of the City of London from 13 to 16 July 1897, the year of Queen Victoria's Diamond Jubilee. Although not officially part of the Association's own activities, the initiative was taken by the Council and the organising committee consisted of officers, councillors, and leading members. Sir John Lubbock served as President, MacAlister as Honorary Secretary-General and Tedder as Honorary Treasurer, while Garnett,

Welch, Jones and Tedder acted as Chairmen, and Brown,
Borrajo, Mason and Knapman as Honorary Secretaries of the
Conference committees. 641 delegates attended the conference,
one-third of them members of the Association. Overseas
representatives came from twenty-one foreign and empire
countries. Thirteen Governments were officially represented
and there were delegates from more than fifty libraries in the
United States.

The 1897 Conference papers provided little that was new on
United Kingdom affairs and the brief domestic controversies on
the already evergreen fiction question and the newer subject of
open access in municipal libraries were perhaps regrettable in
the *international* context assumed. But much useful information
on their own services was provided by some of the overseas
delegates. The presence of so many American representatives,
including Melvil Dewey, meant, inevitably, that library school
training and informal apprenticeship systems for the training of
assistants should be compared and contrasted. Charles Welch
was certainly ahead of his own Association when he said:

An ideal system would be to combine these three methods of
education, – to place a well-educated lad as an assistant in the library
at the age of say, 15, giving him at the same time facilities for keeping
up his education; after four years in the library to send him to the
university for his degree, with which might well be combined the
training of the library school. After taking his degree, should the
individual be so fortunate as to get a couple of years experience of the
book trade, he would probably be fitted as far as training could fit
him, for the post of assistant librarian, with a good chance of a
distinguished career.[77]

There was also generous international applause for the
editor-in-chief and publisher of the then new *Dictionary of
National Biography*, both of whom gracefully acknowledged the
plaudits of the members.

The Second International Conference seems, in retrospect, to
have been a less serious and less earnest affair than its predecessor
of twenty years earlier. But its brilliant social success was never
in doubt. The City Corporation, Sion College and Lady Lubbock

gave receptions; the Marchioness of Bute gave a garden party; the Duke of Wellington invited delegates to Apsley House and the Duke of Westminster to Grosvenor House. Five London Clubs made delegates honorary members and the Conference dinner was at the Hotel Cecil. The high point was assuredly reached when Sir Henry Irving, undoubtedly on MacAlister's* instigation, invited the delighted delegates to a special performance of *The Merchant of Venice* at the Lyceum Theatre when he himself played Shylock and Ellen Terry Portia.[78]

* Irving and Wilson Barrett had nominated MacAlister for membership of the Savage Club in 1887.[79]

References

1. *NQ*, 5th series, 8, p 300.
2. *Transactions, 1883.* 1886, p 1.
3. *Transactions, 1878.* 1879, p 6.
4. *Transactions, 1879.* 1880, pp 32–3.
5. *LAMC* 878.
6. *MN*, 1; pp 86–7.
7. R. Garnett, *Essays in librarianship and bibliography.* 1899, p 324.
8. J. W. Burgon, *Lives of twelve good men.* 1891 (1888), pp 307–320.
9. *LJ*, 3, p 153.
10. *See*, for example, letter from Tedder to Nicholson, 22 December 1897. Bodley mss Misc 67/387.
11. *Ibid* 67/339.
12. H. Ward, *History of the Athenaeum.* P.P. 1926, pp 83–8, 94, 110.
13. H. Wyndham, 'Memories of Henry R. Tedder', *LR*, 15, pp 544–5. *See also* the important LA thesis, *Henry Richard Tedder*, by R. J. Busby, 1974, and particularly Ch 4.
14. London, George Allen, 1899.
15. Published at The Bodley Head. The attractive 'Weekend library' reprint of 1927 includes the introduction by T. E. Lawrence.
16. Carolyn Heilbron gives an episodic account of his life, work and character in her *The Garnett family.* 1961.
17. Williamson, *Poole*, p 111.
18. *Athenaeum*, 3.11.1877, p 567.
19. *LAMC* 878; 18.3.1881.
20. *MFLC* 877.
21. *MN*, 4, p 13.
22. *Ibid*, pp 150–3.
23. *Ibid*, p 40.
24. *LAMC* 878; 12.11.1880.
25. H. R. Tedder, Obituary of Thomas in *L*, 4, pp 73–9.
26. Munford, *Edwards*, p 200.
27. *LC*, 1, p 80.
28. *MN*, 1, p 77.
29. *LAMC* 878, pp 205–6.
30. *LC*, 4, pp 113–6.
31. 'The Education of a librarian', *LR*, 15, pp 381–7.
32. Munford, *Penny rate*, p 33.
33. *LC*, 5, pp 11–16.
34. E. A. Savage, *A Librarian's memories.* 1952, p 169.
35. *Essays in librarianship and bibliography*, p 190.
36. *L*, 2, p 385.
37. *Report of the 15th Annual Meeting of the LA.* 1893, p 42.
38. *LAMC* 881; 3.2.1882.
39. Approved by Council, 10.12.1888.
40. *L*, 3, p 107.
41. J. D. Wilson, 'A. W. Pollard', *Proceedings of the British Academy*, 31.
42. W. A. Munford, *James Duff Brown.* 1968, p 19.
43. *L*, 3, p 449.
44. *LC* 5, p 140.
45. Minutes, 17.3.1890.

46. *LAMC* 881 and 892.
47. Savage *op cit*, p 125.
48. *L*, 6, p 368.
49. Munford, *Brown*, p 62.
50. *L*, 7, p 120.
51. J. D. Brown, "Library progress", *L*. (New series), 1, pp 5–11.
52. Munford, *Brown*, p 32.
53. *Public libraries*, 3rd ed. 1890, p xii.
54. *DNB*, 1912–1921.
55. *L*, 2. *p* 396
56. Published London, A. Smith, 1895, 5 pp.
57. Munford, *Brown*, pp 37–8, 41–4.
58. Bodley, Eng Misc 67/345.
59. First subscription list in *L*, 7, p 167.
60. *Ibid*, p 335.
61. *L*, 10, p 131.
62. *LAM* 877, p 147.
63. *L*, 4, pp 313–8.
64. *Ibid*, pp 319–23.

65. J. Minto, *History of the public library movement in Great Britain and Ireland.* 1932, pp 211–12.
66. Savage *op cit*, p 167.
67. *L*, 9, p 363.
68. *LAC* 896; 13.1.1898, 11.2.1898.
69. *L*, 10, pp 101–111, 129–32.
70. *L*, 5, pp 170–1.
71. Munford, *Brown*, pp 48–9.
72. *LAM* 877, p 141.
73. Second report of the Special Committee on publications, 17.11.1898. (Minute book of Publications committee.)
74. 10.9.1891.
75. *YB* (1895), p 73.
76. Munford, *Brown*, pp 21–2.
77. *Transactions and proceedings of the Second International Conference. . . , 1897.* 1898, p 32.
78. *Ibid*, p 249.
79. *LW*, 1, p 197.

Chapter Four

1898-1914

The history of the LA between 1898 and 1914 is essentially the story of a well-managed but impecunious association striving, above all else, to create better *municipal* libraries. It was impecunious because most municipal libraries were financially hamstrung by the penny rate limit. Although by no means all chief librarians were ill-paid, by the standards of the period, most members of their staffs were well acquainted with poverty. Certainly few of these assistants were members of the Association but then neither were all municipal libraries nor their chief librarians. This situation was seriously anomalous since, at the end as at the beginning of the present period, the Association had to depend on the annual subscriptions of its members for virtually the whole of its income. The legacy of £2000 from Richard Copley Christie, Chancellor of the Diocese of Manchester, who had been President in 1889, was wholly exceptional; it was received in 1911.[1]

Strive as the enthusiasts might, the membership of 582 in 1898 had only risen to 678 in 1913 and the subscription income from £504 to £676. Seen from a different angle, development between 1898 and 1914 is the story of the inevitable conflict between the always prudent manager of the Association's always inadequate financial resources – H. R. Tedder, the Honorary Treasurer and Chairman of the Council – and the younger men who were in fact striving to release librarianship and the LA from what appeared to be many fetters. Both parties to the conflict played important, indeed indispensable, rôles, and both were, ironically enough, to a considerable extent successful. The situation was complicated over the whole period by the 'stormy petrel' activities of MacAlister. On many occasions and over a wide range of subjects he manifested a love/hate relationship with the Council and with the Association. He even resigned his Honorary Fellowship in 1908 and refused to reconsider his decision.[2]

The number of new libraries opened to readers in the United Kingdom of Great Britain and Ireland between 1877 and 1899 had been quite unprecedentedly large. They were, however, nearly all of one type – the municipally rate-supported. Outstanding new examples of other types were rare. In Dublin the National Library of Ireland and in Liverpool the library of the university college began their important lives. In London outstanding new non-municipal ones were those of two City of London Institutes, of the South Kensington Museums, of a handful of Clubs and, of course, of MacAlister's own employer, the Royal Medical and Chirurgical Society. The only other example of outstanding importance and this, admittedly, of such significance that it seemed to dwarf all the others, was the John Rylands. Its neo-Gothic building – never to appeal to all tastes – was, at the beginning of 1899, nearing completion in Deansgate, Manchester, ready for the formal opening in October.[3] Nevertheless, one Rylands, however impressive its building and however magnificent its initial collections of books and manuscripts, hardly heralded a new library situation. Among municipal authorities, on the other hand, changing opinions and some benefaction had substantially improved public library provision – so far as mere numbers of libraries were concerned – and all despite the financial restrictions imposed by the penny rate limit. And the revolutionary changes caused by Andrew Carnegie's grants for municipal libraries came between 1900 and the end of the present period.

The *British library year book* for 1900–1901 gives details of 302 municipal library systems in Great Britain and Ireland; no fewer than 233 of them had opened since 1877.[4] The new municipal impact was, in fact, even more marked than appears

statistically as many of the new libraries had displaced, and many
more were soon to displace, those provided earlier by Mechanics'
Institutes and other local voluntary associations. There was also
a distinct change of emphasis. Some of the most influential
municipal librarians of the period, notably James Duff Brown,
were keenly interested in the promising new idea of the library
as a bibliographical workshop rather than as a museum;
reference has already been made to this. This was controversial,
to be sure, but nothing like as controversial as the drive for
safeguarded open access, also spearheaded by Brown.[5]

The membership of the newly chartered LA at the beginning of
1899 reflected these changes only very imperfectly. Its *Year Book*
for 1899 showed that, of its 497 personal members, no more than
165 were employed by or represented municipal libraries. Yet,
of the 136 libraries in institutional membership, 113 were
municipal. The changes were mirrored more faithfully in the
membership of the council. Eight of the twelve London
councillors and seventeen of the country ones now represented
municipal libraries. And MacAlister's successor as Honorary
Secretary, Frank Pacy, was a London municipal librarian.

The LA in 1899 might seem poised for change. Political change
was in the air. Internationally the Concert of European Powers
appeared in danger of dissolution. British statesmen were
complaining that too many of their near-neighbours – French
ones in particular – seemed to think that British imperial toes
could now be trodden on with impunity. The same British
statesmen, however, had made it impossible for other European
powers to interfere effectively on the Spanish side during that
decaying empire's very recent and disastrous war with the
United States of America. A new Anglo-American relationship
was assuredly possible.

There were signs in 1899 of a long overdue change in the
approach of British national and local authorities to the
pressing social problems of the day. There were many more
signs of change in the literary scene. The new publications of
1898 had included works as different as Bernard Shaw's *Plays,
pleasant and unpleasant*; H. G. Wells' *War of the worlds*; Oscar

Wilde's *Ballad of Reading Gaol*; F. W. Maitland's *Township and borough*; and – it must never be overlooked here because several generations of young librarians had to pay it specially close attention during their professional studies – George Saintsbury's *Short history of English literature*. Despite their individual differences, these books all presented aspects of a new critical approach.

In the editorial of the first number of the LA's new official journal, the *Library Association Record*, the editor, Henry Guppy, of Sion College Library – whose 'manner headmasterly, even governessy, his belief that whatever he was he was by God's grace', [6] irked one rising young librarian, Ernest Savage – this same Henry Guppy explained his aims:

> Our principal design is to furnish members ... more particularly the country members with the full and punctual information respecting the Association's proceedings which they have a right to expect ... But there is another and more ambitious design which we have in view. It is the establishment of a convenient medium of communication, not only between members of the LA, but between librarians in all parts of the English speaking world ... The "Record" will deal with all that concerns the library and bibliographical interests, and when we speak of bibliographical interests we use the term "bibliography" in its broadest sense, as the science of books considered under all aspects. [7]

But whereas *The Library*, for virtually the whole of its life, had been the only British professional journal of significance, the new *Library Association Record* faced rivals. To begin with, MacAlister was still in the editorial chair. As he had written in the last number of the official-organ *Library*:

> I thought I had done my share of work for the library cause and that when I retired from the Honorary Secretaryship of the LA I might also finish the *Library* but there was a volley of appeals that I should not let the *Library* die ... weakly, perhaps, I have agreed. .... I propose to try a new experiment in periodical publication. The new *Library* will be a *Quarterly*, and I think enough *good* stuff can be got together to make a respectable number every 3 months, *but if I have not got it, I'll wait until I have*. .... It may be that more than 3 months may sometimes come between number and number, but each subscriber will get 4 full

numbers complete with title and elaborate index . . . *The Library* in its new form will have 3 distinct sides – Practical Librarianship in its modern and best sense, Bibliography – both archaic and modern, and Literature, in the shape of careful notices of books suitable for libraries.[8]

In the first number of his New Series he went further and stated that he intended it:

to become even more catholic, and will endeavour to justify its name in a new and wider sense, and as a good special library should do, will contain everything about one thing, and will exclude nothing likely to be of use or interest to its readers . . . As regards its special efforts, bibliography and library work, every effort will be made to hold the scales evenly between matters of modern and of antiquarian import.[9]

The Library Redivivus, as MacAlister called it (annual subscription 10*s*) was, however, not the only rival of the *LAR*. The old *Library*'s most important and frequent municipal contributor had decided that the new *LAR* was unlikely to offer sufficient scope for his always active pen. James Duff Brown brought out the first number of a new sixpenny monthly, *The Library World*, in July 1898, informing *his* readers that:

while not neglecting such matters as bibliography, printing and binding it will be primarily a practical magazine, devoted to the urgent needs of the present, and its chief endeavour will be to promote increased efficiency in every department of Library work, and to foster more intimate and useful relations between Libraries and the Public. . . .[10]

In addition, the Library Assistants' Association, founded in 1895 – of which more later – had published in January 1898, the first number of *The Library Assistant*, aimed specifically to report its association's activities but also, and more generally, 'to keep a record of the doings of librarians and assistants and of facts of interest regarding libraries and librarianship'. Potential competition was not limited to periodicals. The LA had as yet only one Branch, the North Western, founded in Manchester in 1896 and centred on it:

designed to consist of all those members of the LA who reside in Lancashire or Cheshire, together with such other members as signify their wish to be included. . . .[11]

It had already more than 100 members and had shown its own special interest in the education of its younger members by arranging 'Summer Schools for the Northern Counties' in 1897 and 1898.[12] But its area was identical with that of 'The Librarians of the Mersey District', centred by contrast, on Liverpool, which had acquired forty members since its foundation in 1887 and charged them annual subscriptions of only 2*s*.[13] The North Midland Library Association, founded earlier, in 1890, centred on Nottingham; its sixty members lived and worked in Nottinghamshire, Derbyshire, Leicestershire, Northamptonshire and Lincolnshire.[14] The Birmingham and District Association had begun its activities in 1895. Both had similarly low subscriptions.[15]

The independent associations and the North Western Branch were admittedly provincial, seeking to provide scope for meetings and discussions comparable with those organised, almost wholly in London, by the LA itself; the Society of Public Librarians was also London-based. By contrast the Library Assistants' Association while, understandably, most active initially in London, had full national potential. The LA up to that date had attracted few members of library staffs other than chiefs and, prior to the London Summer Schools of the 1890s, had seemingly done little for assistants save talk about them. But the Summer Schools brought some of the most far-seeing and ambitious of those assistants together. On 3 July 1895 some thirty of them attended a meeting at the Library Bureau – convened by W. W. Fortune, then of Lewisham Public Library, but soon to join the Library Supply Company, later Libraco Ltd – and formed the LAA. MacAlister was very friendly and James Duff Brown drafted a constitution for them, providing, *inter alia*, for an annual subscription of 2*s* 6*d* for junior members and 5*s* for seniors; the constitution was adopted in July 1895.[16] The LAA's membership grew slowly but it soon began to attract provincial as well as London members and consequently the request for a regular journal was soon voiced.[17]

The LA Council was to be elected in future in accordance with precisely detailed rules and procedures adopted following protest and controversy engendered by the Society of Public Librarians and its peppery Honorary Secretary, C. W. F. Goss; serious electoral irregularities had been alleged. There had been an unpleasant Special General Meeting in February 1898 (fifty-two members present) which repudiated:

the circular issued by Mr Goss, holds that his charges against the Council are deserving of condemnation, and hereby calls on him to withdraw and apologise for the same.[18]

As, however, it would be many years before the Association considered itself able, financially, to pay the rail fares of its country members attending meetings, it was only Londoners who attended regularly. This meant, of course, that members such as Brown, Inkster, Jones, Quinn, Doubleday and Wyndham Hulme (1859–1954), Librarian of the Patent Office, were able to bring much more influence to bear than, say, Ogle, E. R. Norris Mathews (1851–1919), Librarian of Bristol from 1893 to 1919; Alfred Capel Shaw (1847–1918), Librarian of Birmingham from 1898 to 1912; and John Ballinger (1860–1932), Librarian of Cardiff from 1884 to 1909 when he became the first National Librarian of Wales.
Brown's new *Library World* might well complain:

a representative Council can never be obtained which consists of such a large proportion of non attending members.

but it could offer no solution other than the election of more members from libraries on the fringe areas of metropolitan London.[19] The Council meeting normally held during the annual conference week was the only representative meeting of the LA year. Individual councillors and other members tried hard to persuade the Council to pay the return rail fares of country councillors to at least some meetings but limited experiments during 1912 and 1913 were not to be continued during the present period.

The Council was led by its new Honorary Secretary, Frank Pacy, and by its seemingly already evergreen founder member and

73

Honorary Treasurer, H. R. Tedder. At its meeting in May 1898, an attempt had been made to persuade Tedder to succeed MacAlister as Honorary Secretary but he had declined and, following his Presidential year, resumed the Honorary Treasurership. As the Council also began its regular practice of electing him to the Chair each year,[20] his cautious influence was greater than that of any other single member. Frank Pacy (1862–1928) had left Wigan Grammar School at the age of sixteen and, following an exacting apprenticeship in the local Public Library, had become Librarian of Richmond, Surrey, in 1884. In 1891 he had moved to the well-endowed Westminster parish of St George, Hanover Square and, following the creation of the Metropolitan boroughs, was to be appointed the first City Librarian of Westminster in 1905. He was an energetic and assured administrator and an effective speaker whose debonair appearance and exceptional *savoir faire* made him a most acceptable successor to MacAlister.[21] He was to resign, however, in 1901 when, following the refusal of the office by Wyndham Hulme and its tenure for two months only by Basil Soulsby (1864–1933) of the British Museum, Inkster took over. He was to be succeeded, temporarily in 1904 and permanently in 1905, by L. S. Jast (1868–1944) whose period of office was to span the rest of the present period.

To assert that during his period of office as Honorary Secretary, Jast *was* the LA – this would be to exaggerate. His influence was, nevertheless, great and pervasive. He had been born Louis Stanley Jastrzebski, the third son of a Polish refugee settled, as a successful shopkeeper, in Halifax, with his English wife. After initial training in the Halifax Public Library, he had become Librarian of Peterborough in 1892 and remained there until 1898 during which time he abbreviated his surname to the more readily pronounceable Jast; in 1898 he was appointed Chief Librarian of Croydon. His already established friendship with James Duff Brown then matured rapidly, encouraged professionally by jointly held views on the need for modern public library methods including, in particular, open access administration and its natural corollary, close classification; he was also Brown's chief assistant with *The Library World* until appointed the LA's Honorary Secretary. The personal religious beliefs of librarians may be regarded as beyond the scope of the present history; Jast's lifelong membership of the Theosophical Society is mentioned here only because it was so unusual. Brown told him once that he was 'an odd mixture of a canny Yorkshireman and an Eastern dreamer' and the description was always apt.[22]

The LA at the beginning of 1899 had a Charter and it had an emblem, designed for it, at MacAlister's instigation, by the famous artist Alma Tadema.[23] Its other achievements had been limited. Perhaps its most ambitious attempt to improve library administration had been MacAlister's *Manual*. But the pamphlets deriving from that project were already being overshadowed by the independent and unofficial 'Library Series', published by George Allen and edited by Richard Garnett. Its volumes included, in addition to Garnett's own forthcoming *Essays in librarianship and bibliography* (1899) and Henry Wheatley's pioneer *Prices of books* (1898), Ogle's *The Free Library: its history and present condition* (1897); John Macfarlane's *Library administration* (1898), which, despite its excessive emphasis on British Museum practice and on classification and cataloguing, was a most useful addition to the then scanty literature, and F. J. Burgoyne's *Library construction: architecture, fittings and furniture* (1897), a careful study of essential considerations in room arrangement, flooring, lighting, heating, shelving, furniture and appliances.

When MacAlister had been Honorary Secretary, it had been taken for granted that both offices and place for meetings would be at 20 Hanover Square. His resignation in 1898 created accommodation problems which were not easy to solve, granted the LA's limited financial resources. The majority of Council, committee and monthly meetings continued, in fact, to be held at 20 Hanover Square until the end of 1910, immediately prior to MacAlister's own Society moving to new headquarters. During 1905–6, however, there was a period when meetings, following agreement by exchange of letters providing for the use of a hall for monthly meetings and use of committee rooms as required, were held at the London School of Economics. There was even one memorable occasion when McKillop, the School's secretary, complained to Jast about the 'ungentlemanly' behaviour of some librarians who, during the course of a monthly meeting, were alleged to have adjourned to a nearby public house and subsequently returned, in more enthusiastic mood than before. His complaint drew a sharp reply from the Association's Honorary Secretary and then mutual invitations to lunch. The Council's decision to terminate the arrangements with the School at the end of 1906 appears, however, to have been due entirely to difficulties in arranging times for meetings which also suited the School.[24] The member who complained about fellow librarians smoking at monthly meetings – to be told by the Council that this was a matter for chairmen of meetings – might assuredly have made *his* complaint, irrespective of venue.[25]

Office accommodation created different problems. Rooms were rented from Mrs Kate Reilly at her secretarial offices at 24 Whitcomb Street, Pall Mall, from 1899 onwards and, from November 1901, she also became the LA's part-time assistant secretary for an all-inclusive annual payment of £100. The arrangement continued, to the satisfaction of both parties, subject to an increase to £126 per annum as from 1907,[26] until September 1910 when Mrs Reilly regretfully resigned on account of her ill-health and the Association moved out.[27] The storage of some of the LA's accumulating property caused problems during the Whitcomb Street period. In 1901 MacAlister gave notice that the Association's museum and stock of publications would have to be moved from 20 Hanover Square 'as the space occupied is urgently required.[28] Three years later he asked for a check to be made on any property still left there as 'any property not claimed will be disposed of at the discretion of the [ie his] Society'.[29]

In 1910 the National Association of Local Government Officers was also seeking office space; arrangements were made for the two Associations to share accommodation at 24 Bloomsbury Square. Nalgo became the sub-tenant, paying one half of the rental of £130 per annum inclusive, and one half of the upkeep charges, and the LA paid Nalgo £100 per annum, to include the services of a typist at 30s weekly and 'the general supervisory services of their secretary, Mr Hill'[30] The arrangement proved fairly satisfactory, it being found possible to make joint purchases of furniture and an addressing machine[31] but it was difficult to ensure that staff were always available when required for LA purposes. The Association eventually appointed its own full-time clerk at £80 per annum.[32] Both Associations moved to Caxton Hall in mid-1913. The LA rented a room there, with basement storage, for £76 per annum and arranged for 'the occasional use of a large room for Council and Committee meetings'.[33] Nalgo and the LA affiliated in 1913 and the LA appointed Doubleday and Jones its representatives:

to participate in the discussion of any schemes affecting municipal librarians which may be promoted by that body [ie Nalgo.].[34]

The close cooperation with Nalgo provides apt reminder that, until comparatively recently – with good reason – and perhaps even still – with little reason – the LA has had the reputation of being the Public Library Association. During the present period the establishment of more and more municipal libraries, substantially encouraged by Carnegie grants,[35] provided favourable background. Their librarians encouraged the trend; the Council was dominated by their colleagues; and the Honorary Secretaries who followed MacAlister were public librarians. MacAlister who, more than any other man, had built up the status of the Honorary Secretary as Leader of the Council, did not fail to notice it:

The extent to which the workers in libraries of a single class, those under municipal control, predominate in the LA, greatly diminishes its helpfulness in regard to the problems which confront librarians in colleges and universities and all those who deal mainly with professional readers or with students engaged in research work or post graduate studies.[36]

There was another serious disadvantage. MacAlister's successor, Jast, grew to regret the gradual disappearance of the

non-professional element. . . . I see how much we are suffering at this moment from the lack of men of authority and position who are willing to take an active part in our work.[37]

The Councils of the early 20th century felt that there were many ways in which public libraries could be improved and enabled to do better and more effective work. But, first and foremost, since adequate service depended upon adequate financing, the major improvement sought was necessarily the abolition of the penny rate limit. It was true that a relatively small number of local library authorities had been able to raise or abolish their own limits through Local Acts. The LA fought hard and long to help the others. Its continued frustration was due mostly to its failure to obtain Government support; increasingly effective Party discipline made it more difficult for Private Members of Parliament to secure the passing of their own Bills without it. A Bill providing too for simplified adoption of the Acts – also by County Councils – and for the exemption of libraries from rates and taxes, was introduced into the Lords by Lord Windsor, on a second attempt, in 1899 and passed that House but failed to get a second reading in the Commons.[38]

From the beginning of the new century the Bill was in the hands of H. J. Tennant, MP (1865–1935), Liberal Member for Berwickshire until 1918[39] and brother-in-law of H. H. Asquith (later Lord Oxford and Asquith) who became Prime Minister in 1908. He introduced it as a Private Member's Bill in 1903, 1904, 1905, 1907 and 1908[40] but all to no avail. It is to be feared that librarians were frequently more convinced of the need for change than were many members of their own local authorities and, in any case, continued failure is discouraging. In its *Annual Report* for 1908

The Council regret that the members of the Association have not manifested greater interest and enthusiasm . . . unless greater pressure is brought to bear on their Members of Parliament by their constituents . . . it will be impossible to proceed further. . . .[41]

And this despite a Local Conference on the subject in 1906 and in Birmingham, the natural home of municipal enterprise![42] E. A. Savage has also claimed that Tedder and Alderman Abbott, then chairman of the LA's legislation committee, 'bungled' the Association's activities.[43] The classic definition of a camel may, of course, always be relevant.

The controversies between Lords and Commons over Lloyd George's Budget of 1909/1910 bedevilled a new attempt in 1910 to introduce the Bill again in the House of Lords. The question whether a Bill to authorise more Local Authorities to spend more public money was or was not, technically, a 'money' bill, became important. The low water mark of the Association's campaign was reached in April 1912 when:

The President (Sir John Dewar, Bt, MP) reported that as a result of an interview he had had at the House of Commons with Mr Abbott and Mr Jast, he had had a conversation with the Rt Hon John Burns, President of the Local Government Board, in regard to the Bill. Mr Burns's view was that there was not the slightest chance of the Government giving facilities for the consideration of a Libraries Bill during the present year. Mr Burns however, expressed himself in full sympathy with the proposal and stated that he would not lose sight of it; also that as he knows all the merits of the case a deputation to him was not necessary at present.[44]

The Council, nevertheless, pressed on in 1912, 1913 and 1914 with an amended draft, authorising, not the unconditional repeal of the rate limit but its increase to 2*d*: the Bill was not reached in the Commons. In its *Annual Report* for 1914 the Council reported on continued failure but also on signs of more interest among Members of Parliament including the Parliamentary Secretary of the Local Government Board, the Rt Hon J. H. Lewis.[45] The seed had in fact been sown at last: the plant would, however, not bear the fruit so eagerly sought until after World War One.

If the rate limit could not be raised, there were other ways in which the LA could seek to improve the library service and the public library 'image'. At a talk on booksellers' discounts by David Stott in 1892 the speaker had urged public libraries not to seek greater discounts than 25% on the purchase of new books, with an addition of 2½% should the order be larger than £100, and to patronise local book-sellers.[46] The Net Book Agreement, adopted gradually by British publishers at the turn of the century made impossible the granting of any discounts whatsoever.[47] W. E. Doubleday, Librarian of Hampstead Public Libraries, read a paper on the problem in March 1902, and successfully moved a resolution there requesting the Council to approach the Publishers' Association or to take other appropriate action with a view to discounts.[48] The Council unsuccessfully asked the Publishers to receive a deputation later in the year.[49] Four years later a similar request to the Associated Booksellers met with 'a decidedly hostile reply'.[50] The Council next convened a meeting of public library delegates early in 1907; a resolution from the meeting of 150 delegates, chaired by H. R. Tedder, urged the Publishers to grant special terms.[51] The Publishers' Association received a deputation during the following May and appeared sympathetic; they expressed themselves as unable to take any initiative because of the unconditional hostility of the Booksellers.[52] The LA having next publicised its intention of considering the establishment of a book buying agency for public libraries, a conference between its representatives and those of the Booksellers was held in January 1908 – to no avail.[53]

If new books could not be obtained at lower than published prices, there was much to be said for encouraging higher production standards for the net books. The Council set up a Book Production Committee in 1905[54] which, two years later, appointed sub-committees to consider paper, book sewing and publishers' binding, and printing. Ernest A. Savage (1877–1966), who had begun his career at Croydon Public Libraries, had later been Jast's deputy there, and after two years as Librarian of Bromley (Kent) Public Library, became Librarian of Wallasey in 1906, acted as first Honorary Secretary of the parent committee, being succeeded by A. J. Philip (1879–1955), Librarian of Gravesend Public Library. Wyndham Hulme and A. W. Pollard were among other members; non-librarian members included Douglas Cockerell, C. J. Davenport, C. T. Jacobi, and R. W. Sindall. Sub-committee reports were submitted in 1909[55] and in 1913 the Association published *The Library Association Book Production Committee: interim report*. This was a pamphlet of thirty-two pages, exceptionally well printed by the Chiswick Press and sold at 1s. The recommendations given in it were sound, and a request from the Cambridge University Press for a specification for the binding of their magnificent 11th edition (1910/11) of the *Encyclopaedia*

Britannica ensured that the Committee and its report were not uninfluential.[56] Wyndham Hulme and other members of a Sound Leather Committee had also been responsible for *Leather for libraries* published, however, not by the Association, but by the Library Supply Company in 1905.

Ever since librarianship began to become an organised profession, there has been a good case for seeking to help librarians with their book selection. Some of the Association's most ambitious and successful efforts in this field were made during the present period. The lists of 'Best books' of the year past which had been included in the *Library Association Record* from 1904 grew, in 1905, into a separately published *Class list of best books 1905-6*, compiled by a panel of librarian-contributors with, as general editor, H. V. Hopwood (1866-1920), then Wyndham Hulme's deputy at the Patent Office Library.[58] The *Class list* and its successors for 1906-7 and 1907-8 sold disappointingly at first[59] but soon became self-supporting.[60]

Hopwood resigned in 1909 and his annual Lists were discontinued. Various later proposals were considered and arrangements eventually made for 'Best books of the month' lists to be published in the *LAR* and for annual cumulations to be published by Nelson. The arrangement with this publisher had to be abandoned following the outbreak of World War One but the first monthly list appeared in the *LAR* for August/ September 1914.[61] Dr E. A. Baker (1869-1941), who had been Librarian of Woolwich Public Library, acted as general editor; his class editors included Bond for sociology, Tedder for archaeology, Doubleday for history, Prideaux for biography, and Herbert Jones for topography. There was an exceptionally distinguished list of other editors and it was pity indeed that such a promising new venture was launched at such an unhappy time when – as is now obvious – its full potential could not be realised. Had it not been for the outbreak of war other complications were possible. A. J. Philip threatened legal action against the Association on grounds that the lists 'trenched' on those appearing in the monthly *Librarian and Book World*, a library magazine which he had launched in 1910. Fovargue, the Association's Honorary Solicitor, advised the Council to

proceed with their project 'and await whatever action
Mr Philip might take'. [62] As Philip was then a member of the
Council the prospects were intriguing.

The Association – although by no means each of its individual
members – has consistently tried to avoid becoming involved in
book-suppression, much to its credit. One example, at least, of
attempts to encourage it to join the ranks of the censors during
the present period may be noted. In 1909 the Council received a
letter from the Rev Canon Rawnsley, asking it to appoint a
representative on a committee for the suppression of 'noxious
literature'. It was then resolved that the aspiring clerical
gentleman be informed 'that the Council do not consider that the
subject falls properly within the field of the Association's
work'. [63] The *constructive* activities of the National Home
Reading Union were, of course, a very different matter and the
LA became an honorary member of the Union in 1908. The
ground had been prepared by Frank Pacy a few years earlier
when he wrote:

The Union provides lists of books, encourages reading-circles, meets
and dispels incidental difficulties, and is both an educational and an
examining body. The cost of membership is small enough to be no
deterrent to anyone. . . . The coming of the National Home Reading
Union into a connected line with the Public Library would mark an
important advance in the educational usefulness of the latter
institution, and for that reason above others, librarians may be urged
to give their favourable consideration and active assistance to the
contemplated combined attack upon the evils of ignorant and
desultory reading. [65]

Those who have never considered desultory reading to be
necessarily evil may be reminded here that there have always
been librarians who have considered it a highly undesirable
habit in others!

Before the introduction of organised library inter-lending,
between the Wars, postage charges on books did not assume the
importance of later years. Nevertheless, the Association
cooperated during 1907 and 1908 with the Weights and

Measures Association and the British Science Guild to try to
secure reduced postage rates on the publications of societies;
they were unsuccessful.[66] There was a much stronger case for
reducing to a minimum the postage charges on the heavy
embossed volumes read by blind readers. The Association, again
unsuccessfully initially, asked the Post Master General in 1905 to
receive a deputation 'in favour of free postage of books sent to
or from lending libraries for the blind.'[67] Substantially reduced
rates were in fact granted in 1906 and as the national
organisations for the blind, notably the British and Foreign
Blind Association (later the Royal National Institute for the
Blind) and the Incorporated National Lending Library for the
Blind (since 1916 the National Library for the Blind) grew in
strength, so they became better able to argue their own cases.
But the Association continued to show special interest in library
service to blind readers, an interest almost certainly strengthened
by the growing friendship between Jast and the Librarian of the
Incorporated Library, Winifred Austin.[68] Between 1912 and the
outbreak of World War One the LA had a committee on literature
for the blind, with George Roebuck, Librarian of Walthamstow
Public Library and always a good friend to the blind, as
honorary secretary. Detailed information on facilities then
available *via* local public libraries were collected and published in
the *LAR* in 1912.[69] The Association also cooperated with a very
different organisation, the Illuminating Engineering Society,
during 1911. Such matters as direct and indirect lighting, and
the lighting of reading desks, shelves and gangways were jointly
discussed at several meetings; the reports are still of interest.[70]

The important subjects commented on in preceding paragraphs
were all, in some senses, matters of detail for the Association of
the period. Much more important, so it seemed, was the constant
need to keep before library authorities and the general public the
case for good public libraries. The sixpenny pamphlet *The
Establishment of public libraries: some notes for the guidance of library
committees*, published in January 1909, was the work of a special
committee, chaired by Wyndham Hulme, which had successfully
worked over a first draft prepared by James Duff Brown. The
most important advice included was unquestionably the
following:

Shortly after the appointment of the committee, and before any expenditure for library purposes has been sanctioned, the office of librarian should be filled, or an experienced librarian appointed as adviser.[71]

Once a public library service had been envisaged, much was possible if the best buildings and types of service were appropriately publicised. Brown was also one pioneer of the public lecture illustrated with lantern slides; he presented his slides to the Association and they became the nucleus of a useful collection used in particular by Jast, as for example, at a successful public lecture given by him during the Brighton Conference in 1908.[72] By 1913 the fast developing potentialities of the cinema film were also being envisaged, certainly by Walter Briscoe, of Nottingham Public Library.[73] It was also necessary, however, – then as now – for unfavourable press comment to be countered. The 35th *Annual Report* of the Council, for 1912, included the following:

The unfair and often inaccurate nature of certain comments and articles that appear in the Press about Public Libraries has repeatedly occupied the attention of the Council . . . they have appointed a small Committee who will deal with any case on which they think action may be desirable . . . communication in the first instance with Mr Herbert Jones, Chief Librarian of Kensington. . . .[74]

Bearing in mind, too, the importance of imbuing the rising generation with the library idea, the Association welcomed and took the initiative in arranging for joint discussions with the State and Local Education Authorities between 1903 and 1905. The report of the Committee on Public Education and Public Libraries was submitted to the Annual Meeting at Cambridge in August 1905 by its Chairman, H. R. Tedder. Its summarised recommendations were:

i   In order that children from an early age may become accustomed to the use of a collection of books, it is desirable **a** that special libraries for children should be established in all public libraries, and **b** that collections of books should be formed in all elementary and secondary schools

THE LONDON INSTITUTION, FOUNDED BY SUBSCRIPTION A.D. 1805,
FOR THE ADVANCEMENT OF LITERATURE AND THE DIFFUSION OF USEFUL AND POLITE KNOWLEDGE
in the Old Jury, removed to afterwards King's Arms Yard, Coleman Street, and finally settled in Moorfields, where it was opened on the 3rd of April 1819. The first Stone of this
erected after a design by William Brooks, was laid on the 4th of November 1815. by THE RIGHT HON.ble SAMUEL BIRCH, ALDERMAN, and then LORD MAYOR of LONDON
London, Published 2nd June 1819. by Robert Wilkinson, N.o 125 Fenchurch Street.

1. *The London Institution*
Founding home of the LA

2. *20 Hanover Square*
LA Headquarters 1890–1898

3. *Public Library,*
Buckingham Palace Road, Westminster
LA Headquarters 1922–1928

4. Chaucer House
LA Headquarters 1933–1965

5. *7 Ridgmount Street*
LA Headquarters since 1965

6. *E.W.B. Nicholson (1849–1924)*
Founder of the LA

7. H. R. Tedder (1850–1924)
Founding father of the LA
Hon. Treasurer 1889–1896 and 1898–1924
President 1897

8. *J. Y. W. MacAlister (1856–1925)*
Hon. Secretary 1887–1898
President 1915–1919

ii   That the principal textbooks and auxiliaries recommended
      by various teaching bodies, including those directing
      technical studies, as well as University Extension centres,
      the National Home Reading Union, etc, be provided and
      kept up to date in the public library
iii   That the public librarian should keep in touch with the chief
      educational work in his area
iv   That conferences between teachers and librarians be held
      from time to time
v   That there should be some interchange of representation
      between the Library and Education Committees
vi   That the public library should be recognised as forming
      part of the national educational machinery

The report and recommendations were approved, subject to the
addition of two further clauses:

vii   That every library should contain some room in which
      discussions and lectures could be held.
viii That library authorities should be strongly recommended to
      enrol their librarians as members of the National Home
      Reading Union.

The Committee had, sensibly enough, refrained from including
'more ambitious proposals till the library rate is either increased
or the present limitation removed' and, bearing in mind the
primitive quality of most municipal libraries for children and
most school libraries at that time, the recommendations were
assuredly welcome. Nevertheless, remarks made by John
Ballinger, Librarian of Cardiff Public Libraries – already an
outstanding pioneer in this field of service – pinpointed a basic
problem for the years ahead:

the report did not, in any part of it, contain any reference to the
co-operative management of school libraries by the Education
Committee and the Library Committee jointly. That seemed to him to
be fundamental to success, and before the report was circulated some
indication on that point should be included. He thought it had been
satisfactorily demonstrated that school libraries, unless they had the
expert assistance of a public library staff, sooner or later collapsed;

and, on the other hand, they could not be provided out of the public library fund, because the public library rate was limited, but by co-operation of the education authority providing the libraries and the public library officials doing the work of organisation, the result aimed at was achieved.[75]

It is pleasant to note that, amid considerations of many aspects of the public library's future, the Association did not forget one great figure of its past. It was represented at the unveiling of the monument over the grave of Edward Edwards in Niton churchyard in the Isle of Wight in 1902 and encouraged the Manchester Libraries Committee to commemorate the centenary of the pioneer's birth by arranging a dinner at their Town Hall in 1912. Bearing in mind Edwards' chequered association with the great city, the event reflected credit both on the City fathers and on the LA.[76]

London members could continue to keep in touch with LA activities through the monthly meetings. Attendances at these were, however, again declining, or were often disappointingly small. Members in the provinces, where monthly meetings were held only infrequently, had to rely mostly on the annual conferences. The success or failure of these may be judged not only from the printed reports but also through the eyes of Ballinger, who commented on several in MacAlister's new *Library*[77] and, much more through those of James Duff Brown, writing in his own *Library World*. It should also be noticed in passing that Ballinger's series of other *Library* articles during 1908 and 1909 provides the modern reader with one of the best – and most frequently overlooked – accounts of good municipal service during the present period, at his own Cardiff.[78]

Brown was extremely critical of many of the conferences. Thus for 1898*:

* This was the conference at which the Council (5 August 1898) made arrangements for typewriters and operators for the use of members but stipulated 'only male operators'. Ten years later, in *Tono Bungay*, George Ponderevo was to fall for the 'straight little back, softly rounded neck and chestnut hair, very neatly done', of typist Effie Rink. Can the Council have feared similar complications, were old arts and new skills to mingle?

None of the papers were out of the common run and the discussions were even more futile than usual.[79]

For 1899:

The prevailing tones of the Manchester meeting were dullness and depression, caused largely by climatic conditions and a thoroughly uninteresting programme of papers. Not for years had the Council submitted for consideration such an array of deadly dull, undiscussible subjects.[80]

For 1900:

The Conference ... will be remembered chiefly as a highly successful and enjoyable series of social events. ... Fourteen papers were put down for discussion and of these only five had any direct connection with library work.[81]

For 1907:

The largest, best organised and most sociable ever held ... on the professional side, nothing of special importance was accomplished and the ... programme of papers was poor, uninspiring and tame.[82]

For 1909:

In many ways one of the most hospitable of any yet held ... on the social side it was splendid, but on the professional and business side, stale and uninspiring.[83]

For 1910:

On the whole the business side was dull and to a majority of those present, unproductive. ... The annual business was a mere torrent of talk, conducted by the same small ring of individuals who inflict their views on every occasion with unfailing regularity. ... To listen in a hot room to these men talking about nothing is an act of heroism for which every auditor deserves the medal of the Royal Humane Society or the Victoria Cross.[84]

The 1902 and 1903 conferences encouraged Brown much more. For 1902:

The recently concluded Annual Meeting at Birmingham brought into
prominence the fact that a great change has come over the spirit in
which all that concerns librarianship is approached . . . the old time
conservatism which once held the field is rapidly disappearing. . . .[85]

For 1903:

Was in many respects the most important gathering of librarians
which has taken place since librarianship first became organised. The
value and interest of the topics discussed, the joint discussion with
representatives of famous educational bodies, and other features of a
novel kind, all contributed. . . .[86]

The chief topic had been the relationship between state
education and libraries, already touched on.

The 1901 Conference at Plymouth seemed outstanding to
Brown as it was there, at the Business meeting, that MacAlister

in a speech full of point and sparkle, then moved the resolution
standing in his name (expressing the opinion that three London and
five country members of the Council should be ineligible for
re-election for twelve months) after an abortive attempt by Mr Jones
to squash it on a point of order.[87]

In fact, although Jast, among the several speakers to the motion,
was the only one who supported MacAlister, it was declared
carried. The immediate result was that the Honorary Secretary,
Frank Pacy, and three London members of the Council –
Borrajo, Jones and Quinn resigned.[88] The situation reverted to
normal twelve months later.

It may be suggested, in passing, that it is largely because of the
House of Commons that Britain remains a reasonably
'governable' country, and not merely because that House is now
democratically elected – according to generally accepted, if
mostly uncritical British standards of democracy – but because it
is a representative microcosm. It contains among its members
representatives certainly of the social classes but also of the
various levels of intelligence manifest in the nation – a few
brilliant, many clever, many more mediocre and some stupid

enough to beggar literate terms. So too, in the history of the
LA, a reasonably representative Council has necessarily
contributed far more to the success of the Association's activities
than Annual Meetings ever could or can. Until the Charter of
1898 the Annual Meetings had mixed papers and business; after
1898 the Business meeting gradually assumed its modern shape.
But Annual Meetings, by their very nature, are likely to seem far
more successful socially than professionally.

Reference has already been made to what were known, during
the early years of the twentieth century, as Branch Associations
although, as Jast said at a meeting of the Northern Counties
Library Association at Harrogate in 1911, 'They have been
semi-independent, bitterly resenting the slightest attempt to
bring them into line, even with one another'.[89] They also
provided occasional meeting places and local discussion groups
for librarians and others interested in library activities. All of
them, with the solitary exception of the North Western Branch,
consisted mostly of local members who were not, in fact,
members of the LA. At the Council meeting on 16 September
1907, the following statistics were presented:

Name	Total Membership	Total LA Membership
North Western Branch	95	80
Bristol and Western Branch	80	14
Birmingham and District LA	49	18
North Midland LA	66	24
Northern Counties LA	104	36

The Council had resolved, on 14 April 1905:

That it is highly desirable to bring about close relations between
every branch or local LA in the United Kingdom.

but progress was slow and the introduction, from the same date,
of a capitation grant of 2*s* per annum

for each fully subscribing member of the LA being a member of such
local branch

was only very gradually influential. The *Annual Report* for 1906 included the following remarks:

The various provincial LAs throughout the country have been invited to affiliate themselves to the parent Association, under the regulations drawn up by the Council, but the response has not been so prompt and hearty as was expected, in spite of the fact that the regulations have been so reframed as to allow every affiliated body the fullest possible freedom in the management of its own affairs.

From the British Museum in 1907 A. W. Pollard made a strong plea for much closer integration to encourage librarians to become members of the parent body as well as of local branches. He expressed confidence 'that London and the provincial branches when they face facts squarely will infuse new vigour into the LA and send up the membership to over a thousand'.[90] Pollard also saw advantages to London of having a Branch there. E. McKnight and E. A. Savage, surveying the problem from the vantage point of the North West Branch, went further and described the LA as its own London Branch! They made equally strong pleas for more information, more cooperation and more help from London for provincial members, even a measure of devolution and a paid secretary to administer. The overall aim, with which few – be they London or provincial members – would surely have disagreed, would be to make it easier for provincial members to participate.[91]

Jast, whose task it was, and notably during 1909 and 1912, to visit the Branch associations to put over the case for integration, often with little if any local encouragement, felt indeed that federation should be more ambitious; there were also the Museums Association and the Bibliographical Society.[92] But his approach to the provinces in 1912 could be more precise since Branch formation was now easier. Following the Annual Meeting at Exeter in 1910:

Upon receipt of a request in writing from not less than 20 Hon Fellows, Fellows, Members or Associate Members residing in a district, the Council may at their discretion issue a certificate creating a Branch of the Association.

Provision was also made, in the Bye-law revision, for:

a rebate of 4s on the subscription of a Fellow, Member or Associate Member who is also a member of the Branch. Such rebate shall be applied by a Branch for all lawful and necessary purposes connected with its work and objects, and no Branch shall levy any charge whatever upon its members other than local members, who shall pay a subscription to the Branch of not less than the rebate.[93]

The Council had also adopted a tentative scheme of Branch districts for discussion locally:

i   Northumberland, Cumberland, Westmorland, Durham, North Riding of Yorkshire
ii   West and East Riding of Yorkshire
iii Lancashire and Cheshire
iv   Derbyshire, Leicestershire, Nottinghamshire, Lincolnshire, Rutland, Northamptonshire
v   Cambridgeshire, Norfolk, Suffolk, Essex
vi   Shropshire, Staffordshire, Worcestershire, Herefordshire, Warwickshire
vii Gloucestershire, Oxfordshire, Buckinghamshire, Wiltshire
viii Sussex, Hampshire, Dorset
ix   Somerset, Devonshire, Cornwall[94]

Between 1905 and 1906 there were in addition affiliation discussions between the LA and the LAA; they were finally broken off by the LAA by a narrow majority.[95]

No further Branches were formed prior to the outbreak of World War One and the always uneasy and sometimes strained relationship between London and the provinces would continue for some years yet. But a new, most welcome, and potentially powerful Association – the Scottish Library Association – was formally inaugurated in 1908. It had almost 150 members by 1913–14, of whom nearly 100 were employed in Edinburgh, Glasgow and Dundee.[96]

For all members, however, and particularly for the provincial ones, the official journal was outstandingly important. Henry Guppy's four years as editor of the *LAR* (January 1899 to

March 1903) gave general satisfaction. In addition to a variety of articles on librarianship and bibliographical subjects, including select bibliographies, the regular contributions on library notes and news, and causerie, reports of meetings, reviews of professional literature, Fovargue's 'Notes and queries on library law' and, for a time, Ogle's 'Junior Colleagues' Corner', were all promising. The contents aroused little criticism in committee or council although there were occasional controversies including in particular the early one when Jast's first major paper, 'Some hindrances to progress in public library work', read at the 1898 Conference at Southport, causing a discussion there 'which was not always orderly',[97] was only printed following correspondence between author and editor, a strong protest at exclusion by the author at the following year's conference, and a special committee request to the editor to publish.[98] The Publications Committee and Council were in fact concerned, much more, to control the cost of the magazine and to ensure its regular publication. Bearing in mind the many unhappy experiences with *The Library*, the priorities are understandable. It was now agreed that an annual net expenditure not exceeding £150 for production and distribution was acceptable[99]; as adequate advertising revenue was most difficult to obtain, the task of control proved exacting. Regular publication was also difficult. At the committee's meeting on 31st January 1902, Guppy had to promise to bring out the magazine 'regularly again' and in the following August had to be told that the Council was much dissatisfied 'with his proposal to issue double number of *LAR* for August/September' instead of the usual separates.

Guppy moved from Sion College to the new John Rylands in Manchester on his appointment as Joint Librarian there in 1899. Following his early promotion to Chief Librarian, he announced his resignation from the editorship of the *LAR* in its January 1903 number, 'owing to growing demands on his time.' The Council now decided that the *LAR* was to be conducted in future 'under the editorial supervision of the Publications Committee'. Several of its members were to assume responsibility for various sections and general supervision was to be exercised by the committee's honorary secretary; proof readers and an editorial assistant were to be paid and each number was to consist of thirty-two pages except for the large annual issue reporting the conference.[100]

The work of the sectional specialists had obviously to be coordinated if the *LAR* was to have recognisable 'shape'; this essential duty fell to Henry Bond (1871–1917) who succeeded Jast as honorary secretary of the Publications Committee in 1904.[101] Bond, who had been Librarian, successively, of Kendal, Lincoln, and Woolwich, was appointed Chief Librarian of St Pancras in 1906 and, after frustrating and unhappy experience there, moved on to Portsmouth in 1914.[102]

The *LAR* under Bond continued very much on the lines which Guppy had laid down, since the former was a hard-working librarian of quite modest abilities; Guppy's early international aspirations were, perhaps, the chief victims of the change. By 1910 the contents had become standardised to include 'Current views' by various hands in place of editorials, reprinted papers and articles, reviews of professional publications, reports of meetings, including those of the LAA and the Society of Public Librarians as well as of the Branch and provincial associations, notes and news, lists of examination successes, appointments, obituaries and correspondence. Fovargue continued his popular legal notes and the annual meetings were reported in great detail.

The *LAR* had then, as it has always had, many critics. G. T. Shaw (1863–1938), then Master of the Liverpool Athenaeum, but to be appointed Librarian of Liverpool Public Libraries two years later, complained in 1907 that:

1. It contains no section for an authoritative expression of LA opinion on matters affecting libraries and library work.
2. It is not an efficient means of communication between all interested in library work and allied subjects.
3. It is dull, therefore unattractive even to our members.

But he appreciated the difficulties of producing a good regular journal, using only honorary staff, editor and contributors, and could suggest little more than even greater dependence on more

volunteers.[103] It certainly seemed to be even more difficult than
during Guppy's period of office to bring the magazine out on
time each month.[104] The cost of producing and distributing it
was always threatening, too, to increase beyond the maximum
which the Council of the day considered reasonable;[105] income
from advertising remained disappointingly low. But then the
Year Book too, the preparation of which fell to the Honorary
Secretary of the Association rather than to the Publications
Committee, did not appear each year; no issues were published,
for example, between 1910 and 1913.

The Association's educational classes, inaugurated prior to the
Charter, were continued each winter from 1898, lecturers
including Guppy, Burgoyne, Roberts, Quinn and Davis. There
were, however, two quite different complications. The LAA
objected to the classes being open to students other than those
already employed in libraries, 'regarding it as a means whereby
the competition for chiefships would be increased by an excess of
'theoretical amateurs'.[106] This critical approach, as expressed not
only to the LA but also, by letter to the London County Council
had made it difficult for that body to consider the Association's
earlier application for aid entirely dispassionately.[107] The LAA
continued to press its point of view, subsequently with
variations and modifications, quite unsuccessfully. Opposition
to the so called 'open door' was, however, also demonstrated in
the LA's own North West Branch. At the Manchester conference
in September 1899, members decided, by fifty-five votes to
forty-nine, to delete from the Council's Report the paragraph
urging the Branch to discontinue the exclusion from its own
Summer Schools of those not already employed in libraries.[108] It
was therefore almost inevitable that the Association's planning
of its own classes and prevailing critical attitudes should have
contributed to making it all but impossible for university
graduates to be recruited to municipal library staffs. MacAlister's
new *Library* pointed this out in 1903:

In a profession which ought to be a highly educated one it seems
lamentable that a man who postpones entering it until he has taken a
university degree will probably find it not at all easy to get an
engagement.[109]

The second complication derived from the fact that the popularity of the LA classes in common with the Summer Schools seemed to be *undermining* the Association's official examinations. Young students seemed much more willing to take the examinations held at the end of courses of lectures; in 1900 only three candidates sat the official examinations.[110] The Association had certainly begun the process of integration by merging its own Education and Examinations Committees in October 1898 but it took longer to equate syllabuses.

The official examination regulations had been revised in March 19 02. There was no longer a preliminary examination,

but all candidates for the professional examination must have been employed in practical library work during the 3 years previous to their attending any examination.

The Council had, nevertheless, power to suspend this proviso. The examinations were still grouped into three sections: bibliography and literary history; cataloguing, classification and shelf arrangement; and library management. The possibility of reviving the London Summer Schools of the 1890s was also seriously considered; subsequent enquiries indicated insufficient support.

Developments were now influenced, for the first time, by a prominent public figure not a librarian, but a good if always highly critical friend – who was, fortunately, much more far-seeing than most librarians of the period – Sidney Webb. It is at least possible that his initial interest may have been encouraged by Mandell Creighton; the two men had known each other well.[111]

On 10 March 1902, with H. R. Tedder in the Chair, the monthly meeting at 20 Hanover Square was addressed by Sidney Webb, LCC, on 'The library service of London: its coordination, development and education'. The first part of his paper dealt with (mostly municipal) library cooperation, as it was *not*, and as he felt it could be. His suggestions for union catalogues, stock specialisation, readers' ticket interavailability etc, and for regular meetings of metropolitan librarians have long since become part and parcel of the London scene; they all seemed utopian in 1902. In his second part Sidney Webb considered the librarian as a professional man and commented on his technical education in a manner which seemed equally revolutionary:

All candidates for junior posts to have passed some school examination of recognised public character.
No youth should be promoted to anything called a library assistantship or, indeed, to any salary exceeding £50 a year unless and until he has passed the technical examination of the LA.
[In view of the limited number of library posts] it is quite impossible to have a separate institution for the technical education of the library assistant, whether conducted by the LA or by anyone else.
I do not think that professional or any other kind of education should be managed entirely by a professional association. But I have watched with much interest and sympathy the praiseworthy attempts of the Education Committee of the Association to establish technical classes for librarians. The experiment appears to me to have been wisely devised and ably conducted; and no small thanks are due to those public spirited members who have week after week given their time and thought to instructing the junior members of the profession.
It is for the professional association to say what qualifications it wants; to conduct the examination which it exacts as a test of efficiency; and to give the necessary certificates. But education should be conducted by educational bodies, in definitely organised educational institutions, side by side with other students, and in close conjunction with other branches of study. The professional association should be effectively represented on the managing committee; it should undertake a moral responsibility for getting the classes filled, and it may usefully give material aid by founding prizes and scholarships.
We must beware of too narrow a curriculum. I confess that I am somewhat grieved to find that the examination . . . is confined to the three subjects of Bibliography and literary history, Cataloguing, and Library management. . . . If we are ever to attain the goal of a university course of study for librarians, with the opportunity of taking a degree, in which some recognition is given to the librarian's special subjects . . . we must provide for a much wider general culture. . . . It will be easy enough to make out a very thorough three years course quite up to the standard of the medical, legal or any other faculty.

During the discussion which followed most of those present
were critical only of the first part of the paper. But
H. D. Roberts, Chairman of the Education committee,
mentioned that 'another application for aid . . . had been sent to
the London Technical Education Board'.[112] That application was
to prove extremely important with Sidney Webb very closely
involved. A brief account of his wider activities may help
perspective.

Sidney Webb (1859–1947), created Baron Passfield in 1929, had
educated himself – mostly by spare-time reading – to a standard
which astonished his contemporaries and can still astonish. He
had passed by competitive examination into the Civil Service
but, having political ambitions, had resigned in 1892 when first
elected to the then quite new London County Council. In the
same year he had married Beatrice Potter, a wealthy fellow-
member of the Fabian Society, and they had begun that amazing
partnership in social, political and economic research and
publication which made their names famous in every civilised
country. One of his first contributions to London County
Council affairs was to suggest the formation of a technical
education board. He served as its chairman until 1898 and
remained its *eminence grise* for a much longer period. As his wife
subsequently wrote of him:

It is as a committee man that Sidney Webb excels. He is always on the
spot; he thinks twice as fast as his colleagues; he so foresees the drift
of the discussion that he can lie in wait, and open or block the way
according to his aims. He is the ideal draftsman; able to express the
desired conclusion in a dozen different phrases so as to disarm
suspicion and to suit diverse temperaments.[113]

In 1895 Sidney Webb was responsible, more than any other man,
for the foundation of the London School of Economics and
Political Science, created to provide England's capital city with
undergraduate and post graduate opportunities – particularly
for ambitious evening students – comparable with those
available to full-timers at the older universities. At the end of the
century the London County Council was heavily engaged with
the vast slum-clearance programme out of which came

Kingsway and Aldwych. Sidney Webb persuaded it to make a
site in Clare Market available for his new School and encouraged
J. Passmore Edwards, better known as a municipal library
benefactor, to donate £10,000 for the building. This building
was nearing completion when Webb addressed the LA; it was
opened in May 1902 by Lord Rosebery, first Chancellor of the
recently reconstituted University of London. This reconstitution
had been another immense task with which Webb had been
closely associated: the new LSE, which had 443 students in
1901–2, became a School of the University.[114]

On 25 March 1902, William Garnett, Secretary to the London
County Council's Technical Education Board, wrote to
W. A. S. Hewins, the Director of the LSE:

About four years ago the (Library) Association made application for
aid in connection with some of its classes. The Board then offered to
assist the Association provided that the teaching was supplied
through the agency of the LSE, which offered facilities for the carrying
on of the classes at much less cost than would be involved in their
conduct in an entirely separate institution. At that time the
Authorities of the Association declined to comply with the Board's
requirements on the ground that many of their most distinguished
lecturers would not be willing to give their services gratuitously or
for the low fees contemplated if the work were connected with any
institution other than the Association itself, and the negotiations
accordingly fell through. Certain changes have recently been made in
the internal organization of the Association, and the views of the
Association with respect to this question appear now to have
changed. . . . The application was presented to the Technical
Education Board at its meeting held yesterday and I was instructed to
ask the London School of Economics and Political Science to be good
enough to report to the Board as to the extent to which the present
school curriculum meets the requirements of the Library
Association.[115]

Hewins and Webb discussed possibilities carefully and, as was to
be expected, the latter quickly familiarised himself with the
courses of study provided in the four established library schools
in the United States and at L'Ecole des Chartes in Paris. The
Technical Education Board's reference to the LSE made good
sense for, as a later historian commented:

The running in yoke of academic, general and vocational education is no easy thing, but it is what LSE attempts. . . . Certain picturesque groups have vanished.[116]

Other 'picturesque groups', already catered for or soon to be enrolled in 1902, were railway employees and Army officers.[117]

The LA's Education Committee considered progress at its meeting on 22 May 1902:

The report of Mr Hewins referred to, went into considerable detail regarding the present means for the educational training of librarians, but included, as necessary qualifications, a number of accomplishments which the Committee considered to be too advanced for the students who usually attended their classes. The report concluded with the suggestion that the classes might be held at the LSE without further cost to the Association or the Technical Board.

It then successfully recommended the Council:

That the LA cooperate with the LSE in conducting courses of instruction in
1. Bibliography and literary history
2. Cataloguing, classification and shelf arrangement
3. Library management

subject to the following conditions:

1. That the Council of the LA nominate the lecturers
2. That the Council continue to examine and certificate
3. That the classes be open to all comers
4. That the Council and the Governors of the LSE have equal representation on the sub-committee of management. [The LSE had suggested two LA Nominees]

Webb and Hewins represented the LSE Governors initially and the chairman and secretary of the Association's Education committee (Tedder and Roberts) the LA. Tedder's interest in the education of assistants was life-long; he and Roberts were assuredly excellent choices as LA representatives. Cooperation went a stage further: John McKillop, Secretary of the LSE and also its Librarian until 1909, joined the LA's Education

Committee. Roberts gave an introductory talk on technical training, with special reference to the new classes, at a meeting of the LAA held at the LSE on 8 October 1902. James Duff Brown then began as the first lecturer; his course of ten lectures on elementary bibliography attracted thirty-six students, thirty-five of whom were already employed in libraries, thirty-three of them in public libraries.[119] These lectures subsequently formed the basis of his *Manual of practical bibliography* (1906), a small book which proved to be a student's 'must' for more than one generation. Barrett followed in the Lent term with a comparable course on cataloguing, classification and shelf arrangement.

The LA's decision to arrange the LSE classes was not free of controversy. It was attacked by one London assistant as 'hopelessly academic'[120] and others probably shared his opinion, particularly as the fees for lectures in a university college were feared as likely to be higher than those arranged only by the Association itself. But the fees were, in fact, only 17*s* 6*d* for forty lectures and the LA refunded one half of them to each student 'nominated' by one of its members. The LSE Governors also soon showed that, in some respects at least, they were not 'hopelessly academic' by resolving:

That Wednesday afternoon was the most suitable time for the classes if the assistants were required to give up their half holiday, but that Committees and Librarians should be urged to allow their assistants to attend during working hours.[121]

The second session was opened, at the suggestion of the LSE, with an inaugural address by Professor Macneile Dixon, whose Presidential Address at the LA Conference in September 1902 had given much pleasure: it inaugurated what the LSE considered the beginning of 'a very successful School of Librarianship.'[122] Once arrangements for the first LSE classes had been made, the LA Council began to try to equate their syllabuses with those of its own official examinations. In November 1902, the Education Committee thought it desirable to remind its own examiners that many of the examinees in bibliography would probably have attended James Duff Brown's classes; they sent those concerned copies of *his* syllabus.[123] But although a total of thirty students sat the LA examinations in the following month, at centres in Belfast, Gateshead, St Helens and Wigan in addition to London, only eight passed, including three in bibliography. McKillop was understandably critical of the LA's old practice of awarding *pro tanto* certificates for class attendance as distinct from examination success and expressed the opinion that

> it seems to me that the LA is confusing two really distinct things in its desire to improve the intellectual and technical equipment of library assistants ... (i) Certificates that individuals have profited by going through a course of lectures would give unfair advantage to Londoners. (ii) LA diploma comparable with external examinations of the University of London better (and to improve standards of teaching and teaching facilities).[124]

His points were taken and on 30 March 1903 the Council approved and adopted the report of a special sub-committee of its Education Committee, and authorised it to draw up a new and detailed syllabus.

The Sub-committee's report envisaged an organised course of training providing for (annual) examinations, following study in prescribed subjects – to include essay writing on selected aspects – and for a minimum of three years' practical experience. The method of study, as for external examinations of the University of London was to be at student discretion but it would be facilitated by a fully detailed syllabus. Classes should be arranged in large centres of population, 'except perhaps in literary history'; there should possibly also be 'correspondence classes'. Entrance examinations for library posts should be recommended to Library Authorities.[125] The revised regulations and syllabus were to form the basis of LA examinations – admittedly with subsequent changes of some substance – until 1931; some detailed comments may therefore be useful.

Candidates for the full LA certificate or diploma were henceforth to be required:

i   To satisfy the examiners in each of six sections, to be sat separately and in any chosen order (lists of successful

candidates would be divided into honours, merits and
passes)

ii   To submit an acceptable thesis on a prescribed subject

iii To have worked in a library or libraries as a member of an
administrative staff for not less than twenty-four hours
weekly for a minimum of three years.

Just as the method of preparation was to be left entirely to
individual discretion so no textbooks were to be prescribed
although useful sources of information were to be suggested.
There was to be no preliminary entrance qualification and no
examination fees.

Each of the three sections provided for in the earlier syllabus
was now divided into two. The syllabuses for the resulting six
new Sections provided in each case for the writing of an essay on
a special topic to be notified annually in the *Record* January issue
prior to the May examination; the essay was to be prepared and
written at home prior to the examination, except in Section I
where it was to form part of the written examination itself.

The Sectional syllabuses – in broad outline – follow:

i*   *Literary history*
'English literature, especially of the modern period,
including the literature of the British Colonies and the
USA'. The principal authors of one literature in each of the
following groups: **a** Greek or Latin **b** French, German,
Italian or Spanish. Candidates were also 'required to show
an elementary knowledge of Latin, French or German' and
to translate easy unseen passages in the language selected.

ii   *Elements of practical bibliography*
Including outline history; book production, description
and distribution; compilation of bibliographies; guides and
aids; book selection. Candidates for honours were
required to show an elementary knowledge of
palaeography. The essay was to take the form of a select
bibliography.

iii   *Classification*

Both theory and practical applications to be covered and the examination to include 'actual practical classification in addition to answering a set of questions'. Candidates also expected to classify books written in Latin and at least one other language than English. The essay to take the form of a descriptive account of a selected scheme or the classification of a specific topic.

iv   *Cataloguing*
Covering theory, codes of rules, entry making, annotation, catalogues for special purposes, arrangements, forms and printing. As in Section (iii), practical tests to form part of the examination.

v   *Library history and organisation*
Including history, legislation, committees, finance and staff, buildings and fittings, book-buying and accession methods and rules and regulations.

vi   *Practical library administration*
(To be retitled Library routine/Practical library administration in 1900). Covering the routine of the departments and office work.[126]

The changes were generally welcomed. *The Library World*'s view that:

There is no doubt that, in the near future, the certificates of the LA will come to be recognised as the sole passports to position and promotion in libraries. . . .

expressed a widely held and justified assumption, at least as far as public libraries were concerned.[127]

The LSE lectures arranged between 1903 and 1910 continued to prosper. James Duff Brown, however, whose interest in bibliography was limited to its 'practical' aspects – he had little patience with the historical approach – soon switched to practical library administration. His original responsibilities were taken over by, in particular, A. W. Pollard. The two of them duelled over historical bibliography, in the pages of MacAlister's new *Library* in April 1903; one would need to be a very dyed-in-the-wool public librarian to argue that victory lay with J.D.B![128] Quinn joined them as lecturer in cataloguing and Jast in classification. By 1908 McKillop was visualising expansion and more advanced teaching but very realistically:

The annual expenditure of the School on this Department of Library Administration over and above the income from students' fees (and there is absolutely no other source of income) is not less than £100 a year with the present modest dimensions of the teaching, and it is kept down to this figure only by the most painstaking economy and by paying the teachers at about one third of the rates paid to those in other departments [then 30s a lecture]. But more will have to be spent shortly. The present teachers will not consent much longer to lecture at the present scale of fees. Further classes for more advanced students will have to be added, and it is a well-established fact that advanced teaching in any subject not only costs more but draws fewer students than that of an elementary or medium character. . . . In this way it will be possible to develop the existing department into a School of Librarianship which shall command the position in the world which London ought to have.[129]

But the LA Council did not always find it easy to cooperate with the LSE and many problems had to be solved. The School refused to arrange and accommodate the more elementary lectures which numerous London librarians knew to be necessary for their poorly educated assistants, and it declined to teach English literary history to cover Section 1 of the new syllabus. Both LSE decisions were readily understandable, bearing in mind its status as a university college and its specialisation in the social sciences; the LA thought them regrettable. The School suggested that the LA arrange its own elementary classes and eventually in 1911 introductory courses in cataloguing and classification were organised at its offices.[130] To help solve the literary history problem, the LSE referred the Association to King's College, London. King's proved welcomingly cooperative but the assistants who should have been interested failed to register.[131]

The LSE classes certainly provided valuable facilities for London assistants. What of those in the provinces? Once again James Duff Brown led the way. At its meeting on 25 February 1904 the Council were informed that he had agreed to conduct a correspondence 'class' covering Sections (v) and (vi) of the syllabus, provided that sufficient students enrolled. They did so enrol, and soon not only for Brown's 'class' but also for Quinn's in cataloguing, concurrently with his LSE lectures. In 1911, after Brown had resigned his new responsibility, there were twenty-two enrolments for Section (iii); forty-four for (iv); fifteen for (v); and thirty-eight for (vi).[132] Coincidentally, or in consequence, practical interest in the LSE classes began to decline sharply, despite the facts that all the lecturers taught to the new syllabus, and the LA's original intention that correspondence 'classes' were for non-Londoners only. By this date, however, new and promising classes had begun at Liverpool, Manchester and Birmingham. Examination entries also increased substantially. At the May 1907 examinations 155 candidates sat 217 subjects and there were 92 passes; centres had been held at London, Birmingham, Bolton, Bournemouth, Brighton, Cardiff, Carlisle, Glasgow, Leeds, Liverpool, Manchester, Newcastle, Plymouth and Cape Colony. The novelty of the enthusiasm was emphasised, however, by a writer in *The Library World*, who pointed out that up to May 1906 a total of only 126 candidates had passed one or more of the six sections or their predecessors.[133] As for completing the examinations, successful Diplomates were still sufficiently rare to earn special publicity in the pages of *The Library Assistant,* W. R. B. Prideaux being the first in 1906, and F. Dallimore the second in 1908. The latter was then a member of the staff of the Wimbledon Public Library; he was later Librarian of Darlington.[134]

Following the resignation of H. D. Roberts from the LA's Education Committee, consequent on his appointment to the Librarianship of Brighton, the Council

desire to record their deep sense of the valuable services rendered by Mr Roberts during 10 years with conspicuous zeal, ability, discretion and industry and further that they consider that the present success of the educational work of the Association is largely due to his strenuous efforts.[135]

He was elected an Honorary Fellow in the following year. But the 'present success' was by no means complete and apt comment was soon made by E. A. Baker, Roberts' LA successor:

the examination entries show a steady increase but the classes at the LSE have met with a deplorable fall in the number of students attending. Even so, however, there is something to be said on the other side; the classes established by the North West Branch at Liverpool are flourishing and the Birmingham and District Association have started courses of lectures in the practical subjects of our syllabus. Correspondence classes, further, have done better work than ever.[136]

But as Brown, as editor of *The Library World*, had pointed out:

It is public recognition of librarianship as a science which is required if conditions all round are going to be improved. The same old ignorant idea still persists everywhere that librarianship is a mere elementary kind of labourer's job requiring nothing more scientific than the physical ability to hand a book over a counter for which a contemptibly small wage is more than enough.[137]

It may be suspected that some members of the LA Council were never reconciled to classes not completely and entirely under Association control and, indeed, at the end of the first complete year of the LSE lectures, an attempt was made to persuade Andrew Carnegie[138] to 'endow' librarianship with a capital grant of £10,000 to provide a building which would house a centre with lecture and class rooms, library, reading room and museum and accommodation for the LA officers and a resident caretaker. But the attempt was completely unsuccessful.[139] Nevertheless, it could never be claimed that the decline of the LSE classes after 1910 was due to diminished Council support or to diminished official interest. It is possible, of course, that the unsuccessful attempts to use the LSE also for the Association's meetings, already referred to, may have encouraged new prejudices. The announcement, too, of a supplementary class for the 1910–1911 session may have frightened some:

A seminar has also been arranged under the joint direction of Mr Sidney Webb, the Director of the LSE and others on advanced bibliography, the idea being to set students at work investigating the sources of information available in special subjects or in special divisions of economic and political science, prizes being offered for the best bibliographies.[140]

Whatever the reasons, the number of library students registering at LSE dropped from seventy-one in 1909–10 to thirty-two in 1910–11, thirty-three in 1911–12, and only made a poor recovery to forty-four in 1912–13.[141] The School requested a guarantee of 'not less than sixty students' which it was virtually impossible to give. The LA Council included the following in its *Report* for 1913:

Once more it is necessary to appeal to Library assistants in and near London not to allow the classes organized by the Education Committee at the LSE to be abandoned through their neglect . . . it is evident that the decline in the attendances . . . during the past few years is mainly due to neglect of their opportunities on the part of the assistants themselves.[142]

The classes continued however to be held until, following the outbreak of World War One in August 1914, they had to be discontinued as an economy measure. During 1914–15 only seventeen students enrolled.[143]

Now that a more satisfactory scheme of technical education had been introduced, little time elapsed before the question of a professional register was raised. W. R. B. Prideaux (1880–1932), Librarian of the Reform Club, and soon to be the Association's first Diplomate, pioneered the subject, in a paper read at a monthly meeting in October 1905.[144] But he seemed to be moving rather too fast; during the discussion following, the Honorary Secretary, Jast, expressed the view that:

At the present moment there was no need for it – the one strong platform on which they stood was that they were not an Association for purely professional purposes. . . .[145]

Two years elapsed. Librarians doubtless talked the matter over among themselves and a very small minority, led by A. J. Philip, of Gravesend, envisaged instead a new Institute of Librarians.[146]

By the end of 1907 Jast had become convinced of the desirability of a professional register and, as his deputy at Croydon, W. C. Berwick Sayers, was then Honorary Secretary of the LAA – which was overwhelmingly in favour *in principle* – the decision that the two officers read a joint paper on the subject at a joint meeting of the two Associations, and at the LSE, was obviously sound. On 22 January 1908:

They submitted closely knit arguments to support the obvious case in favour, drew helpfully on the experience of other Associations with mixed memberships and professional registers such as the Surveyors Institute and the Institution of Civil Engineers, and suggested that the LA's future membership consist of Honorary Fellows, Fellows (FLA), Associates (ALA), Members and Student Members.[147]

The resulting resolution in favour read:

This meeting of the LA and the LAA records its conviction that the only proper body to hold a professional register is the LA, and in view of the fact that there is a body of opinion, especially amongst library assistants, on the subject, the Council of the Association is requested to consider and publish a report on the whole question in time for it to be considered at the Annual Meeting in 1908.[148]

The Council wasted no time and appointed a special committee which reported back on 17 July, the report being then referred to the Annual Meeting at Brighton.

At Brighton registration was approved in principle, despite some opposition now from LAA representatives – Sayers excepted – who criticised reclassification of the membership and preferred 'a register of all efficient librarians irrespective of membership of any Association, and that the Register should be kept by the LA.[149] This would certainly have made it possible to achieve registration without the obligation of LA membership. One librarian present thought that 'It looks very much as if the tail wants to wag the dog'.[150] Similar expressions of opinion, were, of course, to be heard on numerous occasions in later years.

New bye-laws to implement the revised membership proposals, which had taken into account points raised by the LAA and various members, were submitted to the Annual Meeting at Sheffield in September 1909. Jast moved their adoption, doubtless uneasily aware that his closest friend and collaborator of past years, James Duff Brown, was implacably opposed to 'reclassification of the members'.[151] Prideaux seconded – a nice touch surely – and they were carried.

The most important of the new byelaws, subsequently approved by the Privy Council, provided for:

Fellows
a. Any Member of the LAUK elected within the first year of its foundation
b. Chief Librarians, responsible for the administration of a Library or Library system, and holding or having held office on or before 31 December 1914
c. Librarians of approved status, not holding chief positions and holding or having held office on or before 31 December
d. Holders of the Diploma of the LA and of the complete certificate issued prior to 1901 – may be elected Fellows.

Honorary Fellows
Persons who have rendered distinguished service in promoting the objects of the Association, or whose election in the opinion of the Council will be advantageous to its interests or objects, may be elected Honorary Fellows. Honorary Fellows shall be entitled to the same rights and privileges as Fellows.

Members
a. Librarians, not qualified for election as Fellows, twenty-five years of age or over, and having had not less than six years approved experience, and holding or having held office on or before 31 December 1914
b. Librarians holding four certificates of the Library Association, and with three years approved experience – may be elected Members.

Associate Members
a. Members of Library Committees and other persons

connected with the administration of libraries, or interested in
the objects of the Association, not being Librarians.
b. Librarians not qualified as Fellows or Members.

Student Members
Persons under twenty-five years of age engaged in Library work,
or studying for Librarianship, and not qualified as Fellows or
Members may be elected Student Members. They shall enjoy all
the privileges of Members except that they may not vote or hold
office.

Fellows and Members were to have the right of using the initials
FLA or MLA respectively after their names so long as they remained
subscribing Members of the Association.[152]

There were, subsequently, some differences of opinion between
the LAA and the LA's new Membership Committee as to the
claims of senior members who were not Chiefs to Fellowships.[153]
Few other than Chiefs were in fact admitted and since it was
difficult to argue with conviction that the claims of a deputy of a
large city were weaker than those of a chief of a Puddleby-in-the-
Marsh, controversy was inevitable. The Council 'believed that
no serious case of injustice has occurred'.[154] Be that as it may –
henceforth admission to membership, other than associate or
student membership, was to depend firstly on success at the LA
examinations.

Improved education and professional registration made it easier
for the Association to approach more confidently the Library
Authorities considering or making unsatisfactory appointments.
A. W. Pollard made relevant comments in 1907:

The advantages which the LA offers to its members are of two kinds
(1) corporate, (11) individual. The corporate advantage consists of the
immense improvement in the credit and status of librarians which the
Association has brought about during the 30 years it has been in
existence. It has effected this improvement by steadily holding up the
very highest ideals of the work which librarians are able to perform
for the community and by equally steadily insisting on the necessity
that those who take up this work shall qualify themselves to carry it

out efficiently, and helping them to do so ... It is certainly an extraordinary witness to the enthusiasm of librarians for their work, that the history of the Association may be searched for a whole generation and hardly a trace will be found in it of the urging of any personal pecuniary claims. Librarians are loud in demanding more money for their libraries, but although in proportion to their work they are probably the worst paid body of men and women in the United Kingdom, the question of salaries and pension schemes with which associations of schoolmasters and schoolmistresses are not infrequently concerned, have hardly ever figured on the agenda paper of either the annual or monthly meetings of the LA. The fact, however, remains, that librarians as a class, being miserably underpaid, have very few guineas to spare and that thus there must be a real temptation in countless cases, to take the corporate advantage which the Association has won for all librarians, whether they belong to it or not, as a free gift – a matter of course – and to leave the active support of the Association to others. ...[155]

Viewed in retrospect the LA may have seemed to have been slow and reluctant to begin the necessary task of persuading individual Library Authorities that they must appoint only trained and experienced librarians, and much slower and even more reluctant to persuade them to pay salaries which were adequate and reasonable by the standards of the period. MacAlister's first Conference address, 'Wanted a librarian', previously referred to, had made out a strong case for the appointment only of 'skilled craftsmen' as long ago as 1887;[156] official progress during the present period was still snail-like. Action which might appear to smack of trade unionism was, of course, viewed very differently before World War One than after World War Two. Unsuccessful attempts were made, by individual councillors, to persuade the LA Council to protest to the Local Authority at Sevenoaks in 1906 when the successful applicant for the vacant librarianship would not only be grossly underpaid but would also be responsible, 'at his own expense', for the entire cleaning of the library.[157] James Duff Brown's *Library World* expressed the view that Sevenoaks really needed not a librarian but 'a charwoman with insomnia'.[158] There was a different but equally unsuccessful attempt two years later to encourage the LA Council to protest to the Dundee Authority which had appointed a librarian who lacked both training and experience and was also more than sixty years of age.[159]

By 1911, however, there were signs of change. The LAA's *Report on the hours, salaries, training and conditions of service in British municipal libraries* of that year proved clearly that, while Library Authorities were beginning to take the LA's qualifications much more seriously and were encouraging their own assistants to further education, yet

perhaps the outstanding fact to be deduced is the decidedly inadequate remuneration of the majority of library officials throughout the Kingdom.[160]

A pioneer in this important field was E. A. Savage who, despite much official discouragement, wrote in the same year that

the time is come when the LA and the LAA should combine to draw up a scale of reasonable salaries for properly qualified service in libraries.[161]

He pursued the matter unsuccessfully at the 1913 Conference when Jast, as Honorary Secretary, had to oppose on the unconvincing ground that there were unsatisfactory labour conditions in nearly every calling and that a scale for assistants must also cover chief librarians.[162] Savage subsequently commented on another aspect of official opposition:

At the Bournemouth Conference Dr Baker argued that the Education Committee had nothing whatever to do with the salaries question; what business was it of their's, he asked. I repeat: Certificated assistants, the special product of the LA, should be its special care. Everything relating to libraries, even low salaries, should be the business of the Association and its committees.[163]

The occasion was an unhappy one and was certainly not eased by the refusal to publish Savage's subsequent article, 'A minimum wage for certificated assistants', in the *Library Association Record*; it appeared in *Library World*.[164] The official tide was, nevertheless, turning. During 1911 Chorley Corporation was officially notified of 'the total inadequacy of the salary offered for

the position of Librarian', ie £80 per annum,[165] and a
'respectful' and successful protest made to the London County
Council which, when advertising the vacant post of Librarian to
their Education Office, had stipulated that 'applicants were
restricted to teachers serving under the Council'.[166] Again,
during 1912, Douglas Town Council were approached – as their
Library Committee had recommended the appointment of an
untrained librarian – with a view to them considering 'the claim
of qualified persons who have applied for the post'.[167] The LA
Council, also, at the instigation of the Northern Counties LA,
wrote to the Haslingden Authority, 'pointing out the desirability
of appointing a properly qualified librarian'.[168]

Following the death of James Duff Brown in February 1914,
numerous and varied rumours circulated as to the intentions of
the Metropolitan Borough of Islington when filling the post left
vacant. It was certain that they considered abolishing the post
and making the librarian-in-charge of each of their service points
directly responsible to the Libraries Committee. It was also
rumoured that they were seriously considering appointing a
member of their own body. The LA Council authorised Jast to
write to them 'pointing out the importance of appointing a
trained librarian.'[169] An appointment acceptable to the
Association was eventually made in July 1914.[170]
The quest for satisfactory appointments and satisfactory salaries
led logically to consideration of the need for adequate pension
arrangements. In their absence individual local problems had to
be dealt with, *ad hoc*, by Local Authorities, during the present
period. But, so far as the needs of municipal librarians were
concerned, the Association cooperated, if a little vaguely, with
Nalgo in its attempts – unsuccessful until after World War One –
to secure a firm legal basis for Local Government
superannuation over the whole country.[171]

In the absence of adequate pension schemes librarians normally
died in harness and, if they died unexpectedly early, their families
could easily find themselves in severe financial difficulties. The
Council had tried, from an early date, to build up an Association
Benevolent Fund, despite financial stringencies, but by 1905 this
was 'in a very reduced state'.[172] Nevertheless, payments which

were generous – if judged by the then current full annual
subscription of one guinea – were made in 1913 to the
Bodleian Curators' Fund for the widow of the LA's founder,
E. W. B. Nicholson,[173] a year later to the fund for Mrs
H. E. Johnston, widow of the deceased Librarian of
Gateshead,[174] and, two years later for Mrs James Duff Brown.[175]
Librarians themselves also sometimes fell on hard times, and
occasional payments were made to them as to the Edward
Lings who had begun his library career as Edward Edwards'
'Boy' at Manchester in 1852, had, as first Librarian of Leicester
Public Library, attended the Inaugural Conference of 1877, but
who had been dismissed from that post in 1888 following his
refusal to resign it.[176]

The formation and disappearance of the Association's Museum
has already been referred to. It is one of the surprises of the LA's
hundred years that its own library's history began considerably
later. The *Annual Report* for 1900 included the following
paragraph:

It having been urged upon the Council to maintain a Library for the
Association, it was decided that there would be little hope of
acquiring a collection of any real use by means of chance gifts, and
therefore an appeal was issued for subscriptions towards a Special
Library Fund, the Council undertaking that if a minimum sum of £50
should be raised, to commence the formation of a collection of books
on library economy and bibliography, and to vote a sum of not less
than £10 annually towards the Library Fund. Only a few promises
were received as the result of a circular letter addressed to all
members, so that beyond some gifts of books, notably one of a
number of suitable volumes by Mr Frank Campbell, the proposal has
not made much headway. The Council hope, however, that the
proposal may not be dropped.[177]

Some progress was made, the Library was housed by James Duff
Brown at his Clerkenwell Library from 1902, and members and
students began to find it useful.[178]

Following the organisation of the technical classes at the London
School of Economics, the LA's library also moved there, with
Wyndham Hulme as Honorary Librarian. The organisation and

administration was then taken over by the College Librarian,
B. M. Headicar, and his staff, and the library remained there until
1920. In 1913 the LA published a 'Union class list' of the library
and that of the LAA, prepared by Hulme and Headicar.[179] By then
the Association's library contained about 4000 items, of which
approximately one third were pamphlets, in addition to
periodicals and annual reports of individual libraries. One sorry
comment on the urgent need for library service is contained in
the *Annual Report* for 1910:

One of the greatest difficulties which our lecturers have to contend
with is that many assistants have practically no access to many of the
text-books recommended, either because the libraries in which they
work do not possess them, or because the regulations of the library
preclude the staff using such books . . . a state of affairs which is hardly
creditable to the profession.[180]

But then the children of the traditional shoemaker were
invariably ill-shod.

The cooperation of British librarians with colleagues in other
countries, which had facilitated the foundation of the
Association in 1877, and celebrated its twentieth anniversary,
cannot be described as better than fickle, prior to 1914. Visits
such as those paid by Jast to the United States in 1904 and 1913
were not without limited influence but financial stringencies
discouraged ambitious ventures and visitors to Britain were
much more numerous than British library tourists abroad. The
Council, in 1905, expressed themselves in favour of the
federation of the library associations and bibliographical
societies of the world when this was suggested by the American
Library Association, and in 1909 accepted an invitation to
participate in the 1910 conference of the Institut International de
Bibliographie at Brussels.[181] The success of the Brussels
cooperation encouraged the formation, at the end of the year, of
a committee to follow up the work of the conference, to
welcome foreign librarians and to 'encourage intercourse
between British and foreign librarians'.[182] But, if such activities
were to be productive and successful, they had to be adequately
underwritten financially. By 1914 the committee had ceased to
meet.[183]

There was, however, one example of Anglo-American cooperation of an unusually lasting character, the importance of which can hardly be exaggerated. The Association took continuous official interest in the problems of cataloguing, although not of classification. Since, however, the Honorary Secretary, L. S. Jast, worked so hard to popularise the Dewey Decimal classification, and his old friend, J. D. Brown, even harder to provide British libraries with British substitutes, it may be argued that official achievement in the one art, and unofficial achievement in the other proved equally productive. Be that as it may, the English edition of the Anglo-American cataloguing rules derived from the LA's Annual Meeting of 1902.

Following the 1902 Meeting at Birmingham – when papers on cataloguing and on the LA's own revised rules of 1883 were read[184] – a cataloguing rules committee worked on a revised draft code. The Honorary Secretary, Wyndham Hulme, reported on achievement to date at the Annual Meeting in 1904 and

submitted a proposal by Mr Dewey that the LA and American LA should unite in the production of an Anglo-American code with a view to establishing uniformity in cataloguing throughout the English speaking race.[185]

Dewey's suggestion was cordially approved and Jast took the proposal to the American Congress in the following October; he was rewarded with a unanimous resolution in favour. Much correspondence followed, outstanding differences were resolved, and J. C. M. Hanson, Chairman of the ALA's committee, attended a meeting of the Association's committee at the Glasgow Annual Meeting of 1908. It was finally agreed that, in the few remaining cases of disagreement, both English and American rule forms should be printed together. The English edition of the Anglo-American cataloguing code was published in December 1908; sales soon covered production costs.[186]

The least happy personal event of the present period was the resignation from the Association of one of its best known and most influential members, James Duff Brown, as from the end of 1911. The reasons for it may be ascribed partly to dissatisfaction with LA policy and achievements but substantially to the serious ill-health which led to his death, at the early age of fifty-one, in February 1914. The LA Council proposed Brown's election as Honorary Fellow on 1 September 1913 and reported his acceptance on 17 October. Following his death in the following February the *Record* published a long multi-contributor obituary which is still unique of its kind.[187] In the course of a paper sent by him in January 1912 to the New Zealand Libraries Association for their conference at Wellington in the following April, Brown wrote:

It is perhaps unfortunate that the stagnation of years has been allowed to exist so long that its mere momentum is sufficient to carry it on far beyond reasonable limits, and this stagnation not only affects library authorities, but is even a competent factor in the life of the LA, which for many years past has accomplished practically nothing, either for librarianship at large or the members themselves. Indeed, within recent years, this Association has exercised a reactionary influence, because it is now conducted upon pseudo-academic rather than business lines, which are not calculated to secure the best results. No persistent attempt is made to attract a large and representative membership; the papers read at annual and monthly meetings for years past have been elementary and more or less banal; and the policy of the council has been controlled and directed for some time by men who are not thoroughly well acquainted with library conditions in different kinds of libraries all over the country. They are not thoroughly representative because the country members are not able to attend meetings in London, and they see things through a medium of self-sufficiency, which is not healthy, nor in the best interests of national librarianship. One result of this policy has been that the Association has slowly dwindled or remained stationary in membership, resources and influence, and it is not too much to say that since Mr MacAlister resigned the Secretaryship in 1898, the Association has been one of the least influential in the country. This is an example of the stagnation which a bad standardised policy is sure to induce. There could be no greater contrast than exists between the energetic, virile and successful policy and meetings of the Library Assistants Association and the dull, futile and sleepy methods of the LA, whose sole claim to notice is its production of the stodgiest and most unreadable library magazine ever inflicted upon innocent readers....[188]

Each one of Brown's criticisms was assuredly justified – to greater or lesser extent. It is, nevertheless, still reasonable to maintain that the Association, during those disappointing years prior to the outbreak of World War One, successfully laid some of the foundations for its successes following World War Two.

References

1. 19.5.1911.
2. 18.2.1908; 15.1.1909.
3. *The John Rylands Library, Manchester: a brief descriptive account.* 1958.
4. pp 65–234.
5. Munford, *Brown*, pp 24–38, 41–4, 49, 53. See also Brown, 'Library progress' in *L*(NS), 1, pp 5–11.
6. 'Reference libraries I have known', *LR*, 15, p 155.
7. *LAR*, 1, pp 1–2.
8. *L*, 10, pp 398–400.
9. *L*(NS), 1, p 1.
10. *LW*, 1, pp 1–2.
11. *YB*(1899), p 61.
12. *Ibid.*
13. *Ibid*, pp 22–3. *See also* C. Madeley, 'Librarians of the Mersey District', *LAR*, 22, pp 221–8.
14. *Ibid.*
15. *Ibid*, pp 62–3.
16. M. J. Ramsden, *A History of the Association of Assistant Librarians, 1895–1945.* 1973, Ch 1.
17. *Ibid*, Ch 5.
18. *L*, 10, pp 159–160.
19. *LW*, 1, p 15.
20. E. A. Savage, in his *A Librarian's memories*, 1952, doubts whether he was ever elected Chairman of the Council. The Council minutes record that he was so elected. *See* eg 16.10.1908, 15.10.1909, 2.10.1910, 5.9.1911, 3.9.1912 etc.
21. *Obit* in *LAR*, 30, pp 221–3.
22. A brief account of his life and career will be found in W. G. Fry and W. A. Munford, *Louis Stanley Jast.* 1966.
23. LSE Letters Misc 409.
24. 16.11.1906.
25. 21.1.1910.
26. 18.1.1907.
27. *LAR*, 12, pp 581–2.
28. 10.5.1901.
29. 28.1.1904.
30. 18.11.1910, 17.11.1911.
31. 21.4.1911.
32. 19.1.1912.
33. 20.6.1913, 18.7.1913.
34. *LAR*, 15, p 683.
35. Andrew Carnegie was entertained to dinner by the Association on 2.6.1913. (Council 20.6.1913).
36. *L*(NS), 4, pp 367–8.
37. *LAR*, 13, pp 384–8.
38. 22 *AR* (1899), p 10; 23 *AR* (1900), p 11.
39. *Dod's parliamentary companion.* 1917, 1918.
40. *LAR*, 6, p 497; 7, p 597; 8, p 516; 9, p 679; 10, p 607.
41. 31 *AR* (1908), p 6.
42. *LAR*, 8, pp 265–77.
43. *See* eg his 'Alderman Abbott and the rate limit', *LW*, 55, pp 63–7.
44. 19.4.1912.
45. 37 *AR* (1913–14), pp 8–9.
46. *L*, 4, pp 195–9.
47. F. A. Mumby, *Publishing and bookselling.* 1954, pp 288–9.
48. *LAR*, 4, pp 140–6. Discussion, pp 188–190.
49. 16.10.1902; 18.12.1902.
50. 16.11.1906.
51. *LAR*, 9, pp 269–284.
52. *Ibid*, pp 681–2.
53. *LAR*, 10, pp 608–9.
54. 30.6.1905, 24.10.1905.
55. *LAR*, 11, pp 527–33.
56. *Book Production committee report*, pp 28–9.
57. *LAR*, 6, contains 15 subject lists for 1902 and 1903.

58. *Obit* in *LAR*, 22, pp 27–9.
59. 30 *AR* (1907), p 13.
60. 32 *AR* (1903–9), p 9.
61. *LAR*, 16, pp 441–57.
62. 17.7.1914.
63. 15.1.1909.
64. 20.11.1908.
65. 'Public libraries and the N.H.R.U.', *LW*, 5, pp 169–71.
66. 15.2.1907, 19.7.1907, 17.7.1908.
67. 17.2.1905.
68. Fry and Munford *op cit*, pp 34–5.
69. 21.6.1912.
70. Munford, *Brown*, p 82.
71. 18.1.1907.
72. Fry and Munford *op cit*, pp 32–3.
73. 'Library publicity methods', *LW*, 16, pp 353–8.
74. *LAR*, 15, pp 235–6.
75. *LAR*, 7, pp 547–52, 611–17.
76. 36 *AR* (1912–3), p 11. *See also* Munford, *Edwards, Section 3*.
77. *See eg L*(NS) 4, pp 411–23; 6, pp 428–37; 8 pp 421–36.
78. *L*(NS) 9, pp 66–79, 173–85, 309–22, 353–68; 10, pp 188–200.
79. *LW*, 1, p 51.
80. *LW*, 2, p 101.
81. *LW*, 3, p 85.
82. *LW*, 10, p 121.
83. *LW*, 12, pp 171–7.
84. *LW*, 13, p 97.
85. *LW*, 5, p 85.
86. *LW*, 6, p 85.
87. *LW*, 4, p 105.
88. *LAR*, 3, pp 474–8, 481–5.
89. *LAR*, 14, p 23.
90. *L*(NS) 8, pp 316–336.
91. 'How the Branch associations may help the L.A.', *LAR*, 9, pp 109–119.
92. 'The immediate future of the L.A.' *LAR*, 13, pp 384–8.
93. *LAM* 877, p 235.
94. 21.4.1911.
95. Ramsden *op cit*, pp 61–6.
96. W. R. Aitken, *A History of the public library movement in Scotland to 1955*. 1971, p 230.
97. *L*, 10, pp 272–3.
98. Fry and Munford *op cit*, pp 19–20, 64 (*ref* 25).
99. eg 20.11.1899, 8.2.1901.
100. *LAR*, 5, p 526.

101. 36 *AR* (1912–13), p 8.
102. J. G. Ollé, 'Prayers at Highgate', *LR*, 21, pp 351–6.
103. 'How to improve the LAR', *LAR*, 9, pp 120–5.
104. eg 15.1.1909.
105. eg 18.6.1909.
106. Ramsden *op cit*, p 25.
107. London County Council Minutes, 20.1.1899, pp 123–6.
108. *LAR*, 1, pp 644–7.
109. *L*(NS) 4, p 215.
110. *LAR*, 3, p 503.
111. Beatrice Webb, *Our partnership*. 1948, pp 205–8.
112. Webb's paper, *LAR*, 4, pp 193–203. Discussion, for Roberts', *ref*, p 233.
113. Webb *op cit*, p 6.
114. Janet Beveridge, *An epic of Clare Market*. 1960. *Also* S. Caine, *The history of the foundation of the L.S.E. and P.S.* 1963
115. LSE Misc 409
116. D MacRae, '75 years of L.S.E.', *LSE*. (Special Library Appeal Number. 1973, p 19).
117. Beveridge *op cit*, p 62.
118. *LAR*, 4, pp 558–9.
119. Minute book of Summer School committee, pp 141–2.
120. *L Asst*, 3, pp 110–1.
121. LSE Minute Book of meetings of the sub-committees of the Library Instruction Committee.
122. Letter from LSE to LA, undated, presumably late 1904.
123. 6.11.1902.
124. Letter to H. D. Roberts, 13.3.1903.
125. 30.3.1903.
126. LA *Information relating to the professional examination etc.* 21.12.1903.
127. *LW*, 6, pp 226–7.
128. *L*(NS), 4, pp 144–62.
129. Memo (to LSE Governors) on course of instruction in library administration at the LSE and PS 27.10.1908.
130. 21.10.1910.
131. 15.7.1904, 21.6.1907, 25.10.1907.
132. 19.5.1911.

133. L. Fairweather, 'Professional examinations of the L.A.', *LW*, 9, pp 356–60.
134. *L Asst*, 6, pp 188–9.
135. *LAR*, 8, p 523.
136. *LW*, 14, pp 70–2.
137. *LW*, 13, p 203.
138. *LW*, 10, p 1.
139. *LACOM* 4.6.1903, 22.7.1903.
140. *LW*, 13, p 153.
141. 20.6.1913.
142. pp 12–3.
143. Minutes of the LSE Library Instruction Committee. 9.6.1915.
144. *LAR*, 8, pp 1–6.
145. *Ibid*, p 24.
146. 21.2.1908.
147. Fry and Munford *op cit*, p 32.
148. Ramsden *op cit*, p 68.
149. *Ibid*, p 69.
150. *L*(NS) 10, pp 410–421.
151. Munford, *Brown*, p 83.
152. Minutes of the 32nd Annual Meeting.
153. Ramsden *op cit*, p 72.
154. 35 *AR* (1911–12), pp 11–12.
155. *L*(NS) 8, pp 316–29.
156. *LC*, 5, pp 11–16.
157. 19.1.1906.
158. *LW*, 68, p 211.
159. 21.2.1908.
160. *L Asst*, 8, pp 121–38.
161. 'The salaries of librarians and their assistants', *LW*, 14, pp 33–4.
162. Fry and Munford *op cit*, p 38.
163. *LW*, 14, pp 33–4.
164. *LW*, 16, pp 228–32.
165. 21.4.1911.
166. *Ibid*.
167. 15.3.1912.
168. 20.12.1912.
169. *LAR*, 16, p 361.
170. 37 *AR* (1913–14), p 13.
171. eg 20.6.1913, 24.4.1914.
172. 25 *AR* (1902), p 7.
173. 20.6.1913.
174. 20.2.1914.
175. 21.5.1915.
176. Munford, *Edwards*, pp 99, 110, 129. Letter from City Librarian of Leicester to author, 26.7.1973.
177. 23 *AR* (1900), p 12.
178. 27 *AR* (1904), p 15.
179. 21.6.1912.
180. 33 *AR* (1910), p 8.
181. 19.3.1909.
182. 16.12.1910.
183. *LAR* 16, p 89.
184. *LAM* 877, p 197.
185. *Ibid*, pp 214–5.
186. 27 *AR* (1904), p 10; 28 *AR* (1905), p 9; 29 *AR* (1906), p 9; 30 *AR* (1907), p 15; 31 *AR* (1908), p 10; 32 *AR* (1908–9), p 8.
187. *LAR*, 16, pp 239–262.
188. Munford, *Brown*, p 93.

First Interlude: World War One

Chapter Five

1914-1919

Although complaints that the Association and its Council were 'inactive' during the years of World War One were to be made, at the time, by individual librarians, by groups of them and by the independent journals, the period seems, in retrospect, to have been one of greatly varied and constructive activity of considerable importance for the future. But the LA no longer pursued its objectives in splendid isolation; it had a sympathetic ally of great strength and influence. Some at least of its activities were now to be underwritten – to significant extent – by the Carnegie United Kingdom Trust.

References have necessarily been made earlier to the municipal library grants given by Andrew Carnegie.

In all they amounted to £1¾ million and financed in whole or in part more than half the total number of public libraries which were in existence in 1913.[1]

In 1913 Carnegie, pleased with the success of his other trusts, notably the Carnegie Corporation of New York for the benefit of the people of the United States and Canada, and the Carnegie Trust for the Universities of Scotland, decided to create another for the United Kingdom:

On the 3rd October, 1913, therefore, Mr Carnegie executed a Trust Deed whereby a capital sum of Ten million dollars, approximately Two million pounds sterling, was placed in trust, so that the income, amounting to about £100,000 a year, might be used 'for the improvement of the well-being of the masses of the people of Great Britain and Ireland by such means as are embraced within the meaning of the word "charitable" according to Scotch and English law, and which the Trustees may from time to time select as best fitted from age to age for securing these purposes, remembering that new needs are constantly arising as the masses advance'.[2]

Since Carnegie initially formed the new Trust to continue his benefactions for municipal libraries and church organs, the Trustees began by assuming responsibility for his past promises. They soon found themselves heavily involved, however, with important questions of future policy; they began to formulate it after the most careful and painstaking consideration. From the library angle the seminal early decision was the invitation to Professor W. G. S. Adams, Gladstone Professor of political theory and institutions in the University of Oxford

to report to them in regard to the existing Public Library provision in the United Kingdom with special reference to the extent to which Mr Carnegie's benefactions have been instrumental in furthering the library movement [and] to suggest any further directions in which the library movement might wisely be assisted in future.[3]

Adams' findings need not be covered in elaborate detail here:[4] in brief he found that while approximately 60% of English people, 50% of Scottish and Welsh, and 25% of Irish were served – mostly inadequately – by municipal libraries, residents in the smaller towns and, much more, in rural areas, were still in great need.[5] The Trust then decided that

broadly speaking, the library movement may best be furthered . . . if the question is dealt with under four main heads: **a** Rural library grants **b** Grants for special libraries of a national character **c** Loan charge grants to public libraries **d** Grants for public library buildings.

In the implementing of these objectives close cooperation with the LA would obviously be of great value: the practice of asking the Council to nominate librarians to inspect and report on the validity of applications for grants under heads **c** and **d** was well established before the end of 1916,[6] and continued. Such

124

cooperation was relatively uncontroversial although it must be admitted that some members of the Council tried very hard to persuade that body to agree only to the nomination of small committees of librarians to inspect other librarians' libraries.[7] The Council and the Association's members not only proved receptive also to the Trust Secretary's suggestion of a standardised form of public library statistics but appointed G. E. Roebuck, the Librarian of Walthamstow Public Library, to coordinate them as Honorary Statistician.[8] Similar easy cooperation was possible, under head **b** when the Trust was considering aid to organisations such as the Central Library for Students and the National Library for the Blind. It was likely to be much more difficult in connection with head **a** since both Adams and the Trust soon visualised a new rural service through the eyes of educationalists rather than librarians; to them the most promising administrative bodies were the *existing* Education Committees of the County Councils and not *new* standing committees comparable with the municipal library committees.

The impact of CUKT activities upon those of the LA will be considered in appropriate places in the pages to follow. The scale of the likely impact may be judged – from one angle – by comparing the Trust's annual income of £100,000 with that of the Library Association's which was £850 in 1913[9] and only rose to £900 in 1919.[10]

The LA Council met at Caxton Hall on the afternoon of Wednesday 12 August 1914, eight days after the British declaration of war on Germany. The fourteen members present, with Tedder in the Chair, did not include the Honorary Secretary, as Jast had been holidaying in Switzerland and was finding the unexpected detours on his journey home difficult and time-consuming.[11] The Annual Meeting was to have been held – and for the first time since 1878 – in Oxford with, as President, Nicholson's successor as Bodley's Librarian, Falconer Madan (1851–1935). The Presidency was confirmed but the Council decided – in line with contemporary expectations of a short war – to postpone the conference 'until 1915' and to arrange, instead, for an Annual Business Meeting confined to official matters and strictly necessary business . . . on the date originally announced, Friday, September 4th. . .

and at the Public Library in Buckingham Palace Road, sw, the headquarters of the City Librarian of Westminster, Frank Pacy, who had been appointed to act as Honorary Secretary pending Jast's return.

Business at the Annual Meeting was conducted on normal lines. The retiring President, the Earl of Malmesbury, was thanked; the scrutineers' certificate covering the recent election of officers and Council was received and there was a small amendment to the Bye-laws. The Meeting defeated a motion by an ever increasingly awkward member, A. J. Philip,

That this meeting appoint a Committee to inquire into the working of the Council, with power to call witnesses and examine all documents, and to pay reasonable legal and other expenses incurred. The meetings of the Committee to be open to members of the Association and to the Professional Press for report.

The defeat was overwhelming as only Philip and his seconder voted in favour: Jast, now back from Switzerland, was one of the many speakers against. By contrast, another resolution, carried unanimously, was a sad sign of changing times:

That the members of the LA, representing the principal libraries of the British Empire, in Annual Meeting assembled, desire to place on record their feelings of profound indignation at the wanton and unprovoked act of vandalism on the part of the German Army by the destruction of the City of Louvain, that ancient seat of learning, with its famous University and Library, whereby the world of scholarship has suffered irreparable loss.[12]

MacAlister and Tedder were later to be appointed delegates to a committee 'for the purpose of collecting books to re-establish the Louvain Library', following a letter of invitation from Viscount Bryce.[13]

After its initial stupefaction at the very idea of a European War, the nation's anti-German spirit soon resembled that of a Crusade.

Young librarians, like other young men in other walks of life, began to flock for service in the Armed Forces of the Crown. Soon, alas, the lists of members serving were including the names of those who had died on active service. The oak mural tablet in the British Museum, unveiled in 1924, displays the names of members of the profession to whom it is a memorial.[14] Members in the Forces were regarded by the Association as having 'leave of absence with the subscriptions in abeyance'.[15] Fortunately, from the point of view of the Association's immediate finances, there was a substantial increase in membership during 1914 'in anticipation of the new conditions governing election to Fellowship and Membership after the end of 1914'[16] as the Council put it. During the 1920s at least, young assistants working laboriously for their professional qualifications sometimes referred critically, if occasionally also enviously, to the '1914 FLAS', whose pre-War status had exempted them from like ordeal by examination.

Wartime attendance at the monthly meetings became so disappointingly small that it was soon thought best to arrange them only jointly with those of the Library Assistants Association; after June 1916, the Association withdrew its own recognition even from these.[17] The Branch and provincial associations, on the other hand, were less inactive and more than a little controversy was caused when the Council approved the formation of a new Branch, the North Central,

to cover the whole of the West Riding of Yorkshire and all that part of Lancashire and Cheshire which lies to the east of a north-and-south line drawn to the west of Greater Manchester, and including such places as Eccles, Altrincham and Accrington, which are near to or on such a north-and-south line.[18]

The controversy was due partly to the fact that the area of the new Branch included parts of those of the North Western Branch and of the Northern Counties LA and partly because of the traditional rivalry between Liverpool and Manchester – Jast had moved from Croydon to Manchester and was substantially responsible for the new move. It is at least possible that authority for the change might have been given much less readily had the Council not felt bound to resolve on 19 March 1915

that this Council having had brought before its notice the issue of a circular in the name of a Branch Association asking its members not to vote for certain named candidates, is of opinion that such procedure is contrary to the interests of the Association at large, and expresses the hope that such circulars will not be issued in future.

The offending circular had been issued by the Honorary Secretary of the North Western Branch 'acting by instruction of Mr G. T. Shaw, the President, to its members'. Shaw was also Chief Librarian of Liverpool Public Libraries.

As the members of the Council in 1914 were nearly all older and more senior librarians, few of them volunteered for active service during the early years of the War and, when conscription was introduced in 1916, numbers of chiefs were exempted. Many were in any case by then heavily engaged with duties deemed of national importance, in addition to normal responsibilities, book collecting for camp libraries included.[19] But exemption decisions were local ones, the Council having taken no action, 'there being no likelihood whatever of convincing the authorities that the services of men of military age are essential to keep the libraries open'.[20] Numbers of public library buildings were, in any case, requisitioned for other purposes.

Quarterly Council meetings, in place of monthly ones, were introduced from December 1916 and, although complaints of poor attendances were heard from time to time, those made seem reasonable, current difficulties accepted. Some at least of the rail fares of country councillors were paid during War years and the intelligent decision taken to appoint for the first time an executive committee to act as necessary.[21]

As in other occupations the vacancies caused by the War absences of young men were filled by women, usually recruited 'for the duration', and the LA began a register of temporary appointments available.[22] The changes also had an epoch-making result from the Council's point of view. At the

election of 1915 not only did W. C. Berwick Sayers
(1881–1960) – outstanding authority on classification, local
historian and biographer of Samuel Coleridge-Taylor, and
Jast's deputy and successor at Croydon – become a member for
the first time; the first woman councillor was elected. This was
Miss Kate E. Pierce (1873–1966), Librarian of Kettering Public
Library. Miss Pierce's success followed discussions between
women members and the sensible decision, taken in good time,
to nominate one woman only.[23] The Council has subsequently
had few women members; Miss Pierce was the exceptionally
popular pioneer.

In 1915 the Council invited MacAlister to become President; he
held office until his resignation in 1919. His attitude to his
war-time responsibilities may be summed up in a short extract
from his brief Presidential address:

When I sat down to think what I should say to you, I was immediately
faced by the profound conviction that no one – no man or woman in
these Islands – could possibly feel any real interest at this time in an
address on libraries, librarianship, or even the work of the LA.
Candidly, at this moment, I am not really interested in any of these
things myself, and if I am not, how can I expect any one in my
audience to be interested? Today we have all only one interest, and
beside that overwhelming and absorbing fact all other interests are,
and ought to be, secondary and almost negligible ... I hope – nay I
believe – that there is no one here today who would not, if free to
choose, rather be with our brethren at the front than listening to me
in Caxton Hall. They heard the call, and promptly answered it, and to
us who are left it will be a bitter life-long regret that we could not ...
When peace returns we shall be able to bring our minds back to our
daily round, our common task, to that modest but strenuous service
in the intellectual equipment and spiritual refreshment of the
community to which we are dedicated.[24]

He attended few meetings of the Council until the last year of
his Presidency, of which more later, but his monthly reunions
for LA members at the Royal Society of Medicine were greatly
appreciated by the small number of librarians and assistants able
to attend them. His many services to the wider community
received appropriate recognition with the conferring of a
knighthood in 1919.

Tedder continued in office as Honorary Treasurer throughout the War years and was also continuously re-elected Chairman of the Council until the beginning of 1919 when, in view of the possibility for the first time of a contested election, he declined to be a candidate.[25] Jast stayed as Honorary Secretary until October 1915 when he tendered his resignation on his appointment as Deputy City Librarian of Manchester. It was then unanimously resolved:

That the Council hear with extreme regret the announcement of Mr Jast's resignation of an office which he has filled for ten years to their entire satisfaction. Mr Jast's services to the Association and to the public library movement generally have been conspicuous and unwearied, and deserve the gratitude and warm thanks of the Council as well as of all the fellows and members. The Council feel that every one will recognise with them the loss to the administration of the valuable services of a capable and zealous officer, but they are gratified to know that Mr Jast will continue to exercise in a wider field at Manchester the same professional ability and energy which have hitherto distinguished him. He will carry with him the good wishes of all who have been privileged to work with him. That in recognition of Mr Jast's services to the Association he be nominated for election as an Honorary Fellow.[26]

Pacy was persuaded to take up again the responsibilities which he had given up in 1901; he continued as Acting Honorary Secretary until the Council meeting of 16 November 1917,[27] when he at last agreed to be confirmed in office. It was through Pacy – who volunteered to act as the Association's representative on the Committee of the National Library for the Blind, following that organisation's appropriate request – that the LA was able to arrange for Council and other meetings to be held at the new NLB building in Tufton Street, Westminster, from 1918 onwards. The accommodation was offered free of charge but the Association made a contribution of £25 towards NLB funds in 1919.[28]

The *Library Association Record* maintained regular, if sometimes delayed, and, owing to rising prices, increasingly expensive, publication. But a proposal by Grafton and Co. the new publishers of *The Library World*, that amalgamation should be

seriously considered, was declined.[29] Henry Bond continued as
Editor until 1917 when, faced with personal disasters,
he committed suicide;[30] his duties were taken over by W. E.
Doubleday.[31] It was at Doubleday's suggestion, too, that
the Council tried in 1917 to reopen the question of public
library discounts on net books. The Booksellers 'declined to
discuss the matter'.[32] The classified monthly lists of best books
in the *Record*, the introduction of which had coincided with the
outbreak of War, continued to appear until April 1916. There
was obviously a good case, however, for these useful and
well-selected lists to be published, instead, in a general literary
periodical; approaches were made to the proprietors of *The
Athenaeum*. *The Athenaeum* had been continuously published
since 1828 and had long been regarded – among many good
British literary weeklies – as, if not unmistakeably the best, at
least as *primus inter pares*. It was as natural for the LA to seek to
cooperate with it during the early years of World War One as it
had been for Edward Edwards to pay special attention to its
reviews of the *Report of the Select Committee on Public Libraries* of
1849.[33] The magazine's own list of 'the week's books' was, in
any case, a regular feature. But the War was beginning to take its
toll of literary journals. When *The Athenaeum* changed from a
sixpenny weekly to a shilling monthly in January 1916, 'the
week's books' was displaced by a monthly list classified by
Dewey. The Council were now able to arrange for close
cooperation. From the following May the *Record*'s lists were
discontinued and *The Athenaeum* announced that

Our list of new books will now be prepared in collaboration with a
committee of specialists appointed by the Library Association who
will be responsible for the asterisks distinguishing the works that, in
their opinion, are eminently suitable for purchase by Public Library
Authorities.[34]

If, to a modern reader, the asterisks seem few, the titles thus
chosen provide material for research into the book selection
principles of some librarians sixty years ago. Dr Baker
continued as general editor.

The *Athenaeum* monthly lists appeared regularly until June 1920.

They were fortunate to survive the drastic changes in the proclaimed objectives of the magazine which, from January 1917, was no longer sub-titled 'a journal of English and foreign literature, science, the fine arts, music and the drama'. It became, instead, 'a journal of politics, literature, science and the arts'; within a few months it was an entirely different magazine, devoting much space to politics 'in Aristotle's sense of the term', and more to the admittedly pressing problems of social and political reconstruction.[35] It reverted to its earlier sub-title when it again became a weekly in April 1919, but much of its traditional literary appeal had gone for ever; when it finally amalgamated with the *Nation* in February 1921 it was a mere shadow of its former self. The change to monthly publication in 1916 had also obviously made its columns much less useful for the well-established advertising of library staff vacancies but it agreed to duplicate such advertisements in the weekly *Notes and Queries* free of charge. The LA Council felt bound to recommend libraries to continue to use *The Athenaeum* for this important purpose;[36] there was another reason for such support.

Poole's great indexes to periodical literature, which had been discussed at the American 1853 and 1876 conferences and in 1877 in London, had been continued by supplements, but only up to 1908. Although *Poole* had had American successors, notably the publications of the H. W. Wilson Co, their coverage of British periodicals had been scanty. W. T. Stead's thirteen annual volumes of *Review of Reviews Indexes,* – alphabetical by author – had been published in London between 1890 and 1902 and had covered about 150, mostly British, magazines. But despite their reasonable price of 15*s* a volume, general and library sales had been small and the series had lapsed.

At the Bournemouth conference in 1913, T. W. Lyster (1855–1922), Librarian of the National Library of Ireland, had reminded members of the index need and a resolution had asked the Council to investigate.[37] Following negotiations with the H. W. Wilson Co, which had eventually to be broken off, to the extreme regret of both parties,[38] the Council arranged for the publication of an *Athenaeum* subject index to periodicals. Wyndham Hulme, Chairman of the LA's committee, was

primarily responsible for the early lists, helped by his assistant at
the Patent Office Library, H. V. Hopwood; he also put the
Association quite literally in his debt by providing the
Athenaeum with a private financial guarantee.[39] Lists, published
monthly in the magazine, began appropriately with two on
science and technology in 1915 and with another on education
and child welfare; and continued with music, classical languages
and literature, fine arts and architecture, sports and games. The
total of eleven class lists of November 1915 – April 1916,
covering 13,000 articles from 400 English, American and
Continental periodicals and transactions of learned societies,
were then consolidated and published in a separate volume as
*The Athenaeum subject index to periodicals, 1915: issued at the,
request of the Council of the Library Association.* About thirty
libraries had contributed entries and the arrangement was based
on the alphabetical subject headings of the Library of Congress,
of which, as the general editors rightly claimed in the preface,
'the present work is probably the first printed example'. This
publication, in its turn, was consolidated into *The Subject index to
periodicals: issued at the request of the Council of the Library
Association, 1915–1916,* the preface of which was dated January
1919. This index, like its predecessor, was published from the
Athenaeum office but, to avoid possible confusion – and it must
be admitted that regular readers of that magazine had had many
things to confuse them – its name was omitted from the title
page. These were the only volumes of the LA's *Subject index* to
be published during the war years. Even so, the second
consolidation, with its 29,000 entries from more than 530
periodicals, was a massive task for Hulme and Hopwood. The
Council rendered them no more than bare justice when
expressing the view that 'their ability in the handling of the
difficult and complicated problems which have arisen has only
been equalled by their untiring industry'.[40]
The National Library for the Blind which, as noted above,
provided accommodation for LA meetings from 1918 onwards,
also housed the Subject Index office when this moved from *The
Athenaeum*'s own premises.[41] Much generous and freely given
assistance helped to launch what was to become one of the
Association's most important serial publications. But library
'take-up' was at first disappointingly small. The CUKT supported

these early efforts by buying copies and presenting them to its new rural libraries.[42] Foreign libraries – American ones in particular – were also quick to realise the value of the new Index.[43]

The preface to the second consolidation of the Index included generalisations which were true then and are true still:

There can be little question that, during the last few years, under the stress of war conditions, the want of an organised system for discovering the results of scientific research, for collecting information and ascertaining the trend of public opinion on matters of current interest has been acutely felt. As a result there has been a marked appreciation in the value of bibliography, which henceforward must be recognised as a necessary adjunct not only to scholarship and research, but also to the successful conduct of industry, commerce and administration. The movement, however, will bear little fruit unless these departments are staffed with a new type of official specially qualified to translate into action or practice the data collected, classified and distributed by the bibliographer ... Thus the province of the bibliographer is that of an agent between two principals – the author on the one hand and the promoter, or "projector" as he would have been dubbed in the 18th century on the other. For the efficient conduct of his work the bibliographer must possess a special aptitude and training, the foundation of which will always be the innate love of books. For the acceptance of these principles the Council of the Library Association have been striving for many years past. Their realization now seems to have come within the sphere of practical politics.

The parallel proposal for a lending library of the periodicals indexed – the provision of which was to have been entrusted to the W. H. Smith organisation but which, owing to the many war-time difficulties of the latter, fell to the Central Library for Students, was much less successful.[44] But the LA Council had also been approaching the same major problem from a different angle. At the meeting on 4 October 1916 the Chairman (Tedder) had reported:

that he had had an interview with Sir William McCormick, Chairman of the Advisory Committee of the Privy Council on the subject of Technical Libraries and Collections, who was in sympathy with our movement in the matter and that he hoped for a further interview and discussion of the subject.

Sir William McCormick (1859–1930), as the DNB related, 'was active in the development of the rural libraries, the formation of the Central Library for Students, now the National Central Library, and the School of Librarianship at University College, London'. He had been the first Secretary of the Carnegie Trust for the Universities of Scotland and, in addition to his membership of the CUKT, became Chairman of the University Grants Committee and its predecessor committee and of the DSIR, and its predecessor committee of the Privy Council to which Tedder referred.

Following Tedder's statement Savage successfully moved

that a special committee of the Council be appointed to prepare a report upon ways and means of strengthening public technical libraries in industrial centres.

With Hulme as chairman and Savage as honorary secretary, the new LA Committee soon found itself faced with a variety of problems, some of them unexpected. Its remit was almost immediately extended to include commercial libraries and, as it quickly learnt that the Panizzi Club – founded in 1914 and 'composed of the senior officers of State, University and Professional libraries'[45] – had begun to compile a list of current periodicals 'to be found in Public and Professional libraries in the United Kingdom,[46] cooperation was essential. The Council also referred to it a resolution included in the Workers Educational Association's then recent pamphlet on *Educational reconstruction*:

9. PUBLIC LIBRARIES – That, in view of the importance of extending and developing the work of the public libraries in town and country, it is desirable that they should be brought into closer connection with the general educational system of the country. With this end in view the separate library rate should be abolished and the provision and upkeep of public libraries should be entrusted to the Local Educational Authority as an integral part of the scheme for its area.[47]

The first part of the resolution fell to be supported and the second, equally obviously, to be opposed. Steps had to be taken accordingly and appropriate deputations were arranged.

The interest of the DSIR and of the CUKT in technical and commercial libraries was now sought. It may be noted, in passing, that the LA's own interest, although not completely and entirely new had – up to the present period – been diffused and ineffective. It was also true that, up to the end of 1916, only three municipal authorities in the United Kingdom – the City of London, Manchester and Glasgow – had shown outstanding interest in the subject; Glasgow opened the first full commercial library service in November 1916, thus beginning to meet a need which was being highlighted by wartime conditions and necessities.[48] The DSIR was informed that

The provision of scientific and technical literature in many public libraries is, as a rule, quite insufficient for the needs of students, research workers and others. More liberal provision would increase the number of students and promote their efficiency. Such provision is specially inadequate in industrial centres with a high percentage of working people, whose contribution to the rates cannot suffice to provide the technical literature which is essential to them and to the industries in which they are engaged. It is significant that nearly all the library authorities which have sought, at considerable expense, parliamentary powers to levy an additional rate are authorities in industrial areas.

and advised that

i   the existing statutory limit to the library rate should be removed
ii a national lending library of scientific and technical literature for research workers should be founded (in connection with an existing state library and using public libraries as local agents)

Concurrently the Secretary to the Carnegie Trustees advised a formal approach to them but warned that 'it would be a practical impossibility for the Trust to embark upon a scheme of technical book provision in the libraries of the country'.[49]

Individual members of the LA Committee prepared and submitted to it papers on relevant subjects such as trade catalogues, directories and code books, patents, the training of technical librarians, cooperation with the Board of Trade, and proposals for inter-library lending, the latter by Savage. Then, as if the committee were not sufficiently burdened already, the Council referred to it the task 'of preparing at once a scheme of library development in view of after-war conditions'.[50] The new task was quickly hived off as a sub-committee activity; the concentration was initially on libraries and education and specifically on work with children.[51]

The Interim Report of the Council on the provision of technical and commercial libraries, the cost of which was to be met by the CUKT, was presented to the London Conference in October 1917. It began by reprinting the original memorandum addressed to the DSIR and now recommended specifically

i   that local authorities should afford more generous support to public libraries for the provision of scientific and technical literature

ii   that municipal and other library authorities and institutions should cooperate in issuing union catalogues of technical books, and adopt such other co-operative methods as will make their resources available over wider areas

iii that a State scientific or technical library should publish periodically a descriptive list of selected books in Science and Technology

iv that a more extended use should be made of periodical literature by the increased provision of current indexes and digests[52]

Other suggestions covered many topics including Board of Trade publications, trade catalogues, and the training of librarians for the special services. The Report in particular expressed the important opinion that

the possession of scientific and technical qualifications will not in themselves suffice unless their holder has previously received the foundation of a sound library training.

There was also a final paragraph which may be regarded as a first fingerpost to future activity:

The Council are of opinion that by organizing a body of special librarians within the Library Association and by including a section in the *Record* on Special Libraries (to serve the purpose of the American journal of that name), the membership of the Association might be increased and the interest of members generally awakened to the advantages of specialization.[53]

The LA's 1917 Conference, which was of outstanding importance because of its concern also with work with children and with professional education, debated and passed two resolutions:

In view of meeting trade conditions after the war, commercial libraries should be established in all the great trade centres of the kingdom, as a part of the municipal library system, where business may obtain reliable commercial information, by means of the collection and arrangement for rapid consultation of all Government and other publications relative to commerce; such libraries should act as branches of the Commercial Intelligence Department of the Board of Trade; and such Department should further the work of these libraries in every possible way; in the smaller towns commercial collections should be formed.[54]

The first, set out above, was moved appropriately by S. A. Pitt, City Librarian of Glasgow. The second, which follows, was moved, equally appropriately by Hulme:

Technical libraries are as essential, both to technical education as to manufacture, as the laboratory or the workshop; discovery and invention are stimulated by books; the technical library, therefore, should be established as a department of the public library in all important manufacturing towns, with a special organization, including a librarian trained not only in library methods and in the bibliography of technology, but possessing also sufficient technical knowledge to enable him to act as a medium of information to inquirers.[55]

Delegates spread themselves during the debates, so much so indeed that the size of the printed report caused the Government's Paper Controller to protest.[56] The resolutions which they passed were sent to the Government departments most closely concerned. Little, if anything seemed to happen as a result and, as if to remind the Association at large that progress was much too slow, the new North Central Branch arranged another conference but at the John Rylands Library in Manchester, in October 1918. Here the resolutions passed were as follows:

1. That fully equipped and intensively organized technical and commercial libraries should be formed, under the control of the Municipal Library Authorities, in the half-dozen chief industrial centres of the Kingdom; that these libraries should receive a grant from the Government as a contribution towards their upkeep; that their provision is urgent in the interests of the technical trade of this country; and that these large district libraries should be related to the smaller technical collections in their vicinity.
2. That this meeting urges on the Council of the LA the formation, as soon as possible, of a special Technical and Commercial section of the Association.
3. That the provision of children's libraries and reading rooms, adequately equipped and suitably staffed, is an urgent national need as the only effective way of safeguarding the imaginative life of the child; that the reading rooms should remain, as now, part of the municipal library system; and that the circulation of lending books in the schools should be undertaken by the education authority in cooperation with the library authority.
4. That this meeting of Members of Library Authorities and Librarians, representing all parts of the country, urges on the Government the absolute necessity of the removal of any limitation on the Library rate.
5. That the Council of the LA be requested to arrange immediately for a deputation to the Local Government Board in order to press for temporary relief pending legislation.[57]

The North Central Branch had tried hard to make its locally arranged conference of wide national appeal; its resolutions were referred, rather inconclusively, to the LA's Southport Conference in 1919.

The DSIR did not proceed on the lines suggested by the LA. It preferred, instead, to promote the organisation of technical libraries in conjunction with industries and industrial associations.[58] It also decisively rejected the proposal for a

nationally organised central lending library of scientific and
technical books,[59] a decision which may seem ironic in the light
of the development of the DSIR's National Lending Library of
Science and Technology, one World War later. But the LA's
activities undoubtedly encouraged the formation of new
technical and commercial libraries in the large municipal
authorities. An unpersuasive eight-page illustrated pamphlet,
Proposals for an improved technical library service, published by the
Association in 1919, deserved to make little further impact and
made none. The sub-committee activities on work with children
were even more successful during the next period, being – like
technical and commercial libraries – greatly facilitated by the
abolition of the penny rate limit.

By the beginning of 1919 the financial situation of many, if not
most, municipal libraries had degenerated from straitened to
desperate. Trapped as they were between the Scylla of the penny
rate limit and the Charybdis of sharply rising prices and cost of
living bonus additions to staff salaries, their continued existence
was in jeopardy. The election of a new Government in
December 1918 – though certainly not one of markedly 'liberal'
promise – encouraged the LA Council to urge Local Authorities
to pass resolutions in favour of ending the rate limit; it was soon
reported that 'a large majority' of those replying had complied. [60]
But there was undoubtedly feeling abroad that the Council of the
Association was 'dragging its feet'. 'An informal meeting of the
librarians of London Boroughs and the Extra Metropolitan
Districts' was held at Caxton Hall on 30 April 1919,
G. E. Roebuck acting as honorary secretary. Members attending
were, however, substantially satisfied with Pacy's, the LA
Honorary Secretary's, account of recent Council activity. [61] On
10 May the CUKT addressed a circular letter to all Local Library
Authorities and to all Members of Parliament, of which the key
paragraph read:

Serious though the financial strain has been in the past, the position of
public libraries today is precarious. Unless early and effective steps
are taken to allow each town to decide for itself what annual sum is
necessary to conduct efficiently one of its most popular institutions, it
appears highly probable that many Public Libraries will have to close
their doors or be administered unsatisfactorily. [62]

Agitation continued throughout the summer and autumn of
1919, strengthened by the support of the *Interim Report of the
Adult Education Committee of the Ministry of Reconstruction,* and
Fovargue prepared yet another draft Bill. [63]

At the meeting of the LA Executive Committee on 14 November
1919, Ballinger offered to contact the Parliamentary Secretary
to the Board of Education, and the Committee accepted 'with
great pleasure'. The Parliamentary Secretary was J. Herbert
Lewis (1858–1933) who, as noted earlier, had shown
his sympathy for the public libraries' case in 1914 when
Parliamentary Secretary to the Local Government Board. He
had subsequently given up his Flintshire seat in the House of
Commons and had been returned at the 1918 Election as the
Member for the University of Wales. He had also been
closely associated with the National Library of Wales since its
foundation and was a friend of long standing of the Prime
Minister, David Lloyd George; contact with him by the
National Librarian of Wales, who had previously been the
municipal librarian of Cardiff for many years, was obviously of
quite exceptional value. [64] That value was demonstrated when,
on 28 November, Lewis introduced the amending Bill for which
the LA and public librarians had been waiting for so long. During
the Second Reading, on 2 December, he confirmed that the
Board of Education had 'been receiving most urgent
representations, by deputation and otherwise, from all parts of
the country'. [65] The Government of the country, at long last, was
obviously now in real earnest and brushed aside the opposition
of Sir Frederick Banbury, who had long since become a
Commons' institution 'as an opponent of legislation which
appeared to him to be unnecessary and of change which he did
not regard as progress'. [66] The Bill passed through all remaining
stages on 11 December, passed the Lords with only drafting
amendments and received the Royal Assent on 23 December
1919.*

---

* Students of political irony may note
with interest that the LA's previous
unsuccessful link with the Asquith
'wing' of the Liberal Party, *via*
H. J. Tennant, MP, noted earlier, was
now followed by a successful link with
the Lloyd George 'wing'.

The Act of 1919 not only removed the rate limit in England and Wales. It also authorised the adoption of the Public Libraries Acts, 1892–1919, by County Councils, for the whole or for any part of their areas, and provided that their new powers should stand referred to their Education Committees. The practical implications of the important changes must stand referred, in their turn, to a later chapter.

During the later part of the present period the LA found itself in an increasingly embarrassing financial situation comparable with that of municipal libraries. Various expedients to increase income were explored and the sale of accumulated stocks of its own old publications was not overlooked.[67] But, as ever, financial solvency depended on a satisfactory level of subscriptions. A proposal to increase them was rejected at the Annual Meeting of 1918 but one year later it was agreed that 'The annual subscription for Fellows and for institution Members be two guineas and for Members and Associate Members one and a half guineas'.[68]
The CUKT also made it financially possible, and for the first time, to appoint a full-time paid secretary. E. C. Kyte, formerly Librarian of the Harlesden (Willesden) Public Library, who 'united with library and literary qualifications a creditable record of service during the war and considerable experience as an Education Officer',[69] was appointed to the new vacancy in June 1919.[70]

Before turning to the period of reconstruction following World War One, the progress made up to the end of 1919 in the preparation of a revised system of professional education falls to be considered.

Although the LA/LSE lectures were discontinued soon after the outbreak of war, the LSE Librarian, B. M. Headicar (1875–1958) volunteered to lecture on classification and cataloguing, telling his Director that otherwise 'the work of the student-assistants in the library here in preparation for the examinations of the LA was adversely affected'.[71] Bearing in mind that the lectures, although no longer official, were open to all comers, the LA was displeased and, following a report from its education committee's honorary secretary, Dr Baker, it was resolved, on 19 February 1915 'that the classes originally arranged [ie at the LSE] should be given by Mr J. H. Quinn and Mr W. C. Berwick Sayers at Caxton Hall commencing 17 February, 1915'. Headicar's classes continued until 1919 although those arranged by the LA did not.

The educational situation became progressively more difficult as more and more of the young male assistants passed into the Forces. The correspondence classes were continued for as long as possible but some had soon to be dropped.[72] The total number of candidates presenting themselves for the examinations fell from 332 in 1913 to 302 in 1914, 225 in 1915, seventy-two in 1916, sixty-three in 1917, forty-nine in 1918, and only recovered to seventy-eight in 1919.[73] The substantial decline from 1916 onwards was, however, only partly due to wartime conditions, since in 1915 the Council introduced

a preliminary test in English grammar and composition, and in elementary general knowledge, including English literature ... for candidates who do not hold certain approved (ie school leaving) certificates.[74]

Fifty-five out of 139 passed the preliminary test in 1916 but only eighteen out of sixty-nine in 1917, nineteen out of ninety-one in 1918, and twenty-two out of fifty-three in 1919.[75] Despite these disappointing results, there were also more encouraging portents. In August, 1917 the Summer Schools were revived – not in London – but, at the instigation of John Ballinger, at University College, Aberystwyth, and extending over two weeks.

Students were admitted to the courses at a low fee and were provided with accommodation at the University hostel on moderate terms. A total attendance of 58 students ... rewarded Mr Ballinger's exertions, and the lecturers reported that the interest taken by the students was most encouraging. The President (MacAlister) has given prizes ...[76]

There were thirty-three students at the 1918 School and thirty at that of 1919.

1917 was a momentous year for professional education. When the Fortieth Annual Meeting of the LA was held at Caxton Hall it was generally felt that time and thought could surely now be devoted to the tasks ahead *after* the War. Although the Russian Revolution had already taken one important ally effectively out of the War and the last desperate German onslaught still lay some months ahead, America had declared war and final victory seemed probable at last. The presence at one of the Conference sessions of the Minister of Reconstruction, Christopher Addison, appeared to confirm what had seemed, only recently, to have been forlorn hope; his encouraging address meant much to the delegates.[77]

Reconstruction in general obviously included educational reconstruction in particular; delegates were conscious not only of the obvious needs of those librarians and assistants returning from the Forces and of the generation to follow them; they were also keenly aware of the turmoil of discussion currently associated with the Parliamentary Bill – with its promise of part-time continuation courses for young people – which would become H. A. L. Fisher's great, but never fully implemented, Education Act of 1918.

On the last morning of the Conference Dr Baker opened a discussion on the education and training of librarians. He emphasised 'the total inadequacy of the means at present available', equated training needs with those deemed necessary for teachers, and drew attention to the absurdly small number – 'only about a dozen' who had completed the LA's Diploma *via* the six sectional certificates. He insisted:

we want a syllabus arranged in three grades, an elementary course, the ordinary course leading to the diploma, and advanced post-diploma courses in special branches of library science.

He reported that

a draft scheme for a series of library schools, in various centres in the British Isles is now before the Council. It is proposed that such schools should be established under the same roof or in close affiliation with existing technical schools, university colleges, or similar institutions. There would be nothing to prevent their location in a large library, so long as they were officially connected with the school or college, and recognised by the Board of Education. We are encouraged by the expressed view of the CUKT to hope that substantial aid would be offered us from that quarter.

and moved that 'a system of library schools for the British Isles should be established as early as possible under the control of the LA'. The resolution was carried after some diffused criticism – begun notably by the President (MacAlister) – but coming mostly from those who sought to discuss the subject in wider context.[78] Some of the best contributions came from three women delegates, Miss E. S. Fegan (1877–1975), Librarian of Cheltenham Ladies College and later of Girton, Miss Pierce, and Miss E. W. Austin (1875–1918), Librarian of the National Library for the Blind. Miss Austin's brief contribution deserves quotation in full:

We have spent two hours in discussing a question which was practically already settled, as to whether a library school was desirable or not, whether there was a demand for it. We are agreed we want a library school. We know pupils will be forthcoming if the remuneration is good enough. It seems to me that those who have been criticising Dr Baker's paper, or the idea of a library school, have been taking for their motto, "No advance without security." You will only get your library school by building now and not by looking for difficulties . . . You have not yet had a real word of constructive criticism of the paper, which probably means that the scheme is perfect.[79]

Although A. L. Hetherington, Secretary of the CUKT, who was present, felt bound to point out that 'The Trust is sympathetically interested in all these movements, but on this that is as far as it has gone', It had, however, already gone much further, at least in theory. The 3rd Annual Report of the Trust, signed on 31 January 1917, after commenting on progress with its rural schemes and with the housing of the Central Library for Students – of which more in the next chapter – had included three paragraphs of quite seminal importance:

22 One aspect of the public library movement seems to present features requiring careful consideration by all bodies interested in it.

The importance of the librarian as the vitalising link between the books and their readers seems apt to be overlooked, or – at all events – not placed in its proper perspective. Even if the provision of books is adequate both in quantity and quality to the population to be served, it will be of little avail unless an efficient staff exists for administering it.

At present the attitude of Local Authorities is too frequently to regard the librarian as a person whose sole duty is to hand books over a counter, and to consider that an employee with the slightest qualifications and training is sufficient for the purpose. The term "librarian" is lightly used, and often is applied to an official who is placed in charge of a collection of books, with very meagre knowledge of their contents and still less knowledge of the profession to which he purports to belong. This attitude on the part of some authorities results in a salary being paid which is totally inadequate for the responsibilities of the post. The inevitable result is that the profession as it stands today offers little or no attraction to a person with ambition, and who has a future to provide for. The present statutory rate limit of one penny in the pound, for library purposes, perforce limits authorities – who have not taken special powers to exceed it – to the strictest economy. The provision and upkeep of the building are necessarily first charges, and the provision of books and of an efficient library staff fall to be considered only after these first charges have been met.

23 While, however, a strong case for the reconsideration of present financial limitations can be made out, the elevation of a salary scale will not of itself secure the necessary status of the profession of librarianship, or place the right men and women in its ranks. Probably there is no other profession which demands – under present conditions – such slight qualifications and training from those who enter it. The position might be compared with that of the medical profession more than a hundred years ago. At that time students of medicine were apprenticed to apothecaries and surgeons, and then "walked" the hospitals, picking up the elements of knowledge which gradually equipped them for their career. Today the training of a medical student is a long and exacting one, which has gradually been evolved by the progress of medical science. If a responsible librarian's post has to be filled today, a well-advised authority can at best select a person who has been trained under some Librarian of repute, in other words, one who has been apprenticed to a well-known leader in the profession. There is no systematised course of training which provides a regular supply of qualified librarians, and it is, perhaps a matter for surprise that so much good work has been accomplished in so many of the Library Centres, considering the disabilities of training and of status under which the officials have worked.

24 Classes for librarians have been held at different times and at different centres in the country, and the LA has done a good deal in instituting qualifying examinations, and in issuing certificates of proficiency to those who pass them. But more than this is required. A technical training – based upon a sound preliminary course of general education – is wanted, and this training cannot be secured without providing more than occasional courses of lectures and correspondence classes. Schools for librarians might with advantage be established at the principal centres in the kingdom, co-ordinated with other branches of higher education which are there provided. Schools of this kind would provide the means for the proper study of a complicated subject, and would produce a corps of qualified librarians equipped for the efficient administration of the Public Libraries of the country.

Careful consideration of details would be needed before any professional school of the nature outlined above were established, but something of the kind seems necessary to improve the status of the librarian, and to create a different attitude towards librarianship from that adopted today by those in whose power the financial prospects of the profession largely rest. . . .

The subject of library schools had also not gone unnoticed at the London School of Economics, particularly as Professor Adams had, not unnaturally,

consulted the Secretary and the Librarian here as to their views of the results of the work we have been doing in librarianship during the last dozen years or so. He specially interested himself in the effects on library assistants here of being encouraged to take up work for a degree during the period of their training in librarianship.[80]

In June, 1917, Sidney Webb wrote to Carnegie Trustee Sir William McCormick:

In my view, the Library School ought to be part of a University institution; but then it ought to educate, and train in the best sense, cultivated Librarians, not juvenile assistants, who *merely* fetch and carry books. It ought to be open only to persons of 18 or 19 of fair secondary education; and it ought to provide a quite good undergraduate course of instruction in which the technical elements of Librarianship would play a part (but only a part). There would certainly not be room for more than one such School in the United Kingdom at present, and even that would be small; but it would serve all librarians, and lead on to the care of archives and palaeography, and even to literary and historical research, and not merely aim at making the youthful assistants in the Free Public Libraries more proficient in the handing out of volumes of popular fiction. I should like to see it fed by scholarships covering maintenance, so that the clever and ambitious young librarian from all parts could spend two or three years there, on their way to promotion or transfer to better posts.[81]

A draft scheme for the whole-time and part-time instruction of library students and for the establishment of library schools was submitted by the LA's Education committee to the Council on 21 June 1918; it was already known that earlier in the year a meeting at University College London had received encouraging responses from the Provost and Professorial Board. At the commencement of business at the Council meeting on 16 January 1919 the President (MacAlister) successfully moved

That the President, Honorary Treasurer and Honorary Secretaries with Dr Baker be empowered to negotiate in settling the terms of an educational scheme in cooperation with University College, and that the aforesaid officers, or a majority of them shall have full power to settle terms of such a scheme without reporting to the Council until completed.[82]

The Education committee reported to the Council in the following June:

a A meeting of the joint committee on the School of Librarianship took place at the University of London, South Kensington, on the 14 May, and meetings of a special sub-committee to consider the appointment of a Director took place the same day and on Wednesday the 21 May. The Vice Chancellor, Sir Edwin Cooper Perry, was appointed Chairman, and it was reported that the Carnegie United Kingdom Trustees had granted £1,500 a year for five years for maintenance of the School.

b The Scheme drawn up by the joint committee to establish the School was generally approved, with the amendment that the Joint

Committee for the management should be appointed annually in June. It was resolved provisionally that the School should open on the 1st of October next.

c The Joint Committee were of opinion that a formal instrument should be prepared binding the Council of the LA to defray the expenses of the Library School from the grant made by the Carnegie Trustees.

d At the meetings of the Special Sub-Committee Dr Baker was unanimously invited to allow himself to be recommended to the Senate as Director of the new School at a salary of £400 per annum (part time). His duties to include responsibility for the courses in Library Organization and Book Selection.
In view of the need to bring the existence of the School before Library Authorities we recommend that the Honorary Secretary of this Committee should visit the various Branch Associations and other LAs and to address the members and any representatives of the Library Authorities invited to be present on the subject of the Library School, suggesting methods by which assistance could be granted, leave of absence, and in some cases financial assistance, in order to attend the School; and that his travelling expenses be paid.[83]

Now came drama. The juxtaposition of Dr Baker as Honorary Secretary of the LA's Education Committee and now as Director-designate was too much for a majority of the Council. Although the action taken was considered by the Honorary Solicitor to be 'exactly and in every sense within the terms of the resolution' (of 16 January), a sufficient number of the Council were of opinion that they had not understood it to be so far-reaching and were therefore not bound by it.[84] It was accordingly resolved

That the Joint Committee be informed that the Council of the LA cannot approve of the paragraph relating to the appointment of a Director and are of opinion that this action is outside the terms of reference. They recommend that the appointment be advertised. Further resolved that the expenses of Dr Baker, as recommended, be limited to a sum not exceeding £20.

The President (MacAlister) reacted angrily and immediately and handed in a letter to the Chairman:

With deep regret I inform you that I have no alternative but to hand you my resignation.
I cannot with any self-respect approach the University or the Carnegie Trustees with such a humiliating story of ineptitude and vacillation as today's proceedings will reveal. Both these bodies saw the resolution of the Council, took it in good faith, and acted upon it, and I must leave it to others to undeceive them.[85]

The Council, surely remembering MacAlister's resignations in the past, instructed the Honorary Secretary to ask him to reconsider. But the President had never been in more deadly earnest and summoned a special, and exceptionally well-attended, meeting of the Council on 4 July where he moved (Tedder seconding)

That the resolution passed at the last meeting of the Council with reference to the appointment of Dr E. A. Baker as Director of the School of Librarianship, be rescinded and the decision communicated to University College.
Whereupon Baillie Campbell (in the Chair) read a protest signed by 12 members against any such rescinding.
The meeting declined to adopt the President's motion.[86]

So only one full-time school, and that dependent entirely on the CUKT grant-in-aid, resulted from the war-time deliberations of the Association. It was an important beginning but the controversy over the appointment of the first Director and the realisation that a diploma of university status was now likely to offer effective competition to the Association's own sectional examinations,[87] unnecessarily soured what should have been a cordial relationship from the outset. It is difficult also to avoid the reflection that the Council's agreement to the transfer of the Association's library to University College[88] was motivated not only by a desire to help the new School, but also by satisfaction at its removal from the LSE whose Librarian had carefully tended it since 1912.

In concluding this chapter it is pleasant to recall that war-time problems, pressing as they assuredly were, did not always occupy the minds of all librarians, to the complete exclusion of the transcendental. On 5 May 1916, during the period of the frenzied German attack at Verdun, a meeting of the LA, to commemorate Shakespeare's Tercentenary, was held at the Westminster Public Library in Buckingham Palace Road. Professor Macneile Dixon's inaugural address on 'Shakespeare the Englishman' was followed by a variety of other papers and discussions.[89] For one blissful day the audience of fifty were able to forget 'the heart-ache and the thousand natural shocks that flesh is heir to . . .'.

References

1. W. Robertson, *Welfare in trust: a history of the CUKT*. 1964, p 24.
2. CUKT, 1 *AR*, pp 3–4.
3. *Ibid*, pp 6–7.
4. eg Munford, *Penny rate*, 1951, pp 48–9; Robertson *op cit*, pp 25–30.
5. Munford *op cit*, pp 48–9.
6. 39 *AR* (1915–6). p 381.
7. eg 17.3.1916.
8. 40 *AR* (1916–7), p 12.
9. 37 *AR* (1913–4), p 17.
10. 43 *AR* (1919–20), p 14.
11. Fry and Munford, *L. S. Jast*, p 39.
12. *LAR*, 16, pp 458–464.
13. 30.8.1915.
14. *LAR*, 26, p 35; 27, p 5.
15. 39 *AR* (1915–6), p 368.
16. *Ibid*, p 367.
17. *Ibid*, pp 375–6.
18. *Ibid*, p 381.
19. *LAR*, 17, p 433; 18, p 89.
20. eg *LW*, 17, pp 138–41; 205–8.
21. *LAR*, 20, pp 284–5.
22. 39 *AR* (1915–6), p 382.
23. *LAR*, 17, pp 220–1, 397.
24. *Ibid*, pp 405–6.
25. *LAC*, 915, pp 242–3.
26. 39 *AR* (1915–6), pp 384–5.
27. 40 *AR* (1916–7), p 13; 42 *AR* (1918–9), p 12.
28. 43 *AR* (1919–20), p 14.
29. *LAC* 915, pp 237, 269.
30. Ollé, 'Prayers at Highgate', *LR* 21, pp 351–6.
31. 40 *AR* (1916–7), p 10.
32. *Ibid*, p 13.
33. Munford, *Edwards*, pp 67–72.
34. *Athenaeum*, 1916, p 219.
35. December, 1916, p 569.
36. 39 *AR* (1915–6), p 383.
37. *LAR*, 16, pp 39–47; discussion 15, pp 648–653.
38. Preface to *Athenaeum Subject Index*. 1915.
39. 40 *AR* (1916–7), pp 10–11.
40. 39 *AR* (1915–6), pp 378–9.
41. 42 *AR* (1918–9), p 12.
42. *Ibid*, p 14.
43. 43 *AR* (1919–20), p 11.
44. Letter from H. A. Twort, Librarian of Central Library for Students, dated 14.12.1916.
45. A. W. Pollard's report in *L*(3rd s) 5, pp 95–102.
46. *LAC* 915, p 105.
47. *Ibid*, p 107.
48. J. P. Lamb, *Commercial and technical libraries*. 1955, pp 25–30.
49. *LAC* 915, p 125.
50. *Ibid*, p 147.
51. *Ibid*, p 161.
52. *Interim Report*, p 4.
53. *Ibid*, p 8.
54. *LAR*, 19, pp 467–8.
55. *Ibid*, pp 484–5.
56. *LAC* 915, p 223.
57. 42 *AR* (1918–9), pp 6–7.
58. 43 *AR* (1919–20), p 10.
59. 42 *AR* (1918–19), p 10.
60. *LAC*, 915, p 260.
61. *Ibid*, pp 285–6.
62. CUKT, 6 *AR*, p 26.
63. *LAC* 915, p 323.
64. *Ibid*.
65. *Dod's, Parliamentary companion*. 1919, p 318.

66. Munford, *Penny rate*, pp 35–7.
67. 15.6.1917.
68. *LAR*, 21, p 409.
69. 42 *AR* (1918–9), p 16.
70. *LAC* 915, pp 277–9.
71. Minutes of LSE Committee, 9.6.1915.
72. 19.11.1915.
73. 42 *AR* (1918–9), p 25.
74. 38 *AR* (1914–5), pp 10–12.
75. 42 *AR* (1918–9), p 25.
76. 40 *AR* (1916–7), p 11.
77. *LAR*, 19, pp 430–4.
78. Full report in *LAR*, 19, pp 509–524.
79. *Ibid*, p 523.
80. LSE Director's report to LSE Committee, 9.6.1915.
81. LSE Letter, dated 25.6.1917.
82. *LAC* 915, p 243.
83. *Ibid*, pp 280–1.
84. *Ibid*, pp 290–1.
85. *Ibid*, p 286.
86. *Ibid*.
87. *Ibid*, pp 312, 314 etc.
88. 43 *AR* (1919–20), pp 10–11.
89. *LAR*, 18, pp 273–316; 324–30.

Between the Wars

Chapter Six

1920-1927

When the delegates who had been attending the Forty-third Annual Meeting of the Association began to stream out of Norwich on 10 September 1920 to return to their homes and libraries, they could savour the renewed attractions of normalcy but of a normalcy with improvements. It had been a stimulating conference inaugurated by a pleasant reception in St Andrew's Hall and a performance there, by the Norwich Players, of the *Comedy of Errors*[1]. The adventures of 'these two Antipholus, these two so like, And these two Dromios . . .' might have been watched as symbolising the confusions and prohibitions of the past, now happily resolved. For the financial future now seemed full of promise, certainly for public libraries, and the aspirations of the Association in 1920 were still as municipally centred as they had been at least since the turn of the century. It had seemed sometimes, and indeed right up to the concluding weeks of 1919, that the penny rate limit would remain until 'fowls have no feathers and fish have no fin', to borrow a figure of speech from Dromio of Syracuse. But now the limit had disappeared, as if by magic – at least in England and Wales – and the sorcerer mainly responsible, the Rt Hon J. Herbert Lewis, PC, MP, was not only still Parliamentary Secretary to the Board of Education, but President of the Association as well.

After paying the tributes – naturally expected in Norwich – to Norfolk scholarship over the centuries, and to the writings of

Sir Thomas Browne and George Borrow in particular, the
Presidential address had enlarged on the opportunities for
improved and expanded library services facilitated by the 1919
Act, even after making full allowance for the contrasted
frustrations inevitable during a period of post-war
reconstruction. Lewis had emphasised the need to make life in
country districts more tolerable and fulfilling – especially during
the hard winter months – partly, at least, to halt some of the
population drift towards the towns. He had commented on the
opportunities for the new County Library Authorities to make
their own substantial contributions, on lines drawn by the CUKT
during the War, not only in rural service but also in inter-library
cooperation. He had also drawn attention – and sensibly cautious
attention – to the scope for improving and developing
cooperation between public libraries and those responsible for
formal school education, in the widest interests of the child as
potential life-long reader, encouraging, in fact, the Association
and its members to consider adopting programmes of activity
comparable with those pioneered by Ballinger when Chief
Librarian of Cardiff.[2]

The President's studied caution on the subject of the Board of
Education's influence on public libraries had been in marked
contrast to the arguments in favour of more central guidance,
direction to and control of local libraries, advocated by Frank
Pacy, the Honorary Secretary, in a paper, 'The new opportunity',
which followed. Contributors to the discussion, and Jast in
particular, showed, quite unmistakeably, that the President's
persuasions were much more to their taste than the Honorary
Secretary's directives.[3] But the two initial contributions had
provided an admirable framework for the papers which had
followed on the new Act (by Fovargue); rural problems;
cooperation between urban and rural services – with its
exceptionally far-sighted anticipation of the advantages of the
mobile library by H. Tapley-Soper (1876–1951), City and
University Librarian of Exeter;[4] the Central Library for
Students; service to blind readers; the care and custody of
public records; and the pressing need to provide Scotland and
Ireland with the rate-freedom granted in England and Wales.
Among the remaining papers, the most important had been

Hulme's 'On the Subject Index to periodicals',[5] of which
Herbert Jones, of Kensington, had rightly insisted:

It was the bounden duty of the individual members of the
Association and of every public librarian to see that this first great
literary and bibliographical achievement of the Association was
carried through successfully. Every effort should be made to support
the publication, and not allow this great piece of research work to die
for want of nutrition.[6]

The continued existence of the *Subject index* was extremely
precarious in 1920 and for many later years; of this more later.

The nearest approach to a mirror for the public library picture of
1910 – as it seemed to the Norwich delegates – was the third
edition of James Duff Brown's *Manual of library economy*, of which
the editor, W. C. Berwick Sayers, had been passing the proofs as
the Public Libraries Bill of 1919 became an Act. The new
edition comprehensively updated – so far as this was necessary –
the accounts of public library techniques covered so
painstakingly by Brown in his own greatly improved second
edition of 1907. The *Manual* was still, inevitably, very much a
creature of the penny rate*. But Sayers' *forward* thinking, as
expressed in his new introduction and also in a paper read by
him at a monthly meeting in January, 1920,[7] was still conditioned
by the basic uncertainties of the municipal library's future, since
the shadow of the report of the Ministry of Reconstruction's
Adult Education Committee still lay threateningly, as it seemed,
over the whole scene.

It seemed still a particularly sinister shadow as the Committee
had quoted the Association's views – on the need for municipal
library committees to cooperate with local education
committees, but not to be absorbed by them – only to dismiss
them and to recommend union. The recommendation was,
perhaps, understandable, since the Committee's membership had
been heavily representative of the education interest and
included no librarians.[8] The shadow seemed darker still as the

---

* The rate limit was raised to 3d for   later in 1920; in Scotland there was no
towns in both Scotland and Ireland   rate limit for counties.

new county libraries envisaged in accordance with the provisions of the 1919 Act were to be the responsibility of county education committees. This was a shadow which would not lift until the publication of the report of the departmental committee of the Board of Education in 1927.

During the period 1920–1927 the activities of the CUKT were to be concerned, primarily, with the task of encouraging the County Councils to begin satisfactory library services and to make it easy for them to function economically by concentrating on book-stocks rather than on buildings, profiting from the mistakes long since evident in the earlier policy of their founder. They went further and, by taking major responsibility for the growth of the Central Library for Students and of pioneer inter-lending, endeavoured to maximise the value of their financial help. Their new Secretary, J. M. Mitchell (1879–1940) soon made himself an expert key-figure; he had taken over from Hetherington in 1919.[9]

By the end of 1921 twenty-two English and Welsh, and seventeen Scottish counties had begun library service; by the end of 1925 only five had failed to adopt the Acts and qualify for CUKT grants. The partition of Ireland following the Civil War and the 1920 Treaty of London reduced the LA's responsibilities but was held not to diminish those of the CUKT.[10] Their many disappointments during their pursuit of *impartial* philanthropy in the Emerald Isle which proved *there* to be as complete a contradiction in terms as no matter, must be regarded – not without regret – as outside the scope of this book.

The CUKT expressed the view, in their Seventh Annual Report, signed in February, 1921 that

A most important problem is the supply of competent librarians for these County schemes. The Trustees, after careful consideration, have decided that when more than 100 centres are to be served, the post must be a whole-time appointment carrying a salary of not less than £300 a year. This view is generally approved, and some of the larger and richer counties are offering a considerably larger salary. The point has a special interest for the Trustees in view of the help they have given in the foundation at University College, London, of a School of Librarianship, now in its second year. The spread of the demand for adult education in country areas makes it imperative to attract capable all-round young librarians who, in addition to having a good knowledge of librarianship and general culture, appreciate and can help to direct the aspirations of this new and important class of readers.[11]

But CUKT policy was not always implemented smoothly or easily. As Mitchell explained to an anxious LA Council on 10 September 1924:

The Trustees in their published statements and in letters to Authorities applying for grants have made a special point of insisting upon the importance and the general status of the post of County Librarian. In one or two cases the salary condition has led to the postponement of the scheme. Had the conditions been more stringent it is absolutely certain that the county library movement would have been indefinitely delayed.

It was not indefinitely delayed.

As the county libraries grew, so grew their staffs, although slowly at first, since only the most enthusiastic of the new Library Authorities visualised salaried appointments other than the County Librarian and perhaps a clerk or secretary. The suspicions of the new service held so firmly by many established municipal librarians seemed more than justified when amateurs without previous experience and young diplomates from the University of London School secured some of the new posts. Suspicions were, in a sense, increased when it became apparent that not only were some of the new librarians making decided successes of their responsibilities, they were beginning to sit the Association's examinations and pass them![12] Future possibilities were also suggested, or threatened, when Duncan Gray (1892-1958), who had been appointed County Librarian of Warwickshire and had written one of the pioneer textbooks on the new service, moved on to become the first librarian of the new municipal library at St Marylebone in 1923.[13] But it was true, of course, that he had had municipal experience before going to Warwickshire.

Even the most conservative members of the LA Council had to
agree, eventually, to come to terms with the new county
libraries. During 1925–6 a circular letter was addressed to all
county librarians, inviting them to join the Association; by the
end of that year sixteeen librarians and thirteen Authorities had
taken up membership.[14] The first 'County library notes',
compiled by one of the leaders of the new department of
librarianship, Richard Wright (1891–1976), County Librarian of
Middlesex, appeared in the *Record* of June, 1926; he and another
leader, Miss A. S. Cooke (1895–1971), County Librarian of Kent,
discussed possible developments, *vis-à-vis* the Association, with
Council representatives in January, 1927.[15] Later in the year they
suggested their own sectional organisation; two representatives
on the LA Council, and some form of subscription refund
'sufficient to cover their expenses'. They were advised to form
their own Section informally pending byé-law revision;[16] there
was a further substantial recruitment of new County members,[17]
and Wright and Miss Cooke were themselves coopted to the
Council.[18] By the end of 1927 the scene was clearly set for
county development parallel with that of the much older
municipal library.

It would, nevertheless, still be many years before the
establishments of county libraries became sufficiently large to
make significant impact on the total LA membership figures.
These continued to grow agonisingly slowly – from 781 in 1921
to 832 in 1927. The financial situation indeed seemed desperate
again in 1921; the Council decided on drastic economies[19] and
authorised the Honorary Treasurer to secure bank overdraft
facilities 'of not exceeding £300'.[20] But those rigid economies
and some financial help from the CUKT soon transformed the
situation; increasingly substantial balances were built up and by
1927 the annual surplus of income over expenditure had risen to
no less than £900. Contributions to this surplus were made by
changing the *Record* from a monthly into a quarterly and there
were even more drastic changes in the Association's own
offices.

In January, 1921 the offices at Caxton Hall, which had been
rented since 1913, were given up and a room was found at the

headquarters of the National Council of Social Service, at Stapley House, Bloomsbury Square. The new rent was low; there was more space than at Caxton Hall and the Council could meet in the National Council's library; the Council meeting in December 1920 at the National Library for the Blind was the last to be held there.[21] The Secretary, E. C. Kyte, too, was soon to leave. At the height of the economy drive, a motion 'that the appointment of a paid secretary be terminated at six months from 1 April (ie 1921)'[22] had been tabled. The motion had not been successful but Kyte doubtless sensed continuing uncertainty and resigned in June 1922.[23] He soon went to Canada where he had a distinguished career as Queen's University Librarian, at Kingston, Ontario, until his retirement in 1947.[24]

Following Kyte's resignation and committee discussions, Pacy, who remained in office as Honorary Secretary during the whole of the present period, offered also to accept overall responsibility for the Association's office and to direct and supervise the work of the small salaried staff but only if all these responsibilities were concentrated under his own Westminster roofs.[25] The Council agreed, of course; the Stapley House office was given up and the Association operated until 1927 from the City of Westminster Buckingham Palace Road Library which also became the normal meeting place for council and committee meetings. In 1926, during one of Pacy's spells of illness, the LA Council was to make him a special grant of £200. In his letter of acknowledgment and thanks Pacy referred to 'his keen interest and love of the work'.[26] This was admirably and generously under-stated. His assumption of far more responsibility than could ever reasonably be asked of an Honorary Secretary helped the Association almost beyond accounting and made it much easier to build up financial resources to underwrite the developments to come during the next period of its history.

Pacy's responsibilities were, in fact, soon increased beyond original expectation since Tedder, the veteran Honorary Treasurer, had to seek relief from the burden of the clerical work of his own office.[27] When he died, in August 1924, it seemed as if a whole era had ended; no other surviving member of the Association had been so closely involved with its affairs from the very earliest days, even before the inaugural conference. In his obituary in the *Library Association Record*, Ballinger truly said of him:

In sunshine and in storm, Tedder never relaxed in his devotion. At every annual meeting he was one of the chief figures, and he did his full share of the less attractive work at the monthly Council and Committee meetings . . . his tenure of the office [ie of Honorary Treasurer] has always been marked by judicious care of the Association's precarious finances. . . .[28]

Other tributes were paid in letters to the Editor of *The Times*, following the obituary there on 2 August. Sir Gregory Foster, Provost of University College London:

His counsel and advice were invaluable in the early days of the School and he maintained his faith in its value – as the first school of the kind in this country – very zealously against all opposition. He regarded the foundation and maintenance of the School of Librarianship as an important outcome of his efforts to raise the status and the influence of the librarian in the educational system of the country.[29]

Sir Frederick Pollock, Chairman of the Commission on the Public Records:

He was not only a zealous and efficient, but (what is not a necessary accompaniment) a most agreeable colleague.[30]

Bernard Kettle, Librarian of the Guidhall Library of the City of London, was elected Honorary Treasurer of the Association, to succeed Tedder; he resigned the chairmanship of the Finance Committee to qualify.[31]

Kyte had edited the *Record* until his resignation from the LA's Secretaryship in 1922. The changes in the Association's journal, despite the change from monthly to quarterly publication, virtually enforced by the need for economy, became instead immense improvements, but only because the LA was fortunate enough to secure as new editor, Arundell Esdaile (1880–1956), Cambridge scholar, wit and member of the staff of the British

Museum. Having, in his first editorial, declared war on dullness
and hoped for more general articles and reviews of books,
Esdaile presented his readers with a new cover, wider page, new
and infinitely clearer type-face, generous margins, plenty of
white space and an overall distinction sadly lacking in the *Record*
since its earliest days under Guppy and its predecessor, *The
Library*, in its best days under MacAlister. As example, the
library notes and news feature, now master-titled 'At home and
abroad', made good and frequently amusing reading:

LISBON. The *Biblioteca Nacional* has started a French Section of
which information is given in the *Bibliographie de la France* of 4th July.
It appears to be intended that French publishers shall supply their
new books gratis, in order to stimulate the French book trade in
Portugal, but that so far the beauty of the idea has not penetrated
them, as indeed might have been expected.[32]

and, occasionally, at greater length:

HULL. An unseemly controversy between the Librarian and a
Councillor has certain larger aspects which suggest comment. The
case was this: the Librarian offered to sell to his Committee some
review copies of scientific books. One of that body denounced the
offer as immoral, and this engendered not laughter but heat. The
conclusions we draw are three:-
1. Councillors, like lesser men, should not talk about things they do
not understand. The sale of review copies is a regular and legitimate
practice, as five minutes spent in Charing Cross Road would have
shown. Is a wretched reviewer either to place on his shelves or to
throw into the dustbin every book he receives?
2. The librarian is a public servant, and even under fatuous insults
should not write to the Press in a controversial manner relating to his
office except as the mouthpiece of his Authority. He can always
resign [sic]
3. The common rule that a Library Authority does not buy direct
from its officers may have disadvantages. In this case Hull lost a good
bargain. For the sake of an opportunity it can be judiciously evaded.
But on the whole it is a salutary rule, for the practice would be very
liable to abuse.[33]

It was also superbly ironic that, during a period when the LA as a
whole seemed to respond indifferently save to public library

stimuli, its official organ interpreted its responsibilities
sufficiently widely to regard as newsworthy all kinds of library
and librarian, whether or not in membership, and to have an
obvious *penchant* for the more learned kinds. Not that the public
library interest was ever lacking. Esdaile printed some good
articles and writers and was able on occasion to include
contributions of such outstanding quality as Ernest Savage's
'Plea for the analytical study of the reading habit.[34]

The Association was fortunate and had every reason to be proud
of its journal while Esdaile edited it. Councillors and members
could also be happy because its *quarterly* appearance meant no
unbearable financial burdens upon weak shoulders. The *Subject
index to periodicals,* unhappily, presented the Association with
very different problems.

Up to the end of 1919, as recounted in the previous chapter, only
one consolidated volume of the *Subject index to periodicals* had been
published, and Hulme had himself accepted financial
responsibility for that. His deputy, both at the Patent Office
Library, and with the *Subject index*, H. V. Hopwood, died in 1919
and E. G. Tucker was employed as salaried assistant. Together,
and with the help of their panel of voluntary contributors,
they laboured on with their immense task – until the end of 1920
at the National Library for the Blind and, from January, 1921
onwards, at the National Library of Wales where the ever-
helpful Ballinger offered the fullest cooperation and
support.[35] But, as has been found in other contexts, the best
proved to be the enemy of the good. Hulme's scholarly, even
perfectionist, objectives were much too ambitious for the
finances and organisation available to him. Progress was slow
and costs were frightening. The periodicals of the years 1917 to
1919 were indexed in seven subject parts published between 1920
and 1922; the list of periodicals covered and the author index
followed in 1924. The total cost of completing this three-year
coverage was estimated at £3388 and the estimated receipts – at
an inclusive subscription of four guineas – amounted to only
£1423, leaving an estimated deficit of nearly £2000[36] which, for
an Association whose total annual income from subscriptions
was little more than £1500, was disastrous. It was clear, too, that,

unless the parts issued were much more quickly brought up to date, there would be little chance of enlarging the disappointing subscription list.

The CUKT were approached for help and gracefully responded with

a final and comprehensive grant of £1500 to meet the existing deficit and enable the LA to re-start the work free of debt . . . In offering this grant the Trustees strongly recommend:
a That class-lists should be sold separately as well as in the bulk; only so, they feel, will an extra-library sale be possible.
b That adequate machinery of distribution, advertisement etc. is essential
c That proper provision be made in future estimates for editorial salaries.
The Trustees have been guided in making this proposal by the assurance that the LA has definitely accepted responsibility for the permanent maintenance of the Index, and by the high standard of work which has been set by the devoted labours of Mr Wyndham Hulme and his colleague.[37]

Work proceeded. The periodicals of 1920 were indexed in seven subject (or class) lists published in 1922 and 1923 and those of 1921 in six similar lists published in 1924. But the financial worries were soon renewed and, early in 1923, Hulme was protesting at the LA Finance Committee's attempt to secure complete control of the project.[38] The Council asked its own auditors for a financial report during 1925.[39] Matters came to a head in April, 1926 when the Council, on the recommendation of the Executive Committee – to which Hulme was, at least, nominally responsible – decided that no further class lists were to be undertaken once those for 1922 had been completed and that

an annual volume index, on very much simplified lines, be commenced to cover the year 1926, this to be issued as early as possible in 1927, the annual subscription to be £3 3s. That the list of periodicals indexed be, if possible, reduced to 250 in number. That the interim period be covered by one complete volume, at a price of £6 6s for the three years.[40]

Hulme, who had endeavoured to prevent change on such a scale
by claiming his own copyright and seeking legal support for it,
was unable to suggest how the arrears could be more quickly
overtaken; he surrendered his claims and resigned from the
Subject index in 1926.[41] The Council then appointed a small
controlling committee consisting of Pitt, Powell and Stephen;
one of their first tasks was not to bring out a new *Subject index*
but to pacify the CUKT who were particularly concerned at
the substantial reduction in the list of periodicals proposed for
indexing in future,[42] from the more than 500 on which their
grant had been based to the 250 envisaged. But action, at least on
the lines decided by the Council, seemed inevitable if the *Subject
index* were to survive in any form at all and the LA not to be
bankrupted. Under the guidance of the new committee the first
of a new annual series would appear, certainly not in 1927 as
hoped for but at least in 1928. The missing years were never
covered.

Granted the state of its finances and the burden of the *Subject
index*, it would have been surprising if the Association's other
publishing activities during the present period had been
ambitious. The *Year Book* was issued again in 1921 – for the first
time since the outbreak of World War One – and again in 1922.
In 1924:

L. A. Hand Book – By decision of the Council under this title will be
issued what was formerly described as a "Year Book" presumably
because it was seldom issued either annually or promptly ... As there
is in stock a sufficient number of copies of the 1921 issue of the Year
Book. . . . it has been resolved to restrict the contents of the new
Hand Book to a complete up to date list of the Members, Council,
Committees and Officers.[43]

The *Hand Book*, profiting by this spirited introduction by Pacy,
was published again in 1926 but not in 1927.

Until the very end of the present period the rest of the
Association's publication activities might have been described as
domestic housekeeping. For example, sales were entrusted
to Grafton and Co in 1923, on a 17½% discount basis.[44] Old
publications, of course, were much less attractive to any

bookseller. After another waste-paper clearance[45] the older stocks were removed to the capacious basement of the Chelsea Public Library in 1926 for storage.[46]

One promising sign of new activity must not be overlooked. At its meeting on 8 July 1927 the Council, on the recommendation of its Publications Committee, approved publication 'of a Year Book of Library Studies, provided that a sufficient amount of support be forthcoming'. The advent of *The Year's work in librarianship* – as that volume and its many successors were to be entitled – must, however, await comment in a later chapter.

The Association's monthly meetings in London began again soon after the War and on quite ambitious lines.[47] Attendances quickly fell off again, however, and there were renewed complaints of 'apathy'.[48] A meeting of metropolitan librarians convened by the Council in February, 1923, initially to consider abortive reports of a Royal Commission on London government, decided additionally to request the formation of a new Branch to cover London and the Home Counties, despite differences of opinion as to the number of counties to be included as 'Home' and the objection of Dr Baker that 'a branch at the root would make the Association something like the Tree of Porphyry; all branches without a trunk'.[49] The Council nevertheless authorised formation in the following April[50] and expressed the hope that the monthly meetings might, 'by its energies, re-create the old interest and better attendance'.[51]

The inaugural meeting of the London and Home Counties Branch in October, 1923, was addressed by W. C. Berwick Sayers who, in typically kindly fashion, was critical of the astonishing disparities of public library service in its great area.[52] Those disparities were highlighted in the first (1924) *Report on the municipal library system of London and the Home Counties*, with J. D. Stewart as General Editor. They were indeed very plain to see when analysed under the headings used in the *Report*: constitution and finance, staff, readers and circulation, open access, hours of service, children's libraries, extension work and other information, with a useful appended list of special collections.

The Branch was young, enthusiastic and anxious to begin work on the disparities. It convened a conference of library authorities 'to consider matters appertaining to the coordination of the public library service', much to the concern of the Council who expressed their grave displeasure at the new Branch taking so much upon itself without adequate consultation.[53] 'Coordination', in any case, had been a dirty word ever since the Ministry of Reconstruction's Report in 1919. Some were less easily frightened. Dr Baker had considered the need for coordination in an article in the *Fortnightly Review* of February 1921.[54] This had caused some controversy and more had come from the CUKT's 'Mitchell Report' of 1924,[55] the successor to 'Adams'. But even the possibilities of voluntary, organised inter-lending were only grasped slowly by municipal libraries; encouragement came, at first, mostly from outside the public library field as in a paper read by Professor F. E. Sandbach at the Association's Birmingham Conference in 1925.[56] Such discussions also, inevitably, raised the question of the relevance and importance of the Central Library for Students.

The Central Library for Students had been founded by Albert Mansbridge and the Workers Educational Association at Toynbee Hall in 1916 and had moved to Tavistock Square a year later, thanks to grant-aid from the CUKT. Initially it had been formed to provide book loans for WEA and University Extension classes; it soon began also to lend to individual students.[57] There were obvious advantages in drawing on its stock only after local public library ones had been explored and exhausted; by the end of World War One a few municipal libraries were using it to supplement their own services and were paying small annual subscriptions in recognition.[58] Its continued development was vital to CUKT plans:

The Trustees are at present interested in the Library mainly because of the service which it renders to County Library schemes; it is also, however, extending its usefulness by supplying to the less wealthy municipal libraries books which Library Committees cannot afford to buy. There is therefore reason to hope that it will ultimately become self-supporting on the basis of annual contributions from Borough and County libraries.[59]

The Trustees were optimistic enough to found similar libraries in Edinburgh and Dublin in 1921. Municipal libraries as a whole came to appreciate its indispensable service much more slowly and few in the 1920s were able to visualise it as the possible centre of a future system of organised inter-lending. It seemed to some at least to suggest problems not entirely remote from those of technical and commercial libraries.

The decision of the DSIR to develop technical library facilities *via* industries rather than municipal libraries, referred to in an earlier chapter, meant, inevitably, some parallel growth; the larger municipal library authorities began to provide technical and commercial departments during the final years of World War One and the period now under review. Joint technical and commercial libraries were established at Leeds in 1918 and at Sheffield in 1920; commercial libraries at Coventry in 1918, Dundee, Wolverhampton, Birmingham and Manchester in 1919, and Bristol in 1920; and technical libraries at Coventry in 1918, Manchester in 1922 and Birmingham in 1924.[60] It was also inevitable, however, that the libraries and information departments in the burgeoning industrial firms and research associations would themselves, sooner or later, seek some kind of corporate activity and organisation. A meeting of interested representatives was held at Hoddesdon in 1925; four of them were then invited to attend the LA Council meeting in January. They expressed the wish to be closely associated with the LA; a special libraries section comparable with that envisaged during the war-time discussions with and about the DSIR was again suggested to them. A. F. Ridley, who was acting as first honorary secretary of the new group, read a paper on 'Special libraries and information bureaux'[61] at the 1925 Birmingham Conference. The discussion which followed indicated very clearly the anxiety of LA members to avoid the formation of a separate association and to make fusion easy.[62] The Council went far out of its way to offer easy individual and/or bloc membership. But all to no avail. The Association of Special Libraries and Information Bureaux was formally inaugurated on 29 March 1926, when 'the Chairman, Mr J. G. Pearce (Director of the British Cast Iron Association) . . . added that the new association, while preferring to work separately, was convinced of the need for complete cooperation with the LA'.[63] In modern library folklore the assumption is sometimes made that the LA Council could have easily prevented the formation of a separate ASLIB. Objective study of the records suggests that such was by no means the case. The Council deplored the new association's formation.[64] It could hardly have done more to make it unnecessary, remembering always its then overwhelming interest in municipal libraries.

Many municipal librarians had, of course, taken their opportunities of giving talks on their services to local groups and societies during the years prior to World War One; a few notable figures such as James Duff Brown and Stanley Jast had proved specially brilliant performers. But the abolition of the penny rate limit and the consequential possibilities for development thus encouraged, granted adequate local financial encouragement, engendered, for the first time, a positive drive for public library recognition and publicity. The Association's Council formed its first Publicity Committee; at its first meeting in February 1922 policy was outlined as follows:

i   By every means practicable to influence public opinion to realise the necessity, importance and value of public libraries in the educational and social welfare of the nation
ii   To direct public attention to the fact that the work of public libraries has been hindered by lack of adequate financial support, and that the present cry for 'economy' should not be permitted to starve such institutions and stifle their progress
iii To keep the activities and usefulness of the libraries before the public, and endeavour to advance their status generally[65]

W. A. Briscoe, City Librarian of Nottingham, and G. A. Stephen, City Librarian of Norwich, were among the most active members of the committee,[66] Briscoe acting as honorary secretary. A newcomer on the municipal library scene, L. R. McColvin (1896–1976) appointed Librarian of Ipswich Public Libraries in 1924, in his first contribution to the *Record* wrote:

We do not want to force books and libraries upon any one . . .
However we do believe that any money that is spent in public
libraries will prove to be money well spent from the point of view of
the community, individually or collectively, and we therefore believe
that we must strive our utmost to give publicity to the advantages of
a good library service, convinced that knowledge will bring
assistance.[67]

McColvin's *Library extension work and publicity* (1927) faithfully
reflects some of the best thinking of the period. But Briscoe
himself was much more lyrical:

If – by organised propaganda – we can convince the nation as a whole
that Public libraries are necessary for the education and betterment of
the People – and we can get the unanimous support of the People –
then we shall be able to sing with the fullness of our hearts – Oh,
what a happy land is England.[68]

Extensive lists of lantern slides available for loan were published
in the *Record*[69] and thousands of copies of what were considered
persuasive publicity leaflets were produced by the Publicity
Committee and sold to local libraries, at a small profit to the
Association. One of them, for example – *Education and public
libraries* – included seven quotations on the importance of public
libraries from authorities as varied as H. A. L. Fisher, Sir James
Barrie and W. J. Locke. The new medium of the period – sound
broadcasting – was used by librarians for publicity talks as
early as 1923;[70] Jast became a well known broadcaster from
Manchester on many wider topics also.[71]

It would have been difficult to visualise *worse* publicity for
public libraries than the closing of a library in the heart of
London without provision being made for another to take its
place, remembering always the delayed adoption of the Public
Libraries Acts in most parts of the metropolis. The following
extract from the report of the LA Council for 1925–6 tells an
important story:

There will be noticed in the expenditure a grant of £100 voted to the
Vicar of St Martin-in-the-Fields, in connection with the litigation in
the case of the St Martin's Library. Action was, with great personal
courage and at considerable risk, taken by the Vicar, to restrain the

Westminster City Council from closing the library without providing
another. The judgment against them in the Chancery Court was by
the Council challenged in the Court of Appeal, and the Master of the
Rolls with two Lords Justices, without calling upon counsel for the
relator, promptly dismissed the appeal.

Thus the Vicar, fighting the case single-handed, won and saved the
library originally established for the more particular use of his
parishioners. The most successful litigant, however, does not recover
all his costs. It was brought to the notice of the Council that Mr
Sheppard remained at a substantial loss. Recognising that his public
spirit alone had secured what was more than of local import, indeed a
judgment which has laid down, it is hoped finally, the sanctity of a
public library, the Council has voted £100 towards the expenses of
the case. This great liberality, as he terms it, was gratefully
acknowledged by Mr Sheppard. The Council is confident that the
vote will be approved by all.[72]

And so it was approved. Dick Sheppard is remembered, and
with great affection, by many older people in the 1970s.
Librarians would not wish to forget his special contribution to
the success of the public library cause.

The Net Book Agreement remained a source of frustration to
public library book-buyers during the present period. The
Association's Net Books Committee was reappointed by the
Council in May, 1925 and made yet another attempt to secure
library discounts. But, following a meeting with representatives
of the publishers and booksellers associations at Stationers Hall
in the following September, the Publishers Association found
itself unable to agree to any change.[73] In the light of
developments after World War Two the historian may also
surely note – not least in the interests of irony – that, in the
following year, the Council protested 'at booksellers offering to
undertake services which are an essential part of the duties of the
librarian'.[74] The protest was occasioned by a circular letter sent
to Scottish booksellers by East Lothian Education Authority; it
originated as a notice of motion by Ernest Savage, Principal
Librarian of Edinburgh. Well might established municipal
librarians consider that the new Counties had to be watched!

There was greater success, however, in the field of Government

publications, granted that this problem was much older than
that of net books – certainly as old as Edward Edwards.[75]
Following new representations by the Association, as from
1 April 1924:

The Stationery Office was authorised to supply any Government
publication in future at one half the published price or one half of the
subscription. .... in lieu of the existing arrangements under which a
few publications are presented annually to some public libraries,
other supplies being charged at full price.

The concession, too, applied to:

all public free libraries in Great Britain maintained out of the rates
and to Universities and University Colleges in receipt of assistance
from the University Grants Committee.[76]

This was not regarded by the Council as an adequate concession
but obviously, to most public libraries, it was a welcome relief
'from the really too high cost'.[77]

During this present period examination entrants seeking the
Association's diploma had not merely to obtain the six Sectional
certificates and to show evidence of reading knowledge of Latin
or Greek and of one modern European language; they had also
to submit a thesis displaying original thought or research on
some subject within the purview of the syllabus. The diploma
requirements were in fact so exacting – within the context – that
up to 1927 only thirteen diplomates were listed; their successes,
too, had been spread over the years from 1906 to 1926, an
average of less than one each year.[78] The thesis was, of course,
the main stumbling block to diploma success and hence to
Fellowship of the Association. The Council and its Education
Committee took their thesis requirements extremely seriously.
Several librarians, later to become very well known
professionally, had their original thesis subjects rejected on
grounds of insufficient scope for treatment. One of the more
remarkable cases was surely that of the candidate who suggested
as possible alternative subjects the Picaresque novel, the ancient
minstrels, the influence of the French Revolution on English
literature, the English essay or H. G. Wells: an appreciation. He

was informed that the third-named subject would be accepted, subject to 'American' being substituted for 'French'![79] But the Council's exacting requirements certainly resulted in the compilation of a small number of first class theses; when made available in published form they were distinguished additions to the professional literature of the period. Gwendolen Rees' *Libraries for children* and L. R. McColvin's *Music in public libraries*, both published by Grafton in 1924, may be cited as outstanding examples.

The number of entries for the Sectional examinations soon recovered from the restricting effects of the war years and by 1923–4 had risen to more than a thousand, at which level they remained until the end of the present period; rather fewer than one half of the entrants normally passed.[80] The Association's own preliminary test was abandoned completely by 1927 in favour of the school leaving certificates granted by the various University bodies[81] – a sure sign that junior public library recruits were coming now mostly from the secondary grammar schools – and Nalgo was informed in 1925 that its own preliminary certificate could not be accepted as substitute.[82] The examination fee for each Section was raised from 5*s* to 10*s* in 1921[83] and the Education Committee continued to do its best to authorise a very wide range of examination centres, to ensure, as far as possible, that no candidate had an unreasonably long journey before sitting his or her examination.

The Association's fees for correspondence classes were increased from £1 1*s* to £1 15*s* in 1924 (£3 3*s* for those not in library employment). Tutors were paid a flat fee of £2 2*s*, plus £1 7*s* 6*d* per student taught (£2 2*s* for those not in library employment), subject to a minimum payment of £5 5*s* per tutor.[84] Examiners continued to be paid only £1 for setting each question paper and 1*s* per script marked.[85] Such low fees were perhaps appropriate to what was still, in the 1920s, a lowly paid occupation; they could hardly be claimed as more than nominal recognition of work done. During the economy drive of 1921, an enterprising, if optimistic, member of the LA Council had suggested that examiners' fees should be completely abolished; this suggestion was negatived on the motion of the Honorary

Treasurer (Tedder).[86] Nalgo proposed competitive
correspondence courses in 1924[87] but these came to nothing.
The Association of Assistant Librarians, as the Library
Assistants Association had renamed itself in 1922,[88] introduced
its own correspondence classes in November 1926, in
preparation for the LA exams in May 1927. They were an
immediate success, partly at least because the fees charged
substantially undercut those for the Association's own
courses.[89]

Despite the unfortunate events associated with the foundation
of the pioneer School of Librarianship at University College
London, recounted in the previous chapter, its relationship with
the Association was never bad and continued to improve
through the 1920s. A good beginning was made by the Council
at its meeting in March, 1921 when it was resolved 'that a letter
of congratulation upon the first year's working of the School in
general terms and without criticism should be sent'. Such a
resolution was surely manna to the urbane Pacy. Continued
cordial relationships were made easier, not only because of
the Association's substantial representation on the School's
committee, but also because so many of the part-time lecturers
there were prominent LA members. The Director (Dr Baker) was
discreet in School affairs and the Provost of University College
(Sir Gregory Foster) made a quite outstanding contribution to
cordial relationships when, following a lecture in 1922 at the
School, which he chaired, he said:

The Association had a very difficult task before them. The LA was
step by step bringing about the organisation of the Profession of
Librarianship which, until the Association was founded, was entirely
unorganised. To organise a profession was a difficult matter and took
time.
No doubt the Association had made many serious mistakes, but such
mistakes are inevitable, having regard to the nature of the work
undertaken. The business of all those interested in Librarianship is to
support the LA and to help it discharge its duties more and more
effectively.
The University School of Librarianship has been founded on the
initiative of the LA. In the management of that School the LA has a
very considerable voice, for it nominates seven members of the

School of Librarianship Committee. The foundation of the School marks an epoch in the progress of Librarianship as a trained profession.

It is the intention of the University to work in close cooperation with the Association in the hope that the School may help the Association and the Association the School. The real objects of the School and of the Association are identical. If these objects are kept in mind there can be no clash between the School and the Association.[90]

It was certainly hardly to be questioned that the School was seeking to raise educational and professional standards. In its report for 1923–4 it was stated:

The purpose of the School is to raise the higher ranks of Librarianship to the position of one of the liberal professions. The School is, therefore, encouraging students to take a degree either in Arts or Science before entering in the definite training for the diploma.

The Association recognised this by exempting School Diplomates, from 1925 onwards, from the need to take its own Sectional examinations and thus enabled them to proceed direct to its thesis, if seeking also its own Diploma.[91]

Another interesting educational development originated in the AAL's attempt to persuade the LCC to begin librarianship classes at its evening institutes. Remembering, perhaps, its part in initiating the original classes at the LSE, the LCC seemed reluctant even to appear to compete with the School at University College; it decided instead, in 1926, to grant-aid the School to enable it to offer twenty-five free, evening, places to those employed in librarianship within its own administrative area.[92] But, outside London, lecture and class provision was still ill-provided at this period. The Extra Mural Board of the University of Manchester arranged some lectures[93] and the AAL was also active, at least in some of its divisional areas.[94] The Summer Schools at Aberystwyth were also arranged again each year throughout the period, except in 1923 and 1924. Other short summer schools were arranged by the University College School, and comparable Autumn Schools from 1922 to 1926 by the Scottish Library Association in Edinburgh and Glasgow.[95]

While the educational developments noted above undoubtedly
played important parts in raising standards, there was as yet
little, if any, evidence of financial recognition of examination
success by employing Authorities.[96] Indeed the Council's own
first attempt, in conjunction with Nalgo, to issue a suggested
scale of salaries for chief and other senior officers in Local
Authority libraries seemed hesitant and reluctant.[97] The time for
documentation of this specialised kind was hardly yet ripe. For
some years yet librarians seeking to improve their own salaries
and those of their staffs would have to fall back on the
already time-honoured circularisation of their colleagues before
attempting to persuade their own Authorities to act more
realistically, if not generously. Lacking satisfactory touchstones
in the same context, it was not yet easy for the Association to
protest, other than in general terms, to Authorities advertising
posts at salaries considered grossly inadequate. But occasional
protests were made, as at Tunbridge Wells, Cheltenham and
Chesterfield in 1922.[98]

The LA's interest in activities in other countries soon revived
after the end of the War. Forty members and friends visited the
major libraries of Paris at Easter, 1923, a few staying on for the
Congrès International des Bibliothécaires et Bibliophiles.[99] In
the following year there were visits both to Brussels and
to Holland where the courtesy and liberality of the Dutch
Association were so generous and so appreciated that a
representative was invited to attend the LA's own conference
later in the year as its own guest.[100] L. C. Wharton (1877–1943),
of the British Museum, represented the Association at the
Congrès International at Prague in 1926 when he and the French
representatives proposed a permanent international
organisation;[101] there were to be further developments in the
next period. The most ambitious overseas visit, however,
occurred at the end of the present period, in 1927, when the
Council, aided financially by the CUKT, nominated four delegates
to represent it at the American Library Association's Fiftieth
Congress at Atlantic City. The CUKT's own official representation
included also three librarians, two of them, Cooke and Wright,
being County Librarians. The impressions of some of the
delegates were placed on permanent record.[102]

1927, the halfway year in the Association's century, was up to that date, one of the most eventful. In the country at large it was a year of convalescence – economic, financial, social and industrial – from the General Strike of 1926. It could hardly be described as convalescent politically, since the Conservative Government was determined to get its consequential Trades Disputes Bill on to the Statute book and spent most of the Parliamentary year doing so, opposed by the TUC, the Labour Opposition and some of the Liberal Opposition. It was a year of international wrangling over disarmament and the year of the British decision to sever diplomatic relations with the Soviet Union. It was a year when the President of the National Farmers Union was again complaining of the depressed state of agriculture and the President of the English Chambers of Commerce again explaining that the nation was importing too much and exporting too little. It was the year when the Church of England's new *Book of Common Prayer* was approved by the Lords and rejected by the Commons.

The General Strike provided background for one of the much discussed new novels of 1927, H. G. Wells' *Meanwhile*. Other new novels being eagerly sought by library readers were Sinclair Lewis's study of a mobile American evangelist, *Elmer Gantry*, and R. H. Mottram's chronicle of a relatively stationary English banking family, *Our Mr Dormer*. 1927 was also the publication year of *The Revolt in the desert, The Wandering scholars,* and *Mother India*. It was an exceptionally rainy year; it ended with an unusually cold December.

Although at the beginning of 1927 the Association still had a membership of fewer than 850,[103] it had by then acquired a formidable governing body of no less than sixty-two members; the President, eight Past Presidents, twelve Vice-Presidents, twelve London councillors, twenty Country councillors, four coopted representatives of four of the largest municipal Library Authorities, two coopted representatives of the County Librarians, and the three Honorary Officers.[104] Thirty-four of the total were municipal librarians, including none of the Past Presidents, six of the Vice-Presidents, five of the London councillors and all twenty Country councillors.[105] The contrast

between the proportional representation of the municipal
libraries in London and outside it – to which special reference
has been made earlier – continued.

The Council held its first meeting of 1927 on 14 January,
forty-two members being present. All save ten were municipal
librarians, the exceptions being the President (Guppy), Dr Baker
(University College School), Esdaile (British Museum),
Headicar (LSE), Minto (Signet, Edinburgh), Newcombe
(Central Library for Students), Palmer (Victoria and Albert
Museum), Prideaux (Reform Club), Sanderson (National Liberal
Club), and Twentyman (Board of Education).

The geographical distribution of the municipal librarians
attending was not without interest:

LONDON Burt (Camberwell), Gurner Jones (Stepney),
H. Jones (Ex-Kensington), Kettle (Ex-Guildhall), Quinn
(Chelsea), Stewart (Bermondsey), Thorne (Poplar).
THE NORTH Anderton (Newcastle on Tyne), Ashton
(Blackburn), Gordon (Sheffield), Hand (Leeds), Hawkes
(Wigan), Jast (Manchester), Shaw (Liverpool), Singleton
(Accrington), Sparke (Bolton).
THE MIDLANDS Briscoe (Nottingham), Nowell (Coventry),
Miss Pierce (Kettering), Powell (Birmingham).
THE SOUTH Hutt (Portsmouth), Sayers (Croydon).
THE EAST McColvin (Ipswich), Pollitt (Southend), Stephen
(Norwich).
THE WEST Tapley-Soper (Exeter), Acland-Taylor (Bristol).
SCOTLAND Savage (Edinburgh), Pitt (Glasgow).

Wales was unrepresented at the meeting, Country councillor
Farr (Cardiff) being an absentee as also was his predecessor there,
Past President Ballinger, the National Librarian of Wales. It was
a predominantly middle-aged and elderly council with a
sprinkling of younger members, notably McColvin and Nowell.
Miss Pierce was still the only woman member although she was
soon now to be joined by the County Librarian of Kent, Miss
Cooke.

The most important item of business at this January 1927 Council meeting was the adoption of the recommendations in the reports of the Special Development Committee which had been appointed, on the motion of E. A. Savage, in the preceding July. The major recommendations were:

i   *Increasing membership.* That the system of registration be no longer used as a barrier to ordinary, ie unclassified membership; the membership list and the register to be run, in future, so to speak, in parallel. Since under the bye-laws then existing all members were classified, there had probably been some discouragement to recruitment and certainly anomalies, particularly in the treatment accorded to older librarian members who had not passed any of the LA examinations. There had been, in their case, as the Council frankly admitted, 'differences of opinion even among the Membership Committee themselves'.[106]

ii   *Reduction in size of Council.* That the Council be reconstituted to consist of a President, Past Presidents, three Vice-Presidents, six London councillors and twelve Country councillors. 'London' to be re-defined at a radius of thirty miles from Charing Cross. That arrangements be made to effect the reductions over a period of years and that Past Presidents not attending Council meetings in two consecutive years be no longer members.

iii *Secretary.* A full-time salaried organising secretary be appointed.

iv   *Capital endowment.* The LA to request from the CUKT, five annual grants of £5000 for capital endowment.
     Associated societies. The LA, AAL, ASLIB, and the Bibliographical Society to be asked to form a joint council for questions of common interest; and the CUKT to be approached by them to consider ways and means of acquiring a joint central office.[107]

Some of these recommendations obviously called for bye-law revision; it was decided, in due course, to submit a revised draft, for information, to the 1927 Conference, with a view to approval being obtained at the 1928 Conference. Other recommendations depended for their implementation on the sympathetic support of the CUKT.

9. *James Duff Brown* (*1862–1914*)
Librarian, Islington Public Libraries *1905–1914*

10. *Richard Garnett (1835–1906)*
President 1893

11. *Sidney Webb (1859–1947)*

12. *L. S. Jast (1868–1944)*
Hon. Secretary 1904–1915
President 1930

13. *Frank Pacy (1862–1928)*
Hon. Secretary 1898–1901 and 1915–1928

14. *Miss K. E. Pierce (1873–1966)*
First woman councillor, elected 1915

15. *E. A. Savage (1877–1966)*
President 1936

16. *E. Wyndham Hulme (1859–1954)*
Librarian, Patent Office, 1894–1919

At the next Council meeting, on 8 April, there was promising news about a joint headquarters for the various library societies, including the LA. At a meeting convened by the CUKT, a joint resolution in favour had been passed; the Association's President and Honorary Secretary were now appointed representatives for any further discussions.[108]

The Fiftieth Anniversary Conference, which opened in the United Free Church Assembly Buildings, Edinburgh, on 26 September 1927, was attended by more than 700 British delegates, with a further 100 from overseas, including other European countries, Australia, Canada, India, Japan and the United States. The LA's special relationship with the CUKT was fittingly symbolised by the presence of the Trust's Chairman, the Earl of Elgin and Kincardine – who was also a Trustee of the British Museum – as President. The Trust and the Association had also been joint hosts to many of the overseas delegates during the week prior to the Conference when they had been conveyed from London to Edinburgh in a convoy of motor coaches on a sightseeing tour of British libraries and other attractions by way of Oxford, Stratford, Birmingham, Buxton, Manchester, Leeds, York, Glasgow and Stirling.

The theme of the Conference was 'A national library service', one which, in 1927, suggested aspiration rather than reality.[109] For municipal libraries and the county libraries, as well as the Central Library for Students, the aspirations had been fittingly framed by the publication, three months earlier, of the Report of the Departmental Committee of the Board of Education; its Chairman, Sir Frederic Kenyon, Director of the British Museum, introduced it at a special Conference session. The Report – a sustained plea for local improvement and voluntary cooperation – not only prepared the way for the important developments of the 1930s; it removed the fear of education committee 'takeovers' which had haunted local library committees, their librarians and the LA since the publication of the Ministry of Reconstruction report in 1919. The new Report's recommendations were also sufficiently close to the LA's representations to the committee responsible for them[110] to win eager assent. But then, whereas the 1919 Committee had

included no librarian members, the 1927 one had, in addition to
the Chairman and as well as Mitchell, Secretary of the CUKT,
Ballinger, Pitt, Twentyman and Pacy – all out of a total[111] of
eleven members. Pacy, too, had been responsible for the only
note of dissent in the Report; he had expressed impatience, in a
tersely worded reservation, with merely voluntary sanctions as a
means of improving cooperation among the libraries of the
metropolitan boroughs.[112] Sir Frederic's session was admirably
supplemented by a series of others on cooperation between
urban and county authorities; between the Central Library for
Students and local libraries; between libraries and the BBC; and
between the LA and the associations in other countries.

The Fiftieth Conference had obviously been planned to be,
mostly, an occasion for looking forward. But the fifty years past
were not forgotten; Pacy submitted a paper on the Association's
early days. A very special kind of past *personal* service to the
Association and its members was also remembered when those
attending heard with regret of the resignation of the Honorary
Solicitor, Henry Fovargue whose connection with the LA had
begun even before his appointment as Town Clerk of
Eastbourne in 1890.[113] His contributions, in the *LAR*, to the
'Notes and Queries' on public library law had helped to solve
many problems which loomed large, or small, in their time and
their locality.

The members of the Council assembled for the final meeting of
the year 1927, on 28 October, might well have felt that change
was imminent. There had been, to be sure, but little change in
the names of the councillors returned at that year's recent
elections, only J. E. Walker, Librarian of Fulham Public
Libraries, having taken the place of Burt of Camberwell, and
W. A. Fenton, Borough Librarian of Cambridge, that of Acland-
Taylor, of Bristol. But at the meeting, Pacy, who had borne the
burden of further recent illness, asked to be relieved of the
administration and office work of the Association, while still
prepared to continue as Honorary Secretary. He had carried a
responsibility – entirely in the interests of the Association –
greater than that of any other officer since the foundation. It was
yet typical of the man – who had only eight more months to

live – that he placed himself 'unreservedly in the hands of the Council' and expressed himself as willing to carry on until other arrangements could be made. Frank Pacy deserves to be remembered as a librarian who had done much more than most to ensure that the Association's continued existence through what had been a most testing period was never seriously in doubt. The Council took immediate steps to seek office accommodation and to appoint a full-time paid secretary. An advertisement appearing in the December issue of the *Record* invited applications for the vacancy and offered a commencing annual salary of between £500 and £700[114] which – by the standards of public library salaries of the period – was good. An eventful year for the Association ended momentously with a letter from the Secretary of the CUKT:

December 16th, 1927.
Dear Pacy,
    I am directed to inform you that the Trustees have given careful consideration to the application from your Executive Committee, which has followed upon the decision of the Council to appoint a full-time paid Secretary, to secure premises of their own, and generally to embark upon a policy involving larger expenditure. They are in cordial sympathy with these decisions, and are prepared to accede to the request, though not quite to the amount, or in the form, suggested in your letter.
    The grant offered is as follows:
For 1928: £1000 plus a further sum up to a maximum of £200 on the £ for £ basis in respect of revenue from new subscriptions obtained in that year.
For 1929: £900 plus a further sum up to a maximum of £200 on the £ for £ basis in respect of revenue from *additional* new subscriptions obtained in that year.
For 1930: £800 plus a further sum up to a maximum of £200 on the £ for £ basis in respect of revenue from *additional* new subscriptions obtained in that year.
    The Trustees' quinquennium ends in 1930, and they make a rule of not encroaching upon the funds of a new five-year period. It will, however, be in order towards the end of 1930 to submit an application for a further grant of £700 and £600 for 1931 and 1932, if the circumstances appear to warrant it. The grant in any year after the first is, of course, conditional upon a satisfactory report for the previous year.

The following conditions are attached to this offer:

1. That the Association agree to carry into effect as soon as possible the relevant recommendations contained in the Government Report, which was unanimously approved at the Edinburgh Conference.

2. That every effort be made to give effect to the Council's resolution on the subject of the new Secretary and premises by March 1st, 1928, failing which the offer would be reconsidered.

3. That the post of Secretary be advertised in the general as well as in the Library Press, and that it be made clear that both library and administrative experience will be taken into account.

4. That the Association undertake in due course to make a considered effort to induce the other library groups and associations to come within a single unit; ultimately, if found feasible, housed in a single central headquarters along with the Central Library for Students. (NOTE. This would probably mean a modification of the Charter and perhaps some adjustment of the subscriptions, such as already marks the difference between Members and Associates)

5. That the annual report to the Trustees include a detailed financial statement showing expenditure and revenue for each main activity in order that it may be possible to judge to what extent, and in respect of what items, the position is improving or otherwise.

6. That the Association endeavour during the period of the grant not only to increase ordinary revenue, but to set aside a reserve fund.

The Trustees believe that these six conditions represent the intentions of the Association themselves, and that they will not prove onerous. It is necessary, however, that they should be on record. I am to add that the Trustees have been guided in fixing the amount of the grant by their knowledge of the present financial position of the Association, and by the conviction that it will be possible, with an adequate office staff and increased activity, considerably to increase the ordinary revenue from subscriptions and within a few years to put the Association on a sound financial footing.[115]

Yours sincerely,

J. M. MITCHELL

References

1. *LAR*, 22, p 319.
2. *Ibid*, pp 320–5.
3. *Ibid*, pp 325–31.
4. *Ibid*, pp 331–8.
5. *Ibid*, pp 372–7.
6. *Ibid*, p 376.
7. 'The new prospect: a plea for a policy', *LAR*, 22, pp 12–18.
8. Ministry of Reconstruction. *Third interim report of the Adult Education Committee: libraries and museums.* 1919.
9. Robertson, *Welfare in trust*, p 48.
10. *Ibid*, p 49.
11. CUKT, 7 *AR*, pp 9–10.
12. *See eg* E. J. Carnell, *County libraries.* 1938, pp 77–80.

13. *LAR*, 25, p 141.
14. 49 *AR* (1925–6), p 3.
15. 14.1.1927.
16. Minutes of Executive committee, 2.9.1927.
17. 7.4.1927.
18. 50 *AR* (1926–7), p 9.
19. 18.3.1921.
20. 2.12.1921.
21. 44 *AR* (1920–1), p 16.
22. 18.3.1921.
23. 45 *AR* (1921–2), pp 16–17.
24. *Obit* in *Canadian L.J.*, 28 (Sept./Oct. 1971).
25. *See* 'Report of the special committee appointed to consider future arrangements for the office administration of the Association'. 1922. (*LAC* 920; Appendix.)
26. Letter incorporated in Council Minutes, 6.9.1926.
27. 45 *AR* (1921–2), pp 16–7.
28. *LAR*, 26 pp 141–5.
29. *Times*, 11.8.1924.
30. *Ibid*, 13.8.1924.
31. 23.1.1925.
32. *LAR*, 26, p 190.
33. *Ibid*, p 63.
34. *Ibid*, pp 210–25.
35. 48 *AR* (1924–5), p 10.
36. 44 *AR* (1920–1), pp 9–10.
37. Letter of 21.12.1921.
38. 19.1.1923.
39. Report in *LAC* 920 (between pp 265 and 266).
40. 16.4.1926.
41. Statement in *LAR*, 28, pp 44–5.
42. 49 *AR* (1925–6), p 13.
43. *LAR*, 26, p 35.
44. 19.1.1923.
45. 17.7.1925.
46. 49 *AR* (1925–6), p 12.
47. 44 *AR* (1920–1), pp 6–7.
48. 46 *AR* (1922–3), p 6.
49. *LAR*, 25, p 36.
50. 46 *AR* (1922–3), p 17. *See also* C. W. J. Harris, *Fifty years of progress: the London and Home Counties Branch of the L.A. 1923–1973*. 1975.
51. 46 *AR* p 6.
52. *LAR*, 25, p 225.
53. 23.1.1925.
54. Vol 109, pp 321–333.

55. *The Public Library system of Great Britain and Ireland 1921–1923*. 1924.
56. 'Interlibrary lending', *LAR*, 27, pp 230–41; discussion in *Conference proceedings*. 1925, pp viii–xi.
57. A. W. Pollard, 'The Central Library for Students', *LAR*, 19, pp 372–8.
58. L. Newcombe, *Library cooperation in the British Isles*. 1937, pp 53–4.
59. CUKT, 8 *AR*, pp 11–12.
60. Lamb *op cit*, pp 51–2.
61. *LAR*, 27, pp 242–55.
62. Discussion in *Conference proceedings,* pp xii–xiv.
63. *LAR*, 28, p 108.
64. 49 *AR* (1925–6), p 9.
65. 45 *AR* (1921–2), p 10.
66. L. R. McColvin, *Library extension work and publicity*. 1927, p 66.
67. *LAR*, 23, pp 129–36.
68. 'Public libraries and publicity'. *LAR*, 27, pp 199–208.
69. *LAR*, 24, pp 200–8; 228–30.
70. *LAR*, 25, p 193.
71. Fry and Munford, *L. S. Jast*, p 55.
72. 49 *AR* (1925–6), p 19.
73. 14.9.1925.
74. 16.4.1926.
75. eg Munford, *Edwards*, p 113.
76. *LAR*, 27, p 10.
77. 47 *AR* (1923–4), p 9.
78. LA *Syllabus of information on facilities for training in librarianship*. 1928, p 27.
79. 18.7.1924.
80. eg 50 *AR* (1926–7), p 7.
81. 8.9.1924.
82. 23.1.1925.
83. 1.7.1921.
84. 11.4.1924.
85. 20.4.1923.
86. 1.7.1921.
87. 18.1.1924.
88. Ramsden *op cit*, pp 100–1.
89. *Ibid*, p 107.
90. *LAR*, 24, p 173.
91. *Syllabus. 1928*, p 9.
92. Ramsden *op cit*, p 106.
93. *Syllabus. 1928*, p 9.
94. Ramsden *op cit*, pp 106–7.
95. Aitken *op cit*, pp 225–7.
96. eg 48 *AR* (1924–5), pp 7–8.
97. *LAR*, 24, pp 116–7.

Between the Wars

98. 16.6.1922.
99. 46 *AR* (1922–3), p 16.
100. 18.7.1924.
101. *LAR*, 28, pp 173–6, 287–8.
102. *Some impressions of the public library system of the United States of America,* (CUKT). 1926. Review in *LAR*, 28, pp 127–30.
103. 50 *AR* (1926–7), p 4.
104. *See eg* 45 *AR* (1921–2), p 15; 46 *AR* (1922–3), p 18.
105. 50 *AR* (1926–7), pp 12–13.
106. 48 *AR* (1924–5), p 12.

107. *LAR*, 29, pp 67–9.
108. 50 *AR* (1926–7), pp 10–11.
109. *Proceedings of the 50th Anniversary Conference of the L.A.* Supplement to *LAR*, 30, pp i–xxvi.
110. eg 48 *AR* (1924–5), p 6.
111. Constitution of the Committee, p 2.
112. pp 215–6.
113. *See also* his *Library legislation* (jointly with J. J. Ogle). 1892.
114. *LAR*, 29, p 328.
115. *LAR*, 30, pp 22–3.

Chapter Seven

1928-1939

The period now under review may be divided – for purposes of social background – into two parts. During the first the tendencies engendered by the world economic crisis and the nation's deflationary policy, symbolised by the partial return to the Gold Standard in 1925, combined to create an unemployment problem on a quite unprecedented scale. During the middle and later 1930s unemployment eased as the reflationary influences of the new rearmament programme and of world recovery began to manifest themselves.

The social implications of large scale unemployment are numberless; one of the most obvious palliatives of the early 1930s was the attempt to fill the unsought leisure hours of up to three million people, nearly all men, since it was then still exceptional, in most parts of the country, for married women to occupy salaried posts. The LA, while anxious to help, found itself in a quandary. Lay opinion, which encouraged the opening of clubs and centres for the unemployed, tended to visualise these as necessarily equipped with their own libraries: press and broadcast appeals for discarded books were made, and directed at libraries as well as at the general public. Many librarians, on the other hand, felt, understandably enough, that the most effective book service to unemployed people should be provided locally and by their public libraries. The Association, which at first asked to be associated with the appeals,[1] later took over full responsibility,[2] public libraries frequently being encouraged to act as local collecting depots. The *Record* was able to report:

Well over 40,000 books and periodicals have been sent to the LA by interested persons for distribution to unemployed centres . . . the major problem is the provision of books, constant and adequate, for unemployed centres and clubs where there is no public library service or where the public library service is seriously restricted by lack of funds . . . To library authorities in those more fortunate areas where there is little unemployment we appeal . . . for help for the special areas . . . .[3]

The views of the many librarians who were both uneasy and unhappy were summed up by R. D. Hilton Smith:

Here let me make a protest, an angry protest which should not be necessary, against the practice of sending collections of discarded books to these centres . . . An unemployed man is not an abstraction. He is you and I, thrown suddenly into anxiety for the present and hopelessness as to the future, wondering what on earth is to become of us . . . To my mind, the only justification for sending any collection of books to a social centre is when the readers would have to pay fares which they cannot afford to reach the nearest library. In that event, the centres should be regarded as a service point and supplied with a good selection from the general stock, kept attractive and changed as often as necessary.[4]

During the years of economic stringency the current expenditure budgets of most public libraries were pruned much less than might have been expected but little progress was made in the provision of new buildings.[5] But the situation eased after 1933 and many important new buildings, large and small, were opened during the years prior to the outbreak of World War Two, the new central libraries in Manchester and Sheffield, opened in 1934, heralding changing times. The new buildings, some of which replaced old ones and others providing completely new service points, were significant pointers to change; they seem, in retrospect, rather less important than the phenomenal advances in inter-library cooperation during the same period. Reference to these advances will be made on a later page.

The LA was itself changed almost beyond recognition during this period. Exceptional impetus was provided by a Trust, a constitution, and a man; the man, Ernest Savage, had been primarily responsible for the approach to the Trust and for drafting the bye-laws creating the new constitution.

Frank Pacy died in harness in June 1928 and in the following September Savage was elected Honorary Secretary to succeed him. Some of Savage's many earlier efforts to drive the Association on to greater membership, greater influence and greater power have been referred to in earlier pages; he came now to the post which made infinitely more possible. His initial approach was summed up in two articles in the *Record* introducing the new bye-laws and outlining a programme of development. But before commenting on these articles, it may be convenient to introduce the new bye-laws which were approved at the Annual meeting at Blackpool in September 1928, allowed by the Privy Council without alteration a month later and brought into force as from January 1929.[6] The most important changes resulting were the introduction of graduated subscriptions for both personal and institutional members eg half a guinea for those personal members receiving salaries of up to £150 per annum; one guinea for those with salaries between £150 and £300: no change was made in the basic two-guinea subscription. There was provision also for librarians and institutions overseas to become corresponding members at 15s per annum – effectively an annual subscription to the *Library Association Record*; for life members at 25 guineas and for 'endowment' members at 5 guineas. Sections, 'to attract librarians of non-municipal libraries to join the ranks of the Association in greater numbers', were provided for; and the professional register, consisting of Fellows and Associates, was clearly separated from the membership list. The Council, as governing body, was reconstituted to have three vice-presidents instead of twelve; three institutional councillors instead of four; six London councillors instead of twelve; and fifteen country councillors instead of twenty: each member was to serve for three years instead of one.

Savage's essentially forward-looking approach to the Association emphasised the need for union of the LA and the other library societies, a stronger financial position, endowment, more members, a more realistic publishing policy (eg in relation to the *Subject index*), a monthly *Record*, improvements in publicity, better offices, more and better facilities for training (eg more library schools) and more effective help for the small library.[7] To underline:

We want one efficient Association, embracing all library interests. If we do not win more members the subscriptions must go up again. If we fail to unite we shall continue to be as bankrupt as we have been hitherto. If we neglect to consider sectional interests, and if the branches, sections, and district associations ignore general interests, we may remain disunited for another half century.[8]

Many of Savage's ambitions for the Association were to be realised, wholly or in part. Few, if any, could have been achieved without more satisfactory arrangements for permanent staffing than had obtained hitherto. When Guy Keeling, who had been Secretary of ASLIB since 1924 was appointed Secretary of the LA, at the age of thirty-eight in March 1928, he found the administrative situation – following Pacy's death – to be both complicated and difficult. Pacy's personal administration had resulted in excessive complexity of some records and methods, and extreme paucity of others. This was understandable enough since, in Pacy's capacity as Honorary Secretary, he had taken many decisions for the Association which Keeling rightly felt must now be the responsibility of the Council and its committees.[9] No one could reasonably be blamed since no one man – not even Pacy – could have run the Association fully and efficiently as a spare-time occupation. Change was nevertheless imperative. Keeling began the necessary reorganisation but was unfortunately soon impeded by the chronic ill-health which necessitated long periods of sick leave and, eventually, his resignation, only three years after he had assumed his new responsibilities. Fortunately he had begun to build up the nucleus of an efficient staff, in particular by securing as Assistant Secretary in August 1929 P. S. J. Welsford. Welsford was promoted as Acting Secretary, to succeed Keeling in November 1931, at a salary of £500 rising to £600,[10] a remuneration higher than that then received by most public librarians other than

those of the largest authorities. Aided now by his small staff of
five clerks and assistants,[11] Welsford made easily possible the
Savage-inspired transformation of the Association.

Percy S. J. Welsford (1893–1968) acted as Secretary from his
appointment in 1931, like Keeling at the age of thirty-eight, until
his retirement in 1959. He had had a good deal of business
experience before coming to the LA, much of it under
increasingly difficult conditions in Greece following his
demobilisation from World War One; he soon showed that he
was an accomplished and exceptionally economical
administrator, a most successful office manager and a diplomat
of no mean order, seeming always to be able to make personal
and effective contact with the 'key' man or woman in whichever
other organisation the Association had business with, be it
national or local government, universities, trade unions etc, and
abroad as well as at home. Because he had the highest standards
of personal rectitude himself, he could be, and sometimes was, a
little too critical of librarians and others who seemed to him to
be content with lesser ambitions. He certainly found many
critics himself during his long years with the Association. He
also made many firm and affectionate friends who grew to
appreciate his sterling qualities and were always delighted to see
him; his international acquaintance was vast. The Association's
debts to Percy Welsford were many: his unstinting and
dedicated service shines like a bright light through the present
and later periods.[12]

Integration now began in earnest and the transformation of the
provincial associations into real branches, which had proved
impossible of achievement during Jast's years as Honorary
Secretary prior to World War One, now came in Savage's.
During 1928–9 the Birmingham and District, and
North Midland associations amalgamated with the LA[13] and the
Scottish LA became a branch also as from January 1931, in
accordance with the terms of an agreement providing for its own
special and national status.[14] New branches were formed to
cover Wales and Monmouthshire, and Northern Ireland,[15] the
librarians of the Irish Republic forming their own, independent,
association.[16] The winding up of the always anomalous and

ill-starred North Central branch in 1928 made it possible, once again, for the long-established North Western branch to have a satisfactorily defined area.[17] Progress was indeed so impressive that the Council was encouraged to consider 'mapping out the whole country into areas for Branch purposes'. But this was, on reflection, felt to be 'an ideal to strive for'.[18] The ideal did not become reality until after World War Two.

The Association's sectional development was also notable. The County Libraries, and University and Research Sections were officially formed immediately the new bye-laws made this possible[19] and by 1932 each had more than 200 members.[20] The County Section then developed very rapidly; University and Research progress was inevitably slower since LA membership seemed less important to many members of the staffs of the university and college libraries who, then with much justice, regarded the Association as one primarily for public libraries. Integration with both ASLIB and with the National Home Reading Union was also discussed but came to nothing[21] and the formation of a School libraries section had to wait until 1937.[22]

Sectionally speaking the most important event was the union with the Association of Assistant Librarians[23] which became effective from 1 January 1930. Following much discussion between the two associations and an affirmative poll of the AAL's own membership, it was agreed that it become a Section; the 1929 agreement provided for it to retain its constitution and self-government, students' library and benevolent fund; it also remained responsible for the editing, publication and distribution of *The Library Assistant*. It was now given entire responsibility for the Association's correspondence courses, subject always to these being conducted in accordance with the LA's educational policy. The Association agreed to make an annual payment to the new Section of £30 per hundred members; in return no new members of the AAL only were to be recruited, and existing 'transitional' members, ie those paying only their existing annual subscriptions of 7s, were to be encouraged to become full members of the LA. Arrangements were made for AAL representation on the LA Council and on specified committees.[24]

It is fair to say that the sectionalising of the AAL proved increasingly more controversial than the other unions. Some members of the LA Council soon began to regard it as an impermanent, 'untidy' and altogether unsatisfactory substitute for a Students' section; the voting power of AAL members at LA annual meetings was especially, and understandably, suspect. By 1935 the Council was planning reorganisation to end the AAL's life as a Section and to provide, alternatively, for student membership.[25] New bye-laws[26] were submitted to the annual meeting at Liverpool in June 1939 and were rejected. The 1929 agreement thus remained in operation despite the opinion of the LA's Legal Adviser that the AAL was not a Section. But he contended also that it was merely 'one party to a voluntary agreement enforceable only in honour'.[27] The *de jure* difference was doubtless significant; the *de facto* distinction was, perhaps, less obvious.

The effects of the unions on the LA's membership seemed breathtaking. It rose from 897 in 1928[28] to 1271 in 1929[29] and to 2884 in 1930.[30] The *Annual Report* for 1929–30 reminded members that 'It seems but a short time since the Council estimated as a maximum a membership of 3000; now this figure is well within reach'.[31] It was indeed. The membership rose to 4095 in 1932,[32] 4260 in 1933,[33] 5046 in 1935[34] and to 6039 in 1938.[35]

Two modifying comments on the Association's increased membership are, however, very important. A good deal of it was due to the Council's decision in February, 1929, on the motion of Savage 'that persons should not be permitted to sit for LA examinations after January, 1930 unless they were in membership of the LA; excepting those who had already obtained some sectional certificates'.[36] Secondly, much of the new membership was, initially at least, uneconomic, since the personal subscriptions of half a guinea and one guinea for the lower paid members did not cover the cost of all basic services to them. The situation was also complicated by the need to provide for 'transitional' membership of a significant proportion of the AAL membership as well as that of one of the district associations become Branches. But, overall, the financial situation now seemed infinitely more promising, particularly as it proved easily possible for the Association to earn the CUKT grants promised in their Secretary's letter printed at the end of the previous chapter.

Savage's aspirations for the Association included 'better offices'. Different, if not necessarily better, ones were imperative following Pacy's resignation and in the spring of 1928 the Association moved to 26–7 Bedford Square, sharing premises there with ASLIB and with the CUKT. Although the space available soon proved inadequate to cope with the increasing membership and expanding business, there was also the amenity of a common room where could be obtained 'light refreshments on very reasonable terms'.[37]

The CUKT were approached and the subject of a new headquarters discussed. The Trustees' sympathy was evident but they were even more interested in satisfactorily housing the National Central Library; the possibility of a jointly held building was put to the LA and rejected, on balance of advantage.[38] Various possibilities were then considered to provide both bodies with adjoining but separate offices and in October 1931 the CUKT were able to offer a derelict property in Upper Gower Mews, to be renamed Malet Place.[39] Savage has himself provided interesting insight on the next stage:

A most useful member of the Association's Headquarters committee, he [Arundell Esdaile] was one of the few who wearily tramped London streets looking at numerous buildings recommended by agents with more imagination than truth. I can see him now, bending down to us, his eyes gleaming, his whole face alight with humour, as he shaped an epigram which consigned, with pith and force, each near-ruin to oblivion. But when the Committee saw with dismay the black wreck of a warehouse that the Carnegie Trustees offered he was the only one of us with the vision to see the building as it might be, and as, under a good architect, it became. And when we could not agree on a name for the transformed derelict, he quietly recommended "Chaucer House".[40]

Agreements were signed in December 1931; architects (Gold and Aldridge) appointed in the following February and the

contract let to the successful tenderer (Cheesums) who began
work in May 1932.[41] Chaucer House was opened by Lord Irwin,
deputising for the Prime Minister, Stanley Baldwin, on 25
May 1933. Jast spoke no more than the literal truth when, in
proposing a vote of thanks to the CUKT, he said:

This building has come, as it were, to mark the fulfilment of another
dream of ours . . . namely, the bringing together in one body of all
sections of the profession and of the library calling and of all types
and classes of librarians. That building symbolises this new unity.[42]

Chaucer House provided a members' room, with kitchen, on the
ground floor; council chamber, with folding screen to shut off
part to serve as separate committee room, on the first floor; and
offices on the second, third and fourth floors. The third floor
was let to the Society of Genealogists and part of the fourth to
the Museums Association, two most acceptable tenants.

The members of the headquarters committee responsible for the
acquisition and building of Chaucer House, chaired by Savage,
were able to hold their last meeting on 8 February 1934, 'their
work being quite completed and Chaucer House free of debt'.[43]
The CUKT had contributed £11,970 towards the total cost. But
the Association itself had provided nearly as much, its quota of
£9565 representing an achievement which would have seemed
completely unthinkable only a few years earlier. Its triumph was
surely complete when it was able to repay to the Trustees the
sum of £2000 – lent for 'tiding over' purposes – nearly three
years before repayment became obligatory.

Prudent management of the Association's always too limited
financial resources had enabled it to build up substantial annual
surpluses in anticipation of its headquarters development.
During the years 1927 to 1933 the annual excess of income over
expenditure had averaged more than £850; these surpluses,
added to already existing reserve funds – represented by
investments amounting then in market value to nearly £5000 –
paid the LA's 44% share of the cost of Chaucer House. The
annual surpluses continued from 1934 to 1938 and averaged

£620. They were a very necessary insurance against the uncertain hazards of the future since Savage's hopes of many endowment subscriptions were wholly disappointed and the special headquarters Appeal Fund – launched to replace the reserves – had reached only £2600 by the end of 1937.[44]

Savage's ambitions for the Association, as noted earlier, had included not only union of the library societies, a stronger financial policy and better offices, but also a more realistic publishing policy; a monthly *Record*, and, not obviously linked, more effective help for the small library. Much progress was also made under each of these heads.

The *Subject index to periodicals*, whose chequered history had so bedevilled the Association's finances during earlier years, was now placed, if not on as firm a footing as was devoutly to be wished, at least on a more balanced one. In its *Annual report* for 1927–8 the Council felt able to say:

The number of subscribers to the 1926 *Index* is greater than that to any previous volume, and there has been a steady sale of the earlier volumes and parts. . . . Every effort is being made to ensure that in future the *Index* for a given year shall be issued during the early part of the following summer.[45]

The drastic earlier action in substantially reducing the periodical coverage was certainly subject for criticism[46] but by 1927 the publication was at least almost self-supporting.[47] The editorial office was moved from the National Library of Wales to Bedford Square during 1929–30[48] and, a year later, T. Rowland Powel was added to Tucker's small staff to work on the still missing years 1923–5.[49] He made good progress but, following Tucker's resignation in 1931, was promoted to the main, and current, responsibility.[50] A great deal of credit for the continuing progress was due to G. A. Stephen, City Librarian of Norwich, who acted as honorary secretary of the LA's *Subject index* committee until his death in December 1934, a year after the move to Chaucer House. Yet library subscriptions were still disappointingly small. As Professor H. J. Laski asked those attending the Manchester conference in 1935:

Cannot your own unique bibliographical tool, the *Subject index to periodicals*, secure more than the bare hundred Public Library subscribers for its remarkable merits ?[51]

This, too, despite a very reasonable annual subscription rate of £3 10*s*, a figure which became an even better bargain in 1937 when a location list was included, 'giving particulars of more than 170 libraries in which the periodicals are filed and may be consulted'.[52]

The *Library Association Record* had changed from monthly to quarterly publication in January 1923. It began monthly issues again in January 1931, by which time it was felt that the Association could again bear the necessarily increased cost. That additional cost proved to be substantial although difficult to quantify precisely owing to annual changes, and doubtless improvements, in the detailed presentation of the LA's accounts. Net revenue from advertisements never became buoyant; whereas in 1926–7 the net cost of the *Record* accounted for 19% of the Association's subscription income, it had risen to 22% in 1931 and to 27% in 1938. But the net cost of the official journal is a regular item of expenditure which worries each generation of councillors and members, more even than its alleged 'dullness'.

The format of the *Record* was changed as from January 1934 and it was printed henceforward in double columns and on paper suitable also for half tone blocks. In his first double-column editorial Esdaile made points which are perennially relevant:

The Record is often criticised for dullness . . . the Editor has not seldom found himself in the case of that noble statesman who is reported to have yawned in the middle of one of his own speeches; but if readers suppose . . . that this is because he habitually rejects interesting matter, they are profoundly mistaken . . . It is always much easier and pleasanter to say that the Record is dull than to send in a contribution that will make it less so. The fact is that the Record's public is not one, but several, with certain interests in common, but many more which diverge.[53]

He continued as editor until December 1935 when, following his resignation on medical advice, he was succeeded by

R. D. Hilton Smith (1903–1974), then Borough Librarian of Deptford. The new editor did his predecessor no more than justice when, in *his* first editorial, he wrote:

From its former mediocrity, Mr Esdaile raised it to a level worthy of an Association now growing in numbers and prestige. The resumption of monthly publication in 1931 was a fitting crown to his efforts. He had brought the official journal successfully through one of the most difficult stages in the history of the Association.[54]

Hilton Smith continued in office until beyond the end of the present period; under his direction high standards were maintained, a new layout was introduced, new features such as 'The literature of librarianship', 'Current government publications', and 'Reference library news' were introduced, and at least one old one, 'Current views', revived. His task was made much easier by the appointment of permanent assistant editors from 1934 onwards. Hazel Mews served as Librarian and assistant editor from 1934 until 1936[55] and she was followed by F. J. Cornell whose original appointment to the Association's staff was, however, as Assistant Librarian.[56]

A new publications drive was perhaps symbolised by the decision in 1930 to terminate the seven-year-old agreement with Grafton and Co to act as selling agents; henceforward the Association sold its own publications. One of them, the pamphlet on *Book construction* (1931) was substantially a revised reprint of the *Interim report of the LA book production committee* of 1913; it complemented the *Durability of paper report* of 1930. *Library buildings: their heating, lighting and decoration* (1933) was a small but useful volume reprinting Bournemouth (1932) conference papers. Margaret Burton and Marion Vosburgh *Bibliography of librarianship* (1934) was not only valuable in its own right; it quickly showed up the deficiencies of the Association's own library.

Three publications of the early 1930s had special links with the CUKT. John Minto's *Reference books* (1929; Supplement 1931) received a Trust guarantee against loss of up to £100;[57] the other two were published at direct instigation and with generous financial help. *Small municipal libraries: a manual of modern method,* originally published in 1931 and in a greatly improved and better illustrated revision, incorporating a new chapter on decoration, in 1934, reflected the CUKT's interest in improving service standards in the smaller municipal libraries and may be regarded as closely related to their special book grants made to these libraries up to the middle 1930s. *Small municipal libraries* quickly became, not only an easy-to-use manual for its intended public but, in addition, a first rate introductory textbook for a new generation of young students. *Books to read: a classified and annotated catalogue, being a guide for young readers,* compiled by a committee representing the LA, National Association of Boys' Clubs, National Council of Girls' Clubs and the CUKT, was published in 1931, 'primarily for the use of librarians, teachers and others concerned with the education and training of young readers, as well as for use by the readers themselves'.[58] Edited by Charles Nowell, then City Librarian of Coventry, it listed nearly 5000 titles. The first, and only, supplement, *Books to read, 1931,* quickly followed. A new edition *Books for youth: a classified and annotated guide for young readers,* compiled by a committee of the LA (W. C. Berwick Sayers, general editor), appeared in 1936, the first year for which the Association presented its new Carnegie Medal for an outstanding book for children – to Arthur Ransome for his *Pigeon Post*. The LAR's editorial, introducing the new medal, said:

One of the things most needed in England, where probably more children's books are published than in any other country, was a marking out of really fine work in this field. Quite frankly, many of the books that are written for children are very poor; the field, however, is immense and so, too, should be the opportunities for good authors to distinguish themselves.[59]

The award of the Carnegie medal since 1937 – and its occasional withholding when no book of a single year has been considered sufficiently meritorious – has assuredly been one factor contributing to the immense improvement in the standards of British books for children during the past forty years. It was no doubt inspired by the Newbery medal of the ALA but has acquired distinction in its own right.

Other important publications of the present period were, in
1935, the *County libraries manual,* compiled by the County libraries
section, and effectively superseding the pioneer and then
ten-year-old textbooks by R. D. Macleod and Duncan Gray; and
J. H. P. Pafford's *Library cooperation in Europe*; and, in 1938, even
more outstandingly, R. C. Barrington Partridge's *History of the
legal deposit of books throughout the British Empire*. This book, which
had begun its life as a LA thesis, quickly became a standard
work of which both author and publisher had every reason to be
proud.

It was, however, in annual and series publication that the
Association had its most comprehensive successes. The *Year
Book*, which had been published so irregularly prior to the 1930s,
was now put on a firm basis. The new series commenced in 1932
and continued during the remainder of the present period,
appearing regularly at the beginning of January each year. The
1932 edition contained a calendar of literary anniversaries and
forthcoming dates of LA importance; lists of Council and
committee members, national, branch and sectional; outline
details of past conferences; the Charter, bye-laws and election
regulations; examination syllabuses, lists of textbooks and other
sources of information for students, and the past year's question
papers; lists of the Association's own publications; a very
detailed membership list incorporating the Register; and
Savage's 'Annals of the Association', from the foundation to
date. Successive annual issues included additional features, eg a
list of library associations overseas; lists of addresses of
inter-library-lending interest; notes on cooperation with the BBC
(listening group information etc). The new *Year Book* was
excellent value at its substantially subsidised price to members of
2s 6d.[60] Bearing in mind that the Council's *Report* for 1937
expressed no more than the obvious truth when it said of the
Year Book: 'this has now reached the position of indispensability
to all actively concerned with current library affairs',[61] it may
still be regretted that the average annual sale barely exceeded
1000 copies.

The first annual volume of what had been envisaged in the
previous chapter as a 'Year's work in library studies', appeared

in 1929 as *The Year's work in librarianship, 1928*, edited by Esdaile. It contained sixteen chapters reviewing recorded work of and departments of most major types of library. The intended scope was international and, while the first volume fell short in this respect in numerous ways, there were many improvements in the successive issues up to that for 1938.

The editor of an annual publication comparable with the *Year's work* copes inevitably with many problems. He will seek to have his chapters written by acknowledged experts in their respective fields and he will try to persuade them to submit their contributions by a date not too long after the end of the year under review. Often enough the obvious compilers of individual chapters are already busy people with other pressing commitments. Sometimes a volume may have to be published minus important chapters. It was a remarkable tribute to Esdaile, and to J. H. Pafford, who soon joined him as joint editor, that such a high standard of contribution was maintained and that so much ground was covered each year. The chapter headings and the list of contributors to the *Year's work* for one representative year, 1936, may be quoted as example:

i	General introduction (Esdaile)
ii	National and university libraries (L. J. H. Bradley, London Library)
iii	Special libraries (C. C. Barnard, Librarian, London School of Hygiene and Tropical Medicine; and A. D. Roberts, Birmingham Public Libraries)
iv	Urban libraries (F. Seymour Smith, Hornsey Public Libraries)
v	County and rural libraries (Elsie Cockerlyne, Lancashire County Libraries)
vi	School libraries (Monica Cant, Librarian, Cheltenham Ladies College)
vii	Children's libraries (Eileen Colwell, Hendon Public Libraries)
viii	Library cooperation (Janet Tomblin, South Eastern Regional System)
ix	Professional education (Hannah Smith, Librarian, Leeds Training College)

x   Library buildings (E. J. Carter, Librarian, Royal Institute of British Architects)

xi   Library practice:
a Organisation and routine (W. A. Munford, Dover Public Library)
b Cataloguing (Margaret Taylor (School of Librarianship, UCL)
c Classification (W. C. Berwick Sayers, Croydon Public Libraries)

xii   Library law (A. R. Hewitt, Middle Temple Library)

xiii   Book production:
a Printing and illustration (H. Woodbine, Birmingham Public Libraries)
b Bookbinding: methods and materials (S. Horrocks, Manchester Public Libraries)
c Bookbinding: historical (H. M. Nixon, British Museum Library)

xiv   Historical bibliography (F. C. Francis, British Museum Library)

xv   Bibliography: general and national (J. Vorstius, Prussian State Library)

xvi   Palaeography and manuscripts (C. E. Wright, British Museum Library)

xvii Archives (Irene Churchill and others)

xviii Other matters (J. H. Pafford)

As had been the case with the *Subject index*, too few libraries supported the *Year's work* to ensure its complete financial success, despite the fact that its contributors were unpaid. Librarians who acquired it regularly, as a matter of course, frequently looked forward most to the masterly chapters on 'Library buildings', by Edward Carter appearing in the volumes from 1931 onwards. The Council's *Report* for 1938 expressed general satisfaction:

It is now ten years since the first annual edition was produced and time has shown that its early sponsors were fully justified and that the Council was right in continuing its publication in spite of some discouragement in its infancy.[62]

The 'LA series of library manuals' was an ambitious and largely successful attempt to rewrite the basic professional textbooks. Initial credit for the idea must go to the Librarian of Hampstead Public Libraries, W. E. Doubleday; his approach, as prospective general editor, to the publishers, George Allen and Unwin Ltd, was endorsed by the Council and resulted in an agreement for joint publication.[63] This arrangement facilitated publication, mostly at 10s 6d a volume (8s 9d to LA members). *A primer of librarianship: being chapters of practical instruction by recognised authorities,* edited by Doubleday and Esdaile's *Student's manual of bibliography* appeared in 1931; W. C. Berwick Sayers' *Manual of children's libraries* and John Minto's *History of the public library movement in Great Britain and Ireland* in 1932; Doubleday's *Manual of library routine* and J. H. Quinn's and H. W. Acomb's *Manual of cataloguing and indexing* in 1933; and B. M. Headicar's *Manual of library organization* in 1935. Most volumes were admittedly strongly orientated to specialised public library practice but *Primer of librarianship* included chapters on university, commercial and technical libraries, and *Manual of library organization* was written by a librarian all of whose later experience had been gained at a great non-municipal institution, the British Library of Political and Economic Science at the LSE. The success of the series encouraged the publishers to bring out a supplementary series of shorter 'Practical library handbooks'. This included several acceptable and useful titles but it was not the joint responsibility of the LA.

From the point of view of sheer size and coverage the most ambitious LA publication of the period was *A survey of libraries: reports on a survey made by the LA during 1936–1937,* (1938). This had originated, slightly indirectly, from another of Savage's suggestions:

With the acquisition of Chaucer House came renewed desires for a library of librarianship worthy of the Association ... with the improvement of the library came an increase in the information service ... In April, 1935 the Association was grateful to hear that the (Rockefeller) Foundation had decided to make a grant, part to be expended on the improvement of the library, part to be devoted to the cost of the survey.[64]

The *Survey*, based substantially on tours of inspection by senior British librarians, covered, in addition to Great Britain, Belgium, France, Holland, Scandinavia, Germany, central and north-east Europe, Russia, and the United States. It provided librarians and the Association with a mass of information – inevitably of unequal quality – which had not been readily available previously, the whole skilfully knit into one large volume by Lionel McColvin who had succeeded Savage as Honorary Secretary in 1934, following a short period of office with him, and at his suggestion, as joint Honorary Secretary.[65]

It was unfortunate that the overall success and indeed intrinsic value of the *Survey* should have been jeopardised by the shortcomings of one small portion of its contents but so it was. Great objection was taken, in particular by the Scottish LA, to the part covering public libraries in south-west Scotland, Cumberland and Northern Ireland, for which Miss A. S. Cooke, County librarian of Kent, had been responsible. The Scottish LA was invited by the Council to re-survey the area itself but declined.[66] At the Annual meeting at Liverpool in June 1939:

A motion by Mr A. Ogilvie on behalf of the Scottish LA, repudiating Report 2 (Part 1) in *A Survey of libraries* and instructing the Council to publish and issue to all subscribers, without delay, a new report, embodying the facts contained in the report sheets on which the original survey was based, supplemented by re-inspection of the area, was carried.[67]

The coming of World War Two suspended the controversy and two years later the Scottish LA agreed to let the matter drop.[68]

The Association's successes in the field of its own publications during the 1930s were very real. As the *Annual Report* for 1938 put it:

The (Publications) Committee have been constantly vigilant to encourage the publication of any work which will be a contribution to the knowledge of librarianship, a useful library tool, or a help to students, but at the same time avoiding anything which is redundant or for which there is not a real need.[69]

No small part of the credit was due to W. Benson Thorne (1878–1966), Librarian of Poplar Public Libraries, and chairman of the committee until his resignation at the end of 1937 when the committee reported:

His withdrawal is a severe loss, both to the Committee and to the Council. It may fairly be said that all the major publishing activities of the Association were initiated and brought to successful issue under his direction. His devotion to the work must have engaged the greater part of his leisure for the whole nine years for which he has served. Members of the Committee recognise his initiative, his ready grasp of new needs, his skill and industry and, above all, his friendliness and tolerance in conducting all the meetings over which he has presided. This summing up is quite inadequate but is some earnest of the gratitude of the Committee.[70]

There were indeed many successes: there were also failures. A new series of booklists at the beginning of the period was depressingly unsuccessful and the project was quickly dropped.[71] A later proposal for a 'Bimonthly LA Booklist' was frustrated by the outbreak of World War Two. But the gap had in fact been substantially filled by Sectional activity, by the County Section's 'Readers' guides' pamphlets, of which the first twenty-four, on subjects as different as architecture and building, modern poetry, and physical fitness were published at a minimum subscription of 1*s* per dozen copies of each title;[72] and by the 'Recommended books' supplement to the AAL's *Library Assistant*.[73] The present historian may also be allowed to regret that the Council's suggestion to Savage that he write 'a readable history (of the LA) of about 80,000 words, appropriately illustrated'[74] came to nothing, and that no action could be taken, due to excessive estimated cost, to issue a facsimile reprint of Edward Edwards' *Memoirs of libraries*.[75]

At the beginning of the present period the Association adopted the practice of selling its own publications, other than the *Record*, to members at a cash discount.[76] This initiative set a useful example for booksellers supplying libraries: the LA, following so many earlier disappointments in this wider field, was at last successful. The *Annual Report* for 1932 included the following paragraph:

It was with deep regret that the [Net books] Committee received, in September, the resignation of Mr W. E. Doubleday from the Chairmanship of the Committee. They realize, however, that Mr Doubleday has very ably brought to a successful conclusion his work as the champion of the net book commission, and that in his well-earned retirement it is only reasonable that he should be relieved of further responsibility in the administration of the agreement. At the same time the committee are indeed glad to know that he is always ready and willing to place at their disposal the benefit of his advice and experience. As far back as 1902 Mr Doubleday first became active in the movement to obtain a reduction in the cost of new books to libraries, and from 1928 to 1932 he led the campaign for special terms to libraries. It is largely due to his tactful and efficient leadership that the libraries owe the terms – representing in the aggregate a saving of many thousand pounds a year – under which they are now able to obtain their books. The negotiations were difficult and required delicate handling. Few persons could have carried them through successfully and retained – as Mr Doubleday has done – the respect and friendship of all the bodies concerned.[77]

It was an immense achievement and it was only reached by what seem now to have been exceedingly laborious stages: much deeply ingrained bookseller resistance had to be worn down. As from November 1929 licences issued to libraries in membership of the LA.[78] provided for commissions – but only in the form of books – of 5% on the first £100–£500 spent per annum on books price controlled under the Net book agreement, and of 10% on further expenditure, to be given by the booksellers listed on the licence as authorised to supply.[79] The 10% commission – henceforward available as cash discount – was extended to all the new book purchases of libraries spending more than £500 per annum as from June 1931,[80] and the qualification for the 10% commission was lowered to annual book expenditures of not less than £100 as from September 1932.[81] Books obtained by the booksellers themselves at publishers' discounts of less than twopence in the shilling, plus 5%, were excluded from the scheme.[82] Licences were issued by a Joint Advisory Committee on which the LA, Publishers Association and Associated Booksellers were represented; the committee was indispensable as it proved necessary to ensure that the discount facilities were made available also to non-municipal libraries in membership of the LA, and there were initial difficulties in some of these cases, solved only by the stubborn insistence of the Association's representatives that the agreement be fully implemented.[83]

A motion requesting the reopening of negotiations with the publishers and booksellers with a view to securing more favourable terms than the 10% commission, which was not carried at the Scarborough Conference in 1937[84], was approved at Portsmouth a year later.[85] The Council then decided, in view of the obvious difficulties, to obtain detailed records of the book expenditures of individual libraries for the year ended March 1940.[86] The subject lapsed on the outbreak of war.

In his 'programme' of development for the Association, Savage had stressed the need for 'more and better facilities for training (eg more library schools)'. The theme was developed in his book *Special librarianship in general libraries and other papers* (1939) which has many claims to being the most important addition to the literature of librarianship published during the 1930s, but by Grafton and Co, and not by the Association. More than fifty of its 300 pages are devoted to 'the training of librarians'. Savage argued there that library staffs – at least in the larger public libraries – might usefully be divided into clerical, secretarial and professional, and continued:

If we assume that only about one-third of the staff are librarians we may face the problem of higher professional education with greater hope of solving it. I cannot believe that wholly satisfactory professional staffs will be recruited unless every candidate passes through a library school or college where he receives proficient teaching. The library as a school is less good than in earlier days: the urge for economy is ever pressing, the practice of specialization more usual; staffs are larger, hours shorter, branch libraries are more numerous and more distant; so that the time is nearly past when senior librarians are able to attend personally to the training of subordinates. Apprentices (in fact, if not in name and in law) are still with us, but the masters are busy elsewhere. Count the new employees likely to be absorbed into the service, and people already in librarianship who may be unreservedly encouraged to train at college; and then the task is not beyond practical politics. But if we continue to coax or to force every library employee into a calling as small as ours we cannot offer all of them college training and our younger members, in the future as in the past, must be content for years to accept the status and remuneration of clerks.[87]

He went on to discuss practical training in library schools, primarily in administration and bibliography, each in the widest sense of the term. The overall approach was exceptionally far-seeing for the 1930s since the theory that there was a chief librarian's baton in the knapsack of each young assistant was still common assumption and there were no British library schools other than that at University College London.

It became indeed ever more ironic that the school at UCL which had been established originally on the initiative of the LA should have found it increasingly difficult to 'place' its diplomates, largely because the municipal libraries continued reluctant to employ them; during the early 1930s the difficulties were accentuated by economic depression. Municipal library committees, guided by their chief officers, tended to remain faithful to the principle of informal apprenticeship which Savage had appropriately criticised: the attitude of most younger members of the municipal library staffs was not significantly different from that of the generation which had opposed the Association's 'open door' examination policy thirty years earlier. They objected even more strongly to the initiative of those UCL diplomates who sought to gain practical experience in municipal libraries by offering their services *voluntarily*.[88] The insight displayed by one young assistant – herself a graduate – was unusual:

The root of the resentment which is felt very generally in the public library profession against the incoming graduates lies in the assumption that they are necessarily superior to the normal assistants and that the higher grades should in time be reserved for them. This is manifestly wrong. Many boys and girls who are quite capable of taking degrees do not go to college, many for economic reasons, and some simply because they do not want to.[89]

But in plain fact almost the only graduates on public library staffs in the 1930s – apart from a small number in the largest authorities – recruited *after* graduation – were that tiny minority who had been recruited as school-leavers in the normal fashion and had chosen to qualify 'the hard way' in their own leisure time.

The Association's education committee was of the opinion, by 1937, that the UCL school could place not more than 'from 25 to 35 men and women of good personality each year'.[90] The School raised its admission standards to reduce intake[91] and by 1938 '89% of those completing the course in the previous session found permanent employment within 12 months from the completion of the examinations'.[92] But hardly any went into municipal libraries. The county libraries were more hospitable and more far-seeing; the appointment of a well-known county Librarian, J. D. Cowley (1897–1944), of Lancashire, to succeed Dr Baker on the latter's retirement in 1934, was surely appropriate in the present context.[93]

The Association's own summer schools at Aberystwyth were discontinued after ten successful sessions. They were one of the many debts owed by the LA to John Ballinger; his Honorary Fellowship in 1929 was minimum token of great service.[94] From 1930 onwards a new series of summer schools was arranged in Birmingham. These proved even more popular than their Welsh predecessors and, after 1932, attracted more than 100 students each year, some of them from overseas.[95] The Scottish LA's Autumn schools continued and, until 1934, were held every second October in Edinburgh and Glasgow alternately. They were succeeded by residential summer schools, the first in Edinburgh in July 1936; annual successors from 1937 to 1939 were held at Newbattle Abbey.[96]

The official correspondence courses, administered since the beginning of the period by the AAL, continued to flourish although by the end of it the numbers enrolling were in decline, due to the very substantial increase in the availability of part-time classes in colleges of further education. This development was another of the many remarkable changes during the 1930s. Immediately prior to the outbreak of war part-time classes were being held at no less than five polytechnics and evening institutes in London, and also in Glasgow, Birmingham,

Liverpool, Manchester, Leeds, Nottingham, Croydon, Cheltenham and Folkestone.[97]

The thesis hurdle, which had so limited the number of young librarians proceeding to the Association's diploma, was removed as from January 1929. Henceforward, 'Any student presenting a satisfactory thesis ... will be awarded a Diploma with honours'.[98] The number of diplomates soon began to soar, forty-one new ones in 1931,[99] fifty in 1932,[100] sixty-three in 1934[101] and ninety-one in 1937.[102] Some excellent theses were still submitted, nevertheless; among those subsequently published were, in addition to Partridge *Legal deposit*, already referred to, F. Seymour Smith *Classics in translation* (Scribner, 1930); L. M. Harrod *Lending library methods* (Grafton, 1933); and Miss D. M. Norris *History of cataloguing and cataloguing methods 1100–1850* (Grafton, 1939).

The *Reports* of the Council show that the numbers sitting the sectional examinations increased steadily during the present period, being 1202 in 1928 (556 passes); 1314 in 1929 (696 passes); 1637 in 1930 (784 passes); 1965 in 1931 (976 passes); and 2457 in 1932 (1019 passes). The exceptionally numerous entries of 1931 and 1932 were substantially due to the ending of the sectional examinations. As from January, 1933 the examination structure, assuming a more orthodox modern shape, provided for elementary, intermediate and final examinations. As, however, the elementary covered, *inter alia*, the ground of the old sectional examination in library routine, the intermediate those of classification and cataloguing, and the final those of English literary history, bibliography and library organisation, the difference was more apparent than real. The change even had the disadvantage that students who had preferred, quite reasonably, to sit the examinations in literary history and bibliography before proceeding to classification and cataloguing were no longer able to do so. Examination entries fell back to 1501 (760 passes) in 1933 but quickly recovered to 2267 (814 passes) in 1936 and to 2258 (1026 passes) in 1938. Examinations were held each May and December up to and including May, 1939. The admission qualification continued to be at the matriculation minimum, or equivalent, provided through school leaving certificates,

although exceptions were made in 1934–5 when the
Association's own preliminary examination was revived
temporarily. 117 candidates out of 219 sitting were then allowed
to proceed to the professional examinations.[103]

The limitation of the new intermediate examination to
classification and cataloguing was soon felt to be unsatisfactory
since successful candidates at this level could then proceed to
register as Associates (ALA) after a minimum service period;
from 1935 onwards the Council was working on a revision
which would have included there papers also in library routine
and in bibliography disguised as 'Library stock and assistance to
readers'. But the new draft regulations provided, in addition, for
new minimum ages for entry and for longer minimum service
periods before admission to the Register. They met with much
criticism – notably from the Director of the UCL School, whose
diplomates would have been particularly adversely affected –[104]
and were only approved in part at the Annual Meeting at
Scarborough in 1937; their operation was postponed until 1940
and lapsed when War came. The successful resolution against
the Council in 1937, which was strongly supported by the AAL,
was moved by J. P. Lamb (1891–1969), City Librarian of
Sheffield, a librarian of outstanding north of England qualities,
whose relationship to the Council, of which he was a member,
bore marked resemblance, throughout his career, to the
love/hate pattern so characteristic, in earlier years, of
J. Y. W. MacAlister.

The new age and service regulations had been proposed, at least
partly, to reduce the number of young librarians who, freed
from the thesis handicap, were able to gain the diploma and
proceed, after three years' approved service, to the Association's
highest normal qualification, the Fellowship (FLA), by their early
twenties. It was felt by many, and with much justification, that a
qualification which had to be presented to employing
Authorities as the hallmark of a mature librarian would,
inevitably, be devalued if seen to be obtainable so early in one's
professional career. Indeed the new Register established
following the bye-law revision of 1928 was soon swollen with

FLAS. Their numbers rose from 547 in 1932[105] to 745 by 1935[106] and to 902 by December 1938.[107] As by then there were as many Fellows as Associates, the desire for change was clearly understandable.

Irrespective of the mechanics of the Association's examinations they could all be justifiably subjected to one criticism of basic importance. When a university librarian, B. S. Page, wrote, in a letter to the *Record* in 1937, 'I submit that the examination should be designed with a view to the training of other than public librarians'[108], he was expressing a view which would be accepted as axiomatic only *after* World War Two. His opinion was endorsed by the University and Research Section and sympathetically received by the Council.[109] But the two years remaining before the outbreak of war provided insufficient time for effective change.

It may be asserted, without fear of contradiction, that the LA's achievements in raising professional standards during the period under review were greater, overall, than at any earlier time in its history. Admittedly its most convincing and effective work was done in the public library field. The background against which that progress may be measured was comprehensively surveyed in 1931 in the AAL's *Report on the hours, salaries, training and conditions of service in British municipal libraries,* the 'twenty years after' successor to the 1911 Report discussed in an earlier chapter.[110] The new 'general survey' included the following:

The verity of that improvement in librarianship as a profession which all library workers are conscious of having taken place since 1918, is proved by comparative references to the 1911 and the present reports. Salaries and general status have improved, the hours of work have lessened, a high standard of professional education is demanded by most authorities, a definite standard of general education for entrants to the profession is almost universal, and the conditions under which assistant librarians work have improved with better organization and the better planning of library buildings. This is the impression the observer receives by concentrating on the averages beloved of statisticians. But averages may conceal a multitude of evils. No consolation to a man dying of a fever to know that his *average* temperature during the whole year has been but a fraction over the normal: sandy throat and flaming forehead are inescapable facts; so, junior assistants in the City in Group D who must wait five years before they are allowed a summer holiday of more than six days will find no joy in contemplating the average for that group. Yet an average calculation may be made more than interesting: it reveals an injustice, it brings to light an anomaly; may thus provoke a protest, cause an alteration: in brief be made useful.

Pay and conditions have, then, undoubtedly, improved, yet we must still bear in mind the existence of the all too many libraries where both are lamentably below the average. It is no longer true to say, as the 1911 report states, that libraries "are, in general, inadequately housed, insufficiently provided with books, and the librarians are grossly underpaid"; yet, sadly enough, it *is* a true enough statement to make of some libraries where the hand of progress has been stayed.[111]

There was certainly, as the Report's 'Summary of recommendations' indicated,[112] still plenty of scope for really substantial improvements in salaries, the length of the working week, the number of evening duties, holiday entitlements, assistance with professional education, and many other matters. In pensions, too, since the adoptive Local government and other officers superannuation Act of 1922 had not been implemented by a considerable minority of local authorities. The long anticipated compulsory Act for England and Wales came, however, in 1937.[113]

So much was in fact achieved that there was a quite natural feeling among LA members – and particularly among impatient younger members – that nothing like enough was being done. The idea of 'blacklisting' authorities where salaries and conditions failed to 'measure up' was an obvious corollary; the earlier success of the British Medical Association and the Society of Medical Officers of Health in a comparable field was naturally quoted.[114] The Council's approach was, however, more neatly, and indirectly, linked to 'the art of the possible'. The Honorary Secretary, L. R. McColvin, asserted:

The standard of library service is much higher than the standard of salaries . . . I could, in great justice, make a plea for better salaries for the hundreds of capable and keen people at present receiving far less than their services demand. Instead, I am making a plea for a better library service, and emphasising the fact that without suitable staff progress is impossible.

The plea for higher standards of service was associated with recommendations for better conditions of service, ie maximum weekly working hours of thirty-eight, with twelve days summer holidays for those under twenty-one years of age rising to twenty-four days for chief officers, and *minimum* salary scales, based on those of Nalgo, ranging from £55 to £225 per annum for juniors, to £420 to £510 for chief librarians of the smaller libraries.[115] The salaries suggested seemed utopian enough at the time. There was also severe denunciation of the practice of taking unpaid pupil assistants:-

With the sole exception of foreign and colonial librarians who are resident in the United Kingdom for a limited period, and students during the course of their studies at a recognised school of librarianship, unpaid assistants (pupil or otherwise) should not be allowed to work in rate-supported libraries.[116]

A few months later McColvin felt able to insist:

The LA is doing its utmost to raise the prestige of librarianship and to secure satisfactory remuneration. . . . I would earnestly urge all our members, no matter if it involves present sacrifice, to refrain from applying for patently underpaid posts. . . . the time will come before many years when the LA will be in a position to inform those on the Register that if they apply for posts where any of the conditions of employment are judged to be totally unsatisfactory they will be guilty of "conduct prejudicial to the interests of librarianship", and so liable to be expelled from membership, thus losing their professional status.[117]

In 1937 the Association published 'Recommended salaries for Chief Librarians' providing for minima of £400 for those in urban and county public library Authorities serving up to 40,000/50,000 population and proceeding, by graded steps, to £900/£950 for the larger – but not the largest – Authorities, with a 10% addition for those within the Metropolitan Police area.[118] By the end of 1938 the Council reported that 'Helpful information has been sent to a number of Library Authorities and useful results have been achieved'. There was also some progress to report in a field other than that of municipal service:

The recommendations drawn up in conjunction with the University and Research section regarding the status and emolument of University library staffs are receiving the sympathetic consideration of governing bodies.[119]

A firmer line was now considered possible towards employing authorities appointing professionally unqualified chief librarians. Strong protests were made in 1935 to the London School of Economics and to Tyrone County Library[120] and the Wednesbury local authority was expelled a year earlier following its appointment of a Librarian without experience or qualifications.[121]

The inadequate salary offered in connection with the vacancy for Chief Librarian of West Ham Public Libraries also occasioned a strong official protest a few months before the outbreak of war.[122]

Larger public library problems than the salaries and service conditions of librarians and their staffs also agitated the Association during the 1930s. New legislation was considered necessary for England and Wales, and Scotland; the draft of a new and consolidating measure was completed just before war began.[123] This was, however, relatively unexciting when contrasted with the debate on 'state control', that is, possible government grants and general overall supervision by a Department of State. This controversy did something to split the profession, at least temporarily, since few municipal librarians but many county ones were favourably disposed and the CUKT lent support.[124] A friendly reference in the new *County libraries manual* of 1935 to a 'National library board' was repudiated by the Council.[125] The controversy formed the chief subject for discussion at the Margate conference in 1936 and the Council was then asked to report. It decided, subsequently, in favour of a grant-making body more akin to the University Grants Committee than to a Department of State and with the limited objectives of aiding training, the promotion of cooperation and the strengthening of particular libraries.[126]

Relationships between the LA and the CUKT underwent some
strain through the state control controversy but the Trust was
no longer as influential as it had once been; the LA was beginning
to play its part on a wider stage. It projected the public library
image early in the period with a new publicity poster designed
and presented by the well known artist, Frank Brangwyn;[127]
copies were sold for 15*s* a dozen.[128] The initiation by the BBC of
its new weekly journal, *The Listener*, in 1929 also offered the
opportunity of providing it with annotated reading lists and
book notes[129] but the cooperation was deemed unsuccessful and
soon lapsed.[130] The Association was more fortunate in its
developing relationships with organisations other than the BBC.

At the beginning of the present period the LA had representatives
only on the Joint committee of the UCL school of librarianship;
the Seafarers' Education Service; the British Institute of Adult
Education and the CUKT 'Books to read' panel. More and more
contacts were made during the 1930s and by 1938, the last full
and normal year prior to war, the Council reported membership
also of the Architectural Graphic Records Committee, the
Association of Technical Institutions' committee on libraries,
the Board of Education's adult education committee, the British
Film Institute, the British Society for International Bibliography,
the British Records Association, the National Association of
Boys' Clubs, the National Book Council, the British Red Cross
and Order of St John hospital library committee, the Victoria
League's education committee and the Standing Joint
Committee of Nalgo. It was, in addition, through its
membership of the National Central Library's trustees and of
the National Committee on Regional Library Cooperation,
playing its part in coordinating the activities of the regional
systems whose development during this period covered the
whole of England and Wales, transformed the whole face of
library inter-lending and made the United Kingdom a world
leader in this most important field. Internationally the
Association had been closely connected, from the earliest
beginnings, with the cooperation leading to the foundation of
the International Federation of Library Associations following
its Edinburgh Conference in 1927.[131]

In some respects the most interesting and unusual opportunity of 'promoting' the Association into the wider world came when it was fortunate enough to secure as its President for 1937 William Temple, then Archbishop of York. Temple's long and distinguished service for adult education brought special distinction to the LA. The Presidential badge designed for the Association by Omar Ramsden in 1930 bears as its motto 'Ingenia hominum res publica'. The Archbishop's librarian-predecessors as President during the 1930s – Jast, Pitt and Savage – could assuredly have worn it with no more pride.

From its more assured and influential position the Association now advised and gave evidence over a much wider field than earlier. Interesting examples were the Departmental Committee on Local Government Officers (1930),[132] the Royal Commission on Museums and Art Galleries (1928)[133] and various enquiries of the Board of Education on many kinds of specialised library provided by parts of the education service.[134] By the end of the period, too, it had become increasingly interested in the still neglected subjects of prison libraries[135] and of libraries in teacher training colleges;[136] both types of service offered immense, if different, scope for improvement.

Dr Johnson's old college friend, Oliver Edwards, displayed what Boswell and better judges considered 'an exquisite trait of character' when he remarked that he had in his time tried to be a philosopher but that 'cheerfulness was always breaking in'.[137] Bearing in mind the Charter objects of the Association and its increasingly successful efforts to raise standards of library service throughout the country, the story of its own library would surely test the patience of any library philosopher and – at least up to the middle thirties – justification for cheerfulness of any kind was assuredly lacking. But prior to the opening of Chaucer House in 1933 the library lacked accommodation, it lacked staff and it lacked money.

The library, which had been moved from the LSE to UCL in 1919, following the inauguration of the school of librarianship there, as recounted in an earlier chapter, stayed there for ten years;

during the early months of 1929 it was taken to the Bedford Square offices. The Council's report on it then was depressing:

The books must be examined, re-bound or repaired if necessary, classified and catalogued; and many new books are required before the collection can become a useful reference library. A part-time librarian is necessary immediately and a whole-time librarian must eventually be appointed. The funds of the Association are, however, insufficient for this development. [138]

But the space at Bedford Square was soon required for other purposes and after only two years there the library was moved again, for storage, to a branch of the Birmingham Public Libraries where it was found to be in a deplorable condition. [139] The Council was, at least, refreshingly free of illusion:

The arrears of collecting and organization to be made up are enormous, and some years must elapse before the library will be worthy of the Association which exists to promote libraries and to set standards in librarianship!
The Library of the Association should be in two divisions, **a** a lending library of reference books and material, and **b** a lending library of textbooks for students. Division **a** should be organised as a library of information, with books, reports, documents . . . and plans . . . Division **b** should comprise a sufficient number of the more important of the books recommended in the Education committee's syllabus, so that no young librarian will lack the means of studying for his examination. . . .

One suggestion, nevertheless, had to be rejected out of hand:

A suggestion has been made that students should pay a subscription for textbooks to reimburse the Association for possible decrease in sale of its publications. The Association, however, in its negotiations with publishers and booksellers strongly maintains that public libraries increased the sales of books, and the Council are of opinion that by lending textbooks they will ultimately increase the sale of them. Quite clearly, the Council could not charge a subscription for lending textbooks as long as they stand for the principle of free lending from public libraries. [140]

The library was moved once again in 1933 but this time to its first permanent home on the top floor of the new headquarters at

Chaucer House, a few months after its official opening; Hazel Mews was appointed to the Association's staff as Librarian and assistant editor one year later.[141] The modern history of the library begins then in 1934, just as any librarian should surely have expected! Expenditure on it appears for the first time as a separate heading in the Association's accounts for that year; a sum of some £270 is recorded as having been spent on salaries, furniture and books out of a total expenditure for the year of nearly £10,000.[142] During 1935, 700 books were acquired and a further 800, including thirty sets of completed periodical runs, were re-bound. The whole stock, now of nearly 4000 books, had been slip-catalogued and classified by expanded-Dewey, and thousands of pamphlets, bulletins, reports and plans were being classified and filed.[143]

Miss Mews resigned her post in September 1936 and in the following December D. C. Henrik Jones was appointed as full-time Librarian and Information Officer at the commencing salary – modest by prevailing standards and comparable responsibilities – of £300 per annum.[144] Annual expenditure on books and other library materials also continued to be modest right up to the outbreak of war; even in 1938 and 1939 little more than £100 was being spent each year.[145] But many very useful donations were being received and for the first time in its history the Association's library was attempting a comprehensive service for members. The home reading issues, which had been less than 300 in 1935, rose to 1456 in 1937 and to 2042 in 1939, by which time the total book-stock had risen to more than 7000.[146]

The Rockefeller grant, the Association's *Survey of libraries*, both already referred to, and the appointment of a full-time Librarian and information officer at the end of 1936 made it possible also to begin to provide an adequate information service to members. The Council's *Report* for 1938, the last full year before the outbreak of war, is indicative:

856 enquiries on a wide variety of topics have been answered by letter during the year, while many others were satisfied immediately by telephone and by personal call. The material already collected and classified enables the staff to answer many of the enquiries in a few

minutes, but some involve a considerable amount of time and research ... Eighty-four periodicals dealing with librarianship and bibliography are received regularly as well as a large number of English and foreign library bulletins ... The following is a selection of some of the subjects upon which information has been sought during the year: cooperation with community centres; deposit and delivery stations; deposits by readers; grants for elementary school libraries; home binderies and repair departments; inter-library cooperation; Local Acts; microphotography; poster display; preservation of bindings; prison libraries; projection rooms and apparatus; rating of libraries; staff in relation to issues and population. Much more frequent subjects of enquiry are: planning of libraries; shelving; lighting; heating and air conditioning; budgets; salaries and wages; hours of opening; hours of staff; fines; losses; loan sanctions; rules and regulations.[147]

Here, indeed, was promise of a new era.

References

1. 57 *AR* (1933), p 9R.
2. 59 *AR* (1935), pp 5R, 10R, 17R.
3. *LAR*, 37, pp 471–3.
4. 'English libraries in the depression', *LAR*, 36, pp 435–440.
5. 55 *AR* (1931–2), p 3R.
6. 52 *AR* (1928–9), pp 6R.
7. 'A Programme for the LA', *LAR*, 32, pp 1–13.
8. 'The New bye-laws and why they are necessary', *LAR*, 30, pp 264–7.
9. *Report on work in offices of the L.A.*, Council, 5.4.1929.
10. 6.11.1931.
11. H. Miers, 'Reflections on the Annual Report of the Council', *LAR*, 35, pp 308–14.
12. *Obits* in *LAR*, 70, pp 273–4, 304.
13. 52 *AR* (1928–9), p 6R.
14. 53 *AR* (1929–30), pp 8R–9R; 54 *AR* (1930–1), p 12R.
15. 54 *AR* (1930–1), p 14R.
16. 51 *AR* (1927–8), p 12R.
17. 51 *AR* (1927–8), p 17.
18. 53 *AR* (1929–30), p 14R.
19. 52 *AR* (1928–9), p 6R.
20. 56 *AR* (1932), p 12R.
21. 22.2.1929; 53 *AR* (1929–30), p 8R.
22. 61 *AR* (1937), p 13R.
23. 52 *AR* (1928–9), pp 6R–8R (includes agreement).
24. Ramsden *op cit*, Ch 16; 52 *AR* (1928–9), pp 6R–8R.
25. 5.4.1935.
26. 2.12.1938.
27. 8.4.1938.
28. 51 *AR* (1927–8), p 3R.
29. 52 *AR* (1928–9), p 8R.
30. 53 *AR* (1929–30), p 3R.
31. *Ibid*, p 13R.
32. 56 *AR* (1932), p 9R.
33. 57 *AR* (1933), p 11R.
34. 59 *AR* (1935), p 13R.
35. 62 *AR* (1938), p 17R.
36. W. A. Munford (ed), *Annals of the L.A.* 1965, p 33.
37. 51 *AR* (1927–8), p 3R.
38. 14.10.1930; *LAR*, 33, p 14.
39. *Annals*, p 36.
40. 'Arundell Esdaile', *LR*, 15, pp 474–7.
41. 56 *AR* (1932), p 4R.
42. *LAR*, 36, p 187.
43. 57 *AR* (1933), p 13R.
44. Annual accounts in 61 *AR* (1937), pp 58R–62R.

45. 51 *AR* (1927–8), p 6R.
46. *eg LAR*, 30, pp 71–2.
47. 52 *AR* (1928–9), p 14R.
48. 53 *AR* (1929–30), p 17R.
49. 54 *AR* (1930–1), pp 17R–18R.
50. 55 *AR* (1931–2), p 13R.
51. 'Inaugural address: The uses of the public library', *LAR*, 37, pp 357–61.
52. *LAR*, 40, p 455.
53. *LAR*, 36, p 1.
54. *LAR*, 38, p 1.
55. 8.6.1934; 4.12.1936.
56. 9.4.1937.
57. 5.4.1929.
58. *Preface.*
59. *LAR*, 39, p 1.
60. Annual accounts in *ARs* 1932–9.
61. 61 *AR* (1937), p 17R.
62. 62 *AR* (1938), p 18R.
63. 54 *AR* (1930–1), p 15R.
64. *Intro*, pp 3–4.
65. 18.9.1933; 8.12.1933.
66. 3.2.1939.
67. *LAR*, 41, p 367.
68. Aitken, *op cit*, p 179.
69. 62 *AR* (1938), p 18R.
70. 61 *AR* (1937), p 17R.
71. 5.4.1929.
72. 63 *AR* (1939), p 202.
73. *See* eg F. M. Gardner, 'A co-operative bulletin', *LAR*, 37, pp 25–7.
74. 5.4.1935.
75. 18.6.1937.
76. 9.9.1929.
77. 56 *AR* (1932), p 16R.
78. 21.2.1930.
79. 53 *AR* (1929–30), pp 17R–18R.
80. 54 *AR* (1930–1), p 17R.
81. 56 *AR* (1932), p 15R.
82. 54 *AR* (1930–1), p 8R.
83. 53 *AR* (1929–30), p 18R.
84. *LAR*, 39, p 327.
85. *LAR*, 40, p 356.
86. *LAR*, 41, pp 102–3.
87. p 164.
88. *See* eg S. A. Firth, 'A Forward policy for librarianship', *LAR*, 35, Conference supplement, pp xx–xxii.
89. Mary Walton, 'This graduate problem', *LAR*, 36, p 168.
90. 61 *AR* (1937), p 9R.
91. 60 *AR* (1936), pp 7R–8R.
92. 62 *AR* (1938), p 9R.
93. *LAR*, 36, p 151.
94. 9.9.1929.
95. 54–63 *AR* (1930–1939).
96. Aitken, *op cit*, p 227.
97. LA *Year book* (1939), pp 105–9.
98. 52 *AR* (1928–9), p 4R.
99. 55 *AR* (1931–2), p 10R.
100. 56 *AR* (1932), p 6R.
101. 58 *AR* (1934), p 6R.
102. 61 *AR* (1937), p 7R.
103. 59 *AR* (1935), p 7R.
104. Letter from J. D. Cowley in *LAR*, 39, p 191.
105. 56 *AR* (1932), p 10R.
106. 59 *AR* (1935), p 13R.
107. 62 *AR* (1938), p 17R.
108. *LAR*, 40, pp 39–40.
109. 7.10.1937.
110. Edited by F. Seymour Smith.
111. p 8.
112. pp 28–9.
113. L. Golding, *Dictionary of local government in England and Wales*. 1962. p 377.
114. As in F. Higenbottom, 'The general trend of professional education today', *LAR*, 41, pp 209–212.
115. *LAR*, 36, pp 130–1; 223–4.
116. *Ibid.*
117. Letter in *LAR*, 37, p 242.
118. *LAR*, 39, p 99.
119. 62 *AR* (1938), p 17R.
120. 14.6.1935.
121. *Summary of ... London conference, 1934*, p xxiii.
122. 3.2.1939.
123. *LAR*, 42, p 198.
124. For contrasted views on the controversy, *see* eg report of a meeting at Chaucer House, 13.11.1935, *LAR*, 37, pp 581–4 and E. A. Savage, 'The Board of Education and public libraries', *ibid*, pp 257–64.
125. *LAR*, 37, pp 496–7.
126. *LAR*, 39, p 99.
127. 52 *AR* (1928–9), p 14R.
128. 53 *AR* (1929–30), p 14R.
129. 52 *AR* (1928–9), p 14R.
130. 53 *AR* (1929–30), p 17R.
131. *Ibid*, p 5R.
132. 14.10.1930.

133. 20.1.1928; 20.4.1928.
134. eg 5.4.1935.
135. eg *LAR*, 41, pp 332–6; Council 8.4.1938.
136. 8.4.1938; 21.10.1938.
137. *Life of Johnson*, 17.4.1778.
138. 52 *AR* (1928–9), p 5R.
139. 54 *AR* (1930–1), pp 11R–12R.
140. 55 *AR* (1931–2), pp 6R–7R.

141. 8.6.1934.
142. 58 *AR* (1934), p 31R.
143. 59 *AR* (1935), p 16R.
144. 4.12.1936.
145. 62 *AR* (1938), p 44R; *LAR*, 42, p 216.
146. *LAR*, 42, p 201.
147. 62 *AR* (1938), pp 16R–17R.

Second Interlude: World War Two

Chapter Eight

1939-1945

Whereas the declaration of war in August 1914 had impacted like thunder out of a clear sky, the new declaration of September 1939 had been long expected and seemed, indeed, to relieve almost unbearable tension. During the earlier months of 1939, while politicians floundered – as only politicans can – ordinary citizens were made aware of impending hazards by the expansion of Civil Defence measures – introduced originally as Air Raid Precautions, hence ARP; by plans for the mass evacuation of children and expectant mothers from areas considered specially liable to enemy air attack; and by the introduction, in April, of compulsory military service for young men, originally called 'militia men'.

Although the Association and the National Central Library, jointly, had certainly approached their local authority with a view to proofing a portion of their premises against poison gas attack,[1] up to the time of the Liverpool Conference in June 1939 there had been only occasional references to a possible wartime situation in the pages of the *Record*.[2] At the conference itself only one session was devoted to it. The Presidential address, by Arundell Esdaile, was on quality in reading. Those which followed – on book selection, school libraries, children's books, prison libraries, and the relation of public libraries to adult education and to broadcasting might have been arranged in any other year. The exception, 'The Public Library during times of national emergency or war', by J. D. Stewart, displayed careful thought but was inevitably based on 1914–1918 experience, a foundation which became increasingly evident during the discussion which followed its delivery. It seemed that the greatest fear was that library buildings, and possibly library staffs, might be requisitioned for other purposes.[3] But as the war began, and extended, it was evident that Governmental attitudes were to be in sharp contrast with those during World War One. The harbinger of a new attitude was a thirty-eight-page booklet, *Catalogue of books for the Services,* published at 3*d* by the National Book League in October 1939. This had been compiled originally as 'Books for militia camp libraries', at the request of the War Office and was duly commended to 'every man in the Services', by 'Ian Hay' Beith, then Director of Public Relations at the War Office.

Books for the Services listed some 1200 titles, ranging from A. N. Whitehead's *Adventures of ideas* and Bertrand Russell's *Outline of philosophy* to Karl Marx's *Capital* and Adolf Hitler's *Mein Kampf*, and from George Borrow's *Lavengro* and Herman Melville's *Moby Dick* to Edgar Rice Burroughs' *Tarzan of the apes* and Evelyn Waugh's *Vile bodies*. The list had been the responsibility of a committee of eight appointed by the Society of Authors and the National Book Council but nearly all the selection was in fact undertaken by two members of the LA, F. Seymour Smith and W. A. Munford.[4] Although these two librarians had been nominated, not by the Association but by the National Book Council, the Editor of the *Record*, in relaxed welcoming mood, was encouraged to claim part responsibility for the Association.[5]

Later evidence was also to show that this new war was to be one in which books and libraries were to be more important than in any earlier conflict. In the past some books had been read by some soldiers on some battlefields. Now books were to be read, and in large numbers, not only by the men and women serving in the Armed Forces in all parts of the world, but also by lonely women and children, by land and factory workers evacuated to strange and unfamiliar places, by men and women in civil defence and fire-watching centres and isolated posts, by those spending long nights in air-raid shelters, in fact by a great many of those taking part in or affected by the nation's war effort. Admittedly much of the reading was done because so many of the alternative, peacetime, leisure pursuits had become inaccessible or had ceased. But the reading, manipulation, lending and inter-lending and even the salvage of books gained new significance. Few libraries were ever closed although many were damaged by enemy action. The overall achievement of the profession of librarianship did not lack its own note of irony since so many members of library staffs – men and women – were called upon to perform quite different wartime duties. The irony was nevertheless incomplete since significant numbers of those called away from their normal duties eventually found themselves running, or helping to run, other libraries.

The publication of *Books for the Services* might, indeed, be viewed as symbolic of modified national attitudes. Following approaches by the Association, the new Ministry of Information sought the assistance of public libraries on the outbreak of war for publicity purposes;[6] the need to maintain and indeed to extend their library services was impressed upon local authorities by the Board of Education a year later.[7] Library buildings were requisitioned for other purposes only very rarely, although new buildings not yet occupied were sometimes taken over, as at Colchester. During World War One the library service of the country had been harassed much more by HM Government than by the enemy; the situation was completely reversed during World War Two. Between 1939 and 1945, and particularly in 1940 and 1941, many library buildings and notably in London, in the industrial areas of the midlands and north, and in the towns on the east, south-east, south and south-west coasts were seriously affected by air-raid damage.[8] The LA itself did not escape. Chaucer House was damaged, and the neighbouring NCL building very seriously damaged by fire following enemy action in April, 1941. Chaucer House might have been completely burnt out had it not been for the prompt action of its senior porter, E. A. Hornsby, who gallantly fought the fires alone until help was forthcoming; thanks to him, damage was slight. The incident fortunately occurred during the period when most of the LA staff had transferred to temporary accommodation made available at the Public Library at Launceston in Cornwall. It was thus easy for all available space at Chaucer House to be placed temporarily at the disposal of the sadly stricken NCL.[9]

The elections for the LA Council, the last for six years, had been held, rather later than usual, during the Autumn of 1939. J. D. Stewart (Librarian of Bermondsey Public Libraries) and Gurner P. Jones (Librarian of Stepney Public Libraries) were re-elected as London members, joining J. D. Cowley (Baker's successor as Director of the University College School), F. Seymour Smith (Librarian of Finchley Public Libraries), R. D. Hilton Smith (Librarian of Deptford Public Libraries), and E. Sydney (Librarian of Leyton Public Libraries). The country councillors elected or re-elected were J. P. Lamb (Librarian, Sheffield Public Libraries), J. Revie (Birmingham Public Libraries), J. F. Smith (Librarian, Liverpool Public Libraries), H. Farr (Librarian, Cardiff Public Libraries), and Miss E. Gerard (Librarian, Worthing Public Libraries).[10] They joined Miss A. S. Cooke (Librarian, Kent County Libraries), Duncan Gray (Librarian, Nottingham Public Libraries), G. V. R. Hayward (Librarian, Norwich Public Libraries), J. Ross (Librarian, Bristol Public Libraries), F. J. Boardman (Librarian, Rotherham Public Libraries), L. Chubb (Librarian, Ipswich Public Libraries), A. J. Hawkes (Librarian, Wigan Public Libraries), C. Nowell (Librarian, Manchester Public Libraries), and A. G. Mackay (Librarian, Midlothian County Libraries). The Honorary Officers were L. R. McColvin (Librarian, Westminster Public Libraries) as Honorary Secretary, and H. M. Cashmore (Librarian, Birmingham Public Libraries) as Honorary Treasurer. Alderman J. S. Pritchett (Recorder of Lincoln) served as Honorary Legal Adviser; he would be succeeded three years later by J. Parker Morris, Town Clerk of Westminster. The three Vice-Presidents were L. Newcombe (Librarian, National Central Library), R. J. Gordon (Librarian, Leeds Public Libraries), and H. E. Craster (Bodley's Librarian). The Past-Presidents serving on the Council were L. S. Jast (Nowell's predecessor as Librarian of Manchester Public Libraries), Sir Frederic Kenyon (formerly Director of the British Museum), J. M. Mitchell (formerly Secretary of the Carnegie Trustees), E. A. Savage (Librarian, Edinburgh Public

Libraries), W. C. Berwick Sayers (Librarian, Croydon Public
Libraries), and Dr William Temple, Archbishop of York.[11] The
Association was to be fortunate in having as its President, for the
whole of World War Two, Arundell Esdaile, whose 'sparkling
wit and lively imagination'[12] alone made him a notable successor
to the wartime President of 1915–1918, J. Y. W. MacAlister.

Wartime conditions soon made it difficult to convene meetings
of the Council which could be representatively attended, and at
the meeting held on 25 October 1940 an Emergency
Committee, consisting of the Honorary Officers and chairmen of
the standing committees, was appointed to exercise most of the
Council's duties and responsibilities other than post-war
planning. This Committee, which held its first meeting on
4 April 1941, became in effect, and with the approval of the
Privy Council, the governing body of the Association until
1945.[13] It met at Chaucer House on average five times each year;
not surprisingly those of its members whose professional skills
were deployed in or near London made the best attendances. Its
activities were denounced as undemocratic by ex-Honorary
Secretary E. A. Savage, in articles published in the *Record* and
Library World. These articles, and especially the *LW* series
entitled 'Divagations of an old busybody',[14] were great fun for
readers and undoubtedly helped to maintain professional morale
during difficult times. Since, in a democratic society, there are
likely to be nearly as many concepts of democracy as there are
citizens in the society, Savage's criticisms would have been
completely apt and valid, *given peacetime conditions*. It says much
for the aplomb of the Council and of its Emergency Committee
that official refutations of the Savage line were rare.[15]

Despite wartime difficulties membership of the Association
continued at a satisfactory level. It rose in fact to 6747 by the end
of 1942,[16] had fallen back to 6048 by 31 December 1944[17] and
recovered to 6510 by the end of 1945.[18] But apparent
near-stability masked exceptionally high turnover figures; new
members and reinstatements during the war years totalled 4734,
and removals because of non-payment or death 4651.
Remembering that an estimated 2000 members of the
Association left their posts to serve in the Forces or to

undertake other work deemed of national importance,[19] and that vacancies were filled mostly by temporary appointments, these high figures are understandable. Remembering also that many of those left in their peacetime posts acted also as virtually full-time officers in local Civil Defence, Food and Fuel control capacities and in the Information Service, the loyalty of members to their Association was remarkable. The LA was able to reciprocate by taking up the question of local salary improvements in more than 200 cases.[20]

Full payment of subscriptions was required unless confidential applications for reduction were successfully made.[21] As so many members temporarily stationed in remote corners of the world managed to keep up their subscription payments, despite all impediments, it would have been exceptionally difficult to exempt from payment those with perhaps less reason or excuse. But the problem of unpaid subscriptions remained controversial until the end of the war.[22]

Prudent management of unexpectedly satisfactory subscription income enabled the Association to weather the war years without financial strain and, indeed, to set aside satisfactory reserves; its portfolio of investments, which had been valued at £11,500 at the end of 1939 had increased to £17,000 at the end of 1945.[23]

Despite all difficulties, not least among them the evacuation of most of the staff to Launceston from 1940 to 1943, services to members were maintained at a good level. The December 1939 examinations were the only ones to be cancelled. The 1868 entries (789 passes) of 1940[24] had certainly fallen to 1154 (663 passes) in 1944[25] but basic continuity was never in doubt. The achievement is even more remarkable when it is remembered that entries, and successful ones at that, included those made by men and women serving in the Forces and sitting in accordance with arrangements made with their local commands.

Association publications were naturally affected. The promising flow of new professional literature, which had been such an important feature of the scene in the 1930s, came to an end but the serials continued, with the notable exception of the *Year's work in librarianship.* The *Library Association Record* continued monthly publication, becoming thinner from 1941, using smaller type-face from 1942 and incorporating the Council's *Annual report* from 1939 to 1944. Its editor, R. D. Hilton Smith, resigned on account of Service duties overseas, in August 1941, and the heavy additional responsibility was shouldered by L. R. McColvin until the end of the war. The *Year book*, shorn of the list of members, was published each January and the *Subject index* also continued to appear. In this case, however, publication dates were less predictable due substantially to the return of its staff to its erstwhile home at the National Library of Wales in Aberystwyth, to paper shortage, and to war damage at its printers.[26] The Association also continued to award the Carnegie Medal for an outstanding book for children although it was withheld in 1943 and 1945 when no titles published during those years were considered suitable. Eric Linklater's *The Wind on the moon,* the 1944 award, remains perhaps the outstanding example of the Association's wartime commendations.

The LA's contribution to the nation's war effort, while still limited, was considerably greater and more effective than during World War One. The transfer of children's books – with or following the children – from the area of one local authority to that of another consequent on the official evacuation scheme was, naturally enough, a matter primarily for the local authorities concerned but the Association acted as coordinator and under its auspices a quarter of a million books were transferred.[27] There was also, at least initially, some success in dealing with the new libraries established for members of the Services. The beginnings were promising and the Association was able to coordinate its own initiatives with those of the Lord Mayor of London's Committee; two librarians, J. D. Cowley and John Wilkes were appointed to direct. But Civil Service and War Office procedure have deep tap roots; Cowley and Wilkes resigned as soon as they found that their recommendations were ignored, and the Council severed its official connection.[28] One unofficial point of view is interesting:

From the first there was opposition to real librarianship and later the authorities refused to allow what they called "educational" books to be circulated except through the Education Service. This made everything impossible and what promised to be the greatest educational movement in the history of the British armed forces dwindled into a supply stores for fiction and other light fare, no doubt useful but quite uninteresting to librarians or educationalists.[29]

Nevertheless, as noted above, in many localities members of the Association subsequently found themselves involved in the day to day activities of Service libraries.

Under wartime conditions and in a beleaguered island necessarily anxious to recycle as much raw material as possible, the disposal of *old* books could seem more important than the acquisition of *new* ones. The ever increasing paper shortage made local waste paper drives appealing, attractive and apparently easy; much important material in the form of books, local records, periodicals and other material was doubtless lost for ever during the first flush of uninstructed national enthusiasm. Local libraries were soon asked to help and the Association's Emergency Committee rightly insisted that:

Whilst they are willing to ask all members to collaborate in the salvage drive, they can only do so if they are satisfied that adequate machinery and safeguards exist to prevent the destruction of any book which would do better service by being used as a book.[30]

This eminently sensible approach was agreed to by the Ministry of Supply[31] and, during subsequent salvage drives, members of local library staffs were intimately involved. It was thus possible for books collected to be treated as waste paper only if considered unsuitable for library stocks or as ephemeral reading material for members of the Services.[32]

The salvage drives were important, not only intrinsically, but also because they led to the formation of the Inter-Allied Book Centre, to aid in library restocking. The Centre, directed by the veteran librarian, B. M. Headicar, was accommodated in a building capable of housing one and a half million books, opened by the Minister of Education, R. A. Butler, in September 1944.[33]

Two other contributions made by the LA to the nation's war effort concerned books and bookbinding. The Association played some part in the successful opposition to the Government proposal to bring books within the scope of the new Purchase Tax provisions of 1940[34] and, but less successfully, in seeking to impress on the Board of Trade the serious consequences to the public library service if further skilled men on the staffs of firms of library bookbinders were called up.[35]

The satisfactory maintenance of the Association's annual income and the less than normally diffused control – by the Emergency Committee – made it relatively easy for a few members of the governing body – L. R. McColvin in particular – to devote much more time than might otherwise have been possible to the important question of post-war planning. References have been made in earlier chapters to the pervasive, complementary, influence of the Carnegie United Kingdom Trust on library development and it was appropriate that the Trust should have acted, once again, as catalyst. Paragraph 16 of the Council's *Annual Report* for 1941 provides a succinct record:

Arising out of a request from the CUKT that the LA should collect information and make recommendations regarding evacuation, reception and badly-damaged areas such as would enable the Trust to decide whether financial aid should be made available, the Emergency Committee considered that constructive proposals for the benefit of the library service could be made in connection with such an investigation and that the proposals might take into account possible post-war conditions and be consistent with a long-term policy. Consequently it was first decided to issue a questionnaire to all libraries, calling for information as to the effect of the war on the public library service and, later, the Honorary Secretary, Mr L. R. McColvin, was invited to undertake a Survey of the public library system and to prepare two reports, one on immediate wartime problems and the other on post-war developments. The invitation was accepted by Mr McColvin, and the Westminster City Council generously agreed to release him for a period of six months in order to carry out the work. The Survey and the reports have now been completed and members will shortly have the opportunity of considering the results of the enquiry.

R. F. Vollans, who subsequently became McColvin's Deputy at

Westminster, has left a pleasant account of the making of the
McColvin Report:

From October 1941 McColvin visited libraries up and down the
country and with Percy Welsford [the Secretary] and members of the
Council, attended meetings which were convened at each Branch and
also at Leeds, Newcastle and Exeter for members in areas where no
branch existed. Miss Joyce Howard [Percy Welsford's secretary] who
joined the LA at Launceston in February, 1941, kept hearing of an
Honorary Secretary called "Mac" and, as a new girl, wondered what
he was like. "When he came to Launceston", she said, "it was like a
rushing, mighty wind in our quiet backwater; rapid talk, quick
movement, flashing eyes behind glasses – and writing to match the
man. He wrote the report mostly in trains on scraps of paper (even
obtained from the toilet in those hard days of paper shortage . . .)" In
the introduction to his report, McColvin paid tribute to the work of
P. S. J. Welsford, Secretary of the LA and D. C. Henrik Jones, its
Librarian . . . he had discussed most things in the report with them
and made full use of their ideas and their wide knowledge of British
librarianship. In fact, he said, "If the work and thought and
enthusiasm that have gone to its making were to be justly
proportioned, they should be named as co-authors . . ."[36].

The McColvin Report, *The Public library system of Great Britain: a
report on its present condition with proposals for post-war reorganization*,
consisted of four parts:

i   The purposes and value of a library service
ii   Present conditions
iii Proposals for the future
iv   Libraries in wartime

It was an attempt – and a most successful one – to present the
arguments in favour of good service; to consider development
up to the date of assessment; and to suggest means by which an
extremely 'patchy' achievement, particularly in the areas of many
of the smaller authorities, might be substantially improved.

The factors deemed responsible for an unsatisfactory situation
were all of special interest to the Association as well as to public
libraries:

i   Unsuitable, unqualified and ineffective personnel
ii   Apathy on the part of the public due to the absence locally
of opportunity to understand and appreciate the values of a
good library service sufficient to make them seek it
iii   Failure of such public interest as does exist locally to make
effective impact upon apathetic local authorities
iv   The limitations of local financial resources
v   Limitations due to the insufficiency of the local unit of
service in relation to population, etc
vi   The lack of coordination between the various local
authorities responsible, and the duplications and omissions
arising therefrom

The generalisations thus formulated prepared the way for
Part III of the Report.

In Part III the proposals for reform were based on certain
principles deriving logically from the several factors considered
responsible for the shortcomings:

i   Complete coverage throughout the kingdom
ii   A proper relationship between demand and supply
iii   A full appropriate supply of books at all stages in the
proposed network of libraries
iv   Proper management
v   Services to be properly coordinated
vi   Some form of national central body to guide, coordinate
and encourage the development of local services
vii   The library service to remain nevertheless a local service
and not directly under the control of central government
viii   The widest possible vision

When the McColvin recommendations were first known, it was
reasonable to assume that the most interesting proposals seemed
to be those for the 'suitable service unit'. The plea for large ones
was immediately criticised, not merely – as to be expected – by
representatives of the smaller units anticipating supersession but
also by at least one retired representative of one of the larger
ones anticipating substantial confirmation, E. A. Savage of
Edinburgh:

I am amused at the idea of the library service commanded by 90-odd
"brass hats" – or Gauleiters is perhaps the better word, for it suggests
efficiency, abject subordination, electric obedience, whereas "brass
hat" suggests Blimpishness. Imagine the scene one fine summer
morning. Gauleiter Dombey, iron man that he is, sighs for the sun
and the breeze and the wild flowers. He orders out two high-powered
Gauleiterish cars. Poor little librarian Bob Cratchit, drowsing in an
empty library erected, according to plan, where it was not wanted, is
shot out of his chair by the long blast of two Gauleiterish horns. He
takes a flying leap to the door and gets there just in time to make a
passable hatstand salute to his particular share of the Mighty Ninety.
But his High Mightiness is not alone. There are two cars, filled with
global men who have got fat in easy chairs and soft-seated cars, from
which they order other poor silly devils to work. There they are – the
Deputy Gauleiter (who has come to take notes for the Gauleiter), the
Superintendent of Branches (who tells the Deputy Gauleiter what
notes to take), the Transport Officer (in command of the Chauffeurs),
the Chief of the Accessions Department (to explain to the Gauleiter
why no new books have reached little Bob Cratchit), the Secretary
and Treasurer (to pay for the lunches and drinks of the inspecting
phalanx), the Superintendent of Buildings (to draw up notes for the
specification of the repair of a leaky tap that wee Bob Cratchit
reported last year), the Assistant in Charge of Work with Children (to
inspect the twelve juvenile books on the shelves), each of these
magnates accompanied by his professional assistant . . . and his
non-professional assistants . . .[37]

The creation of larger service units comparable with and
sometimes identical with those suggested in the McColvin
Report was one of the most important features of the
reorganisation of local government, in Greater London in the
1960s and outside it in the 1970s. It is still too early to make an
adequately objective examination of the changes, of McColvin's
aspirations and of Savage's fears.

McColvin's proposals for the reform of professional education
are now seen to have been even more far-reaching in their
implications, not least because they were to be relevant in the
context of far more than public libraries, in fact of *librarianship as
a whole*. It may in fact be convincingly argued that the McColvin
Report, limited as it appeared to be to public libraries, became,
nevertheless, one of the seminal documents preparing the way

for the reorganisation of the Association, to enable it to become at last, *de facto* as well as *de jure*, the professional association for all librarians.

In his Chapter 17, 'Staff-recruitment, training, grading, salaries', McColvin dealt firstly with the need for a division of library staff into professional and non-professional, arguing, rightly, that the old public library theory that every junior assistant had a chief librarian's baton in his knapsack had never been wholly true and could not possibly be true in the context of larger service units. Then came the all-important question of the education of the professionals. The old system of part-time and correspondence tuition must give way to full-time courses in full-time schools of librarianship. The pioneer London school – closed at the outbreak of war – must be reopened, and other schools initiated to cope, long-term, with the education of the professionals, but, at the outset, to enable those returning to librarianship from other, wartime, occupations to make good the lost years. And these new schools must be ready to receive their first students as demobilisation began.

To the layman outside librarianship the McColvin Report could be judged in the light of its own very notable and individual merits. Within the profession it was necessary to begin to integrate it with the thinking of the Emergency Committee, of the Council and of the Association's membership at large. That process began immediately although hesitantly at first.

Anxieties were in fact expressed as soon as news of the Report's completion began to circulate. At the meeting of the Emergency Committee on 20 March 1942 resolutions were reported from both the Association of Assistant Librarians and the London and Home Counties Branch calling for the Report to be referred to Branches and Sections before any submissions were made to outside bodies. When the Council met in the following September to give the Report preliminary consideration, it was obvious that, while the magnitude of McColvin's achievement was fully appreciated and valued, some of his more drastic recommendations had frightened the more timid members and greatly disconcerted others. An unsuccessful attempt was even made to persuade the Carnegie Trustees to publish the Report: it could at least be argued that a wartime enquiry from the Trust – which was now much easier to answer – had really begun it all! McColvin himself was in no doubt and successfully argued that it should be published, *complete*, by the Association and presented, like the Adams Report of 1915, as *the views of one individual*. The whole membership of the Association might then feel that the Council was taking them fully into its confidence. The Council reluctantly summed up its courage and allowed itself to be persuaded. The McColvin Report was published by the Association one month later, became the subject of leading articles in the *Times* and *Manchester Guardian* and quickly gained further publicity in a wide range of periodicals.[38]

The LA Council's committee, appointed to consider the McColvin Report and the comments of Branches and Sections upon it and to produce the Association's 'recommendations for post-war reorganisation', consisted of the Honorary Officers and Messrs Nowell, Sayers, Lamb, Sydney, Irwin, Revie and Henderson. Their report was submitted one year later by their Chairman (Sydney) and was approved subject to further consideration of points made and queries raised.[39] It was then published as a sixteen-page pamphlet, *The Public library service: its post-war reorganization and development: proposals by the Council of the LA.*

It was obvious enough that a sixteen-page pamphlet could only cover the ground of the McColvin Report if detailed recommendations were changed into generalisations. The *Proposals* were therefore a series of generalisations appropriately prefaced:

By the facilities it affords for wide and unfettered reading the public library enables every man not only to enlarge his mind with the refined pleasures of great literature, but in particular (at present a vital need), to secure that understanding of social and economic forces and conditions without which there can be no true realization of the democratic ways of life. Because of its essential freedom, its wide range, its hospitality to all phases of thought and its infinite adaptability the public library can serve each man according to his requirements and safeguard his development against the dangers of modern standardizing influences.

and concluding:

The post-war world will need and demand a better library service than has yet been fully envisaged by local or national authorities. It will ask not merely the improvement of the best elements while the remainder lag behind but that everywhere, for all men, there may be sound, generous, convenient and well-organized provision.

'Four conditions of paramount importance' were set out:

i   The provision of adequate services by suitable library authorities must be made compulsory

ii   There must be an appropriate department of the central government responsible for guiding, encouraging and coordinating the work of local library authorities and insisting upon their efficiency

iii All local authorities must be rendered financially able to attain efficiency

iv   The composition and size of local government areas must be such that the best results are made possible

'The essential requirements of any system of library service' were:

i   An adequate service must be available to everyone, irrespective of where he may reside . . .

ii   Every accredited person must be enabled freely to borrow books from or consult them in any public library regardless of his place of residence or employment

iii The library service must be so organised and provided that it can meet all the legitimate requirements of the community for books and information. . . .

iv   . . . Libraries should not be controlled by committees charged also with the responsibility for other functions, such as education, nor by sub-committees of such committees

v   Libraries must be staffed by capable and experienced chief officers with sufficient suitable and qualified assistants

It may be noted, *inter alia*, that the Association's policy now provided for the central control that had been criticised so relentlessly in the 1930s; that it visualised a satisfactory authority area of between one quarter and three quarters of a million population; that library staffs should be divided into two main categories composed of technical staff (librarians) and service staff, and that full-time Schools of Librarianship were to be created.

The *Proposals* won immediate applause *and* criticism from the Association's members. The criticisms were felt by at least one member of the Committee responsible for the *Proposals* to 'all cancel one another out'.[40] The major controversies concerning them had nevertheless to be postponed until the war had ended and the members serving in the Forces were back in peacetime positions.

At the meeting of the Council which had approved the *Proposals* it was also agreed, on McColvin's resolution, that 'The Council appoint a Planning Committee' and set the following terms of reference:

i   To make known the terms of the Memorandum of
     Proposals and to secure their implementation
ii   To give further and more detailed consideration to certain
     more important aspects of post-war organisation such as
     a Post-war professional education **b** School libraries, work
     with children **c** The relationship between the public library
     service and adult education **d** Cooperation between the
     public library service and non-rate supported libraries –
     inter-library loans, etc **e** Restoration of war-damaged
     libraries at home and abroad **f** The post-war supply of
     books, including consideration of deficiencies due to war
     conditions **g** Salaries and conditions of library staff **h** The
     future organisation of the LA **i** Any other relevant matters

The Planning Committee, whose membership amalgamated those of the Emergency and Post-War policy committees, was given power to act in respect of i and to recommend in ii. It was also authorised to appoint sub-committees and to coopt to them.[41] Much of the work of this committee and of its sub-committees came to fruition only after the war; some must be glanced at before this present chapter ends.

Planning achievements up to that date and future prospects were usefully reviewed at a weekend conference of members of the Council and of Branch and Section officers at Wadham College, Oxford, held a week before Christmas 1944. Among the papers read P. S. J. Welsford's on 'International and overseas contacts' was specially interesting as it forcefully reminded those present that, despite wartime problems and difficulties, contacts with overseas libraries and librarians had not ceased. It was a reminder in particular of three aspects of the Association's achievement. The work of many libraries had been coordinated to provide much special reference and other material for the use of the planning staffs of the Allied Forces preparing for the reoccupation of the Continent of Europe; there had been much valuable cooperation with the American Library Association, notably after the Americans had established their 'Committee on devastated libraries' in 1940; and there was great promise in the growing cooperation between the Association and the British Council which had

accepted the principle that all its libraries abroad must be managed by qualified librarians, and it has now set up a sub-committee specially to consider the further development of library services abroad and throughout the British Empire.[42]

The outstanding contribution to the success of the Wadham Conference was, however, made by Raymond Irwin, County Librarian of Lancashire and soon to be appointed the new Director of the University College School, on 'Professional education'. He reiterated in his paper the important points that the old system of spare-time professional education had had its day and that the major part of basic training in future must be undertaken in full-time schools which would be urgently needed, in any case, to meet the re-training needs of the demobilised staffs. The various types of possible school had been carefully considered with special reference to the UCL School, to the American schools and to the various institutions offering part-time courses during the 1930s. New schools closely connected with the universities were obviously highly desirable but had had to be ruled out since university resources were likely to be already stretched to the limit and as the Association considered it essential – at least for the time being – to retain complete control over both syllabus and examinations. As the principals of a number of colleges of further education had proved willing and cooperative, new schools of librarianship – initially to offer one-year courses – were planned to open in their institutions in September 1945. It was also obviously essential that the UCL School should reopen without delay.[43]

Mr Irwin now formally introduced the new examination syllabus prepared by the Post-War Policy Committee and approved by the Council. This owed much to the rejected revision of 1937 and provided, for the first time, a satisfactory substitute for the old Intermediate examination, now to be termed the Registration examination, preparation for which would form the basis for the new one-year School courses. The new syllabus was to provide for:

i   Entrance examination consisting of four 1½-hour papers on **a** rudiments of library administration and procedure **b** elementary classification and cataloguing **c** elementary reference material and methods and **d** choice of books. This was to be taken following one year's practical experience working in a library and was not to be prepared for by special courses of study

ii Registration examination, providing for six three-hour papers on **a** Classification **b** Cataloguing **c** Elementary general bibliography **d** Assistance to readers in the choice of books **e** Library organisation and administration **f** History of English literature

The new Registration examination was to cover, therefore, not merely the cataloguing and classification of the old Intermediate but such 'a substantial core' of professional training as could reasonably be equated with one year's full-time attendance at a library school.

After passing the Registration examination and having had at least three years' service, to which the year at School would contribute appropriately, the young librarian was then to be entitled to register ALA and to describe himself/herself as a 'chartered librarian'. The chartered librarian was in fact to be the standard product of the future, the new nomenclature boldly proclaiming to the outside world the existence of a profesional register. Since, in the future, as in the past, all sorts of libraries might risk appointing all sorts of amateur librarians, the importance of devising, at long last, a satisfactory and *legally enforceable* distinction between a librarian and a chartered librarian was obviously difficult to exaggerate.

If the chartered librarians of the future were to progress from ALA to FLA, they must now needs face the rigours of the new Final examination which, unlike the Registration, could be taken in parts, but ultimate success in which could hardly be expected before the age of 25 or 26. The Final examination, for which, at least initially, full-time courses were not envisaged, was to be divided into seven parts with three-hour papers on General bibliography and book selection, Library organisation and general librarianship, Library routine and administration of public, university and college, or special libraries, and Literary criticism and appreciation. (Providing also alternatives to English literary history, eg the literatures of special subjects or subject groups such as technology or music.) There were to be two three-hour papers on a subject chosen from one of the following: Palaeography and archives, Library work with young people, Advanced classification and cataloguing, or Historical bibliography. There was also to be an essay or thesis. of from 5000 to 10,000 words, on a subject to be chosen by the candidate and 'germane' to his professional work, and a final *viva voce*.[44]

If the Council had achieved nothing else during the war-time years, by its insistence on library school attendance – equated with a syllabus attempting genuinely to provide, really for the first time, for the professional education of all librarians and not merely those working in public libraries – and the invention of the 'chartered librarian', it had deserved well of succeeding generations. Prophets are seldom honoured, however, in their own homes, their own countries or their own times. Ever-growing dissatisfaction with the allegedly undemocratic activities of the Council, and of its Emergency Committee in

particular, came to a head when a Special General Meeting of
LA Members was requisitioned. The meeting was held at
Chaucer House on Thursday 21 June 1945, six weeks after the
victory of the Allied Forces in Europe.

As in other organisations the question of the ability of the
General Meeting to *instruct* the governing body, ie the Council,
had been raised from time to time but always inconclusively. The
motions now submitted at the Special General Meeting were
drafted on the optimistic assumption that instruction was
possible. When Sir Parker Morris, the Honorary Legal Adviser,
ruled to the contrary ('No Council would disregard the views of
a General Meeting but it should be made clear that the General
Meeting has no power to instruct the Council'), they were each
prefaced by the qualifying phrase 'That in the opinion of this
meeting. . . .' In view of the general feeling that the Council and
its Emergency Committee had done too much too quickly, the
introductory remarks of the President (Esdaile) that 'the six
years since the last Annual General Meeting had been the busiest
in the history of the LA' seemed apt and more than a little ironic.

The first motion, moved by Mr F. M. Gardner (Librarian, Luton
Public Libraries) was 'That the projected syllabus be withdrawn
for further consideration and that arrangements be made for
one-year courses on the present Syllabus for the Intermediate
and Final Examinations'. He argued that there was little
evidence that library schools could be established sufficiently
quickly to enable leisure-time study for the Association's
examinations to be ended and that the new syllabus would
injure all students, and not merely the ex-Service ones, by
raising standards too quickly. The discussion which followed
displayed much division of opinion. Although one contributor
argued that 'The new Final is extremely difficult and the
Registration examination is a disgrace', many were obviously
prepared to agree that the new syllabus was a great improvement
on the old and the new Registration infinitely better than the old
Intermediate. McColvin contended that the new syllabus was
not more difficult than the old but 'better balanced and more
like other professional examinations'. He continued:

We are presented with a magnificent opportunity to get started without any financial expenditure. We shall never get this opportunity again unless we have another war. We opened negotiations and immediately it was clear how education experts regarded the Intermediate. It was obvious that we had to have a new Syllabus if we were to have a full-time course. We recognise that there are hard cases in the Forces and we have extended the old Intermediate to meet these cases and will examine thoroughly any other cases which may arise . . . It has been said we should have had university schools. Of course we wanted them . . . It was made clear that taking the situation as a whole the universities would have such enormous commitments after the war that they were quite unable to open their doors to library courses. It is asked if grants are sufficient. The answer is yes. Far from it being necessary for local authorities to add to grants it may be a disservice to a candidate as it might lead to a reduction in the Government grant . . . Eight Technical Colleges are willing to provide Schools as soon as we are ready with the candidates for them. . . . The Ministry of Education have been in the discussions from the beginning and have made it quite clear that they will recognise the courses and make appropriate grants and the Ministry of Labour has also been consulted and gives its full approval. We want the new Syllabus *now*. It will be the greatest mistake if you turn it down now!

A contribution such as this could hardly fail to persuade and Mr E. Cave (Southampton Public Libraries), moved an amendment – which subsequently became the substantive motion – calling for the old and new syllabuses to run concurrently for three years. This was carried by a substantial majority after members had refreshed themselves with lunch.

The second resolution, moved by Mr T. E. Callander (Librarian, Coulsdon and Purley Public Libraries), was carried after only brief discussion:

That this meeting requests the Council to take the necessary steps to resume power to hold an Annual General Meeting, and to call such meeting before 31st December, 1945.

Mr A. Smith (Librarian, Newark-on-Trent Public Libraries) now moved:

This meeting is of the opinion that all resolutions of the Council or

Emergency Committee regarding the removal of members in the Forces from membership on account of unpaid subscriptions should be rescinded, and that all such members be reinstated from the date of their removal.

It was soon evident that opinion was notably divided, between those who felt that special consideration, including, if necessary, suspended membership, should be given to all members in the Forces, and those who thought that 'it was quite simple to arrange for accounts to be paid and the great majority of members on service are having their salaries made up and are financially better off'. This third motion was again carried by a large majority.

Finally Mr W. E. C. Cotton (Librarian, Scottish Central Library for Students) moved, and it was carried by a large majority:

That in the opinion of this meeting no further steps should be taken to implement the proposals in *The Public library service: its post-war reorganization and development* until this report has been approved by an Annual General Meeting.[45]

It was all but inevitable that, after six years of war, the LA members, *disessociated* as never before – many by physical distance and many more psychologically – from the central government of the Association should have felt and should have expressed exceptional lack of confidence in the Council. The 'generation gap', too, was liable to become particularly divisive when the minds of so many of the younger members had been force-developed in unaccustomed environments. Walter Bagehot once wrote:

We know at least, that facts are many; that progress is complicated; that burning ideas (such as young men have) are mostly false and always incomplete. The notion of a far-seeing and despotic statesman, who can lay down plans for ages yet unborn, is a fancy generated by the pride of the human intellect to which facts give no support . . . A wise and constitutional monarch attempts no such vanities. His career is not in the air; he labours in the world of sober fact; he deals with schemes which can be effected – schemes which are desirable – schemes which are worth the cost. . . .[46]

The Library Association was indeed fortunate that, during the years of World War Two, it had in L. R. McColvin an influential Honorary Secretary who dealt with 'schemes which can be effected – schemes which are desirable – schemes which are worth the cost'. The ideas of many of the young men and women present at that memorable meeting in June 1945, may indeed have been 'burning'. They seem, nevertheless, and in retrospect, to have been notably more reactionary than those of the Council and Emergency Committee. The two contrasted points of view had, of course, to be reconciled, although not in this present chapter.

References

1. 8.4.1938.
2. eg *LAR*, 40, pp 510–2.
3. *LAR*, 41, pp 307–8.
4. Letters from Maurice Marston (Secretary of National Book Council) to present author, 7.6.1939; 27.7.1939.
5. *LAR*, 41, pp 569–70.
6. *Ibid*, pp 460–1.
7. *LAR*, 43, p 122.
8. *See*, eg W. A. Munford, 'England's southern ports in the War', *LR*, 10, pp 54–6.
9. EC, 6.5.1941. (EC = Minutes of Emergency Committee.)
10. *LAR*, 42, 3.
11. LA *Year book* (1940), pp 3–4.
12. *LAR*, 42, p 107.
13. EC, 10.6.1941.
14. *LW*, vol 44 onwards.
15. But *see LAR*, 44, pp 64, 100.
16. *LAR*, 45, p 114.
17. *LAR*, 47, p 148.
18. *AR* (1945), p 5R.
19. EC, 27.9.1944.
20. L. R. McColvin, 'The LA in wartime and after', *LAR*, 47, pp 213–23.
21. *AR* (1945), p 4R.
22. *See* eg 20.3.1941.

23. *ARs* 1939–45.
24. *LAR*, 43, p 125.
25. *LAR*, 47, p 148.
26. 25.10.1940.
27. *LAR*, 42, p 196.
28. 25.10.1940.
29. *LW*, 43, p 66.
30. EC, 9.1.1942.
31. *Ibid*, 20.3.1942.
32. See *LAR*, 45, pp 6–7, for an account of a representative salvage drive, in this case at Bristol.
33. EC, 26.7.1944; *LAR*, 47, p 147.
34. 25.10.1940; *LAR*, 42, pp 219–20.
35. EC, 8.11.1941.
36. *Libraries for the people*. 1968, p 23.
37. *LW*, 45, pp 58–9.
38. *Ibid*, p 25.
39. 23.9.1943.
40. C. Nowell, 'The L.A. in Wartime', *LAR*, 47, pp 24–30, particularly p 29.
41. 23.9.1943.
42. *LAR*, 47, pp 133–8.
43. *Ibid*, pp 3–11.
44. *Ibid*, pp 12–13.
45. *Ibid*, pp 126–32.
46. *The English constitution*. 1867, p 72, in *Worlds Classics* ed 1928.

A History of The Library Association, 1877–1977

Since World War Two

Chapter Nine

1945-1949

The years following the end of World War Two were inevitably those of recovery and reconstruction. But the period now under review proved also to be one of preparation for important steps forward.

The months of 1945 remaining after the peace celebrations had been concluded were difficult and unsettling. Many citizens were leaving their wartime occupations and returning to their home towns, members of library staffs included.[1] They were faced by acute shortages of virtually every commodity in everyday use – other than money – books included.

Although the immediate post-war scope for the LA Council seemed nearly limitless, two priority objectives were, firstly, the adoption by the membership at large and particularly by the Local Authority members, of *The Public library service: its post-war reorganization and development* and, secondly, the breathing of life into the new schools of librarianship and the new examination syllabus. The membership of the Council now intent on these activities differed to some extent from that which had piloted the Association through the War years. Esdaile's invaluable Presidency ended with 1945 and with a richly merited Honorary Fellowship.[2] H. M. Cashmore succeeded him for 1946, the latter's office as Honorary Treasurer being assumed by Raymond Irwin, the new Director of the UCL School. McColvin continued as Honorary Secretary and Sir Parker Morris as Honorary Legal

251

Adviser although the latter was soon to be succeeded by
J. Waring Sainsbury, Town Clerk of Kensington.[3] New
councillors obtaining seats at the first elections since 1939
included Miss M. F. Austin (Librarian, Hertfordshire County
Libraries), F. G. B. Hutchings (Librarian, Leeds Public
Libraries), E. Wisker (Librarian, Gillingham Public Libraries)
and W. A. Munford (Librarian, Cambridge Public Libraries).[4]
Public library control, which had been so marked in pre-war
years, was obviously still strongly emphasised.

The Public library service proposals, in which the Minister of
Education (Ellen Wilkinson) had promised interest but no
speedy legal implementation,[5] were formally presented to the
Association's membership at the Blackpool conference in
May 1946, being introduced in 'sectional' sessions by the
appropriate chairmen of committees prior to final consideration
at the Annual General Meeting when approximately 700
members were present. They were then adopted subject to
amendments – successfully moved by F. M. Gardner and, at least
to that extent, a dissenting member of Council.*

Paragraph 18a, which was entirely withdrawn, provided, in the
absence of a new Government Department responsible, *inter
alia*, for public libraries, for overall influence and control by the
Board of Education. Paragraphs 12–16, withdrawn for further
consideration and consultation with local authorities – and never
resubmitted – covered 'The Local Authority' and the larger units
envisaged. Debate was animated and the amendments approved
by substantial majorities. The new *Regulations and syllabus of
professional examinations* were also formally received and
provision made, *via* a motion moved from the floor, for the
temporary reintroduction of an Association preliminary
examination in lieu of School Certificate for the benefit of
wartime recruits wishing to continue in the profession and who
would, otherwise, have been unable to sit the examinations.
There was also a reminder, from the President of the Scottish

* Mr Gardner's Authority, Luton
Borough Council, had also been
skirmishing inconclusively with the
LA Council over the latter's allegedly
cavalier attitude to most of the
resolutions passed at the Special
General Meeting in June 1945.

Library Association, that the reform of Scottish public library
law and the removal of the rate limit in that country were still
pressing problems.[6]

The well-attended annual dinner was notable for the
introduction to the members – in the temporary guise of the
proposer of the toast 'The Library Association' – of James
Wilkie, Mitchell's successor as Secretary of the CUKT, following
the latter's retirement in 1939.[7] Mitchell's friendship for and
association with the LA were, incidentally, soon to be
commemorated by the Mitchell Memorial Fund, providing study
loans for qualifying librarians and a plaque in Chaucer House.[8]

The UCL School reopened in September 1945 but it proved
impossible to inaugurate any of the new ones until the
following year.[9] Those opened in 1946 were at Glasgow, under
W. B. Paton; Leeds under N. E. Dain; City of London College
under D. A. R. Kemp; Loughborough under R. Stokes; and
Manchester under J. C. Harrison, all directors being practising
librarians.[10] Schools at Brighton and Newcastle began work in
1947 and another School in the London area at Spring Grove
Polytechnic in 1949. Most of the new Schools were admittedly
still very small by the end of the present period, with fewer than
forty students each. The numbers in attendance at Autumn 1949
were:

Brighton   25
Glasgow   28
Leeds   34
London   98
Loughborough   62
Manchester   38
Newcastle   15
Spring Grove   10
(Total   310)

Of these approximately one-third were on Ex-Service grants and
about a half from local authorities, the remainder being either
private students or those from overseas on British Council
scholarships and the like.

Naturally enough a steadily increasing proportion of students sitting the Association's professional examinations came from the new library schools. But the AAL correspondence courses, part-time classes, arranged as in pre-war years at local colleges of further education, and the revived summer schools still accounted for the majority of entrants. The total number of examination entries increased from 1813 (924 passes) in 1945[12] to 3941 (2131 passes) in 1947[13] and to 6197 (2844 passes) in 1949,[14] suggesting, not only a substantial clearance of wartime 'bottlenecks' but also a vigorously expanding profession. The very large total for 1949 was, however, at least partly due to the 'threat' of another syllabus revision to become effective in 1950.

Full-time students at a school of librarianship are likely to enjoy a less 'isolated' period of study and training than those attending part-time day or evening classes and a *much* less isolated experience than those relying on correspondence tuition. One of the features of this pioneer period of library school development was a considerable upsurge of professional enthusiasm, allied to a new critical approach to the 'external' system of examining – for which the Association was still wholly responsible – comprehending a wide variety of approaches including the drafting of examination papers and the 'control' of examiners, and the choice of textbooks available to students. A substantial revision of the syllabus was in fact already under discussion as early as 1947, meetings of the school directors, tutors and examiners being held, initially, to discuss the first year's experience of the new system.[15] The Association's new Education Officer, B. I. Palmer, also began regular visits to each school to ensure full contact and cooperation.[16] The LA owed a special debt to the chairman of its Education Committee during this pioneer period; F. G. B. Hutchings' task was never easy and frequently exceptionally difficult.[17]

Membership continued to rise steadily throughout the period. It was 6510 at the end of 1945,[18] 7823 at the end of 1947[19] and 9481 at the end of 1949; during the last year the number of new members recruited and of former members reinstated was the highest ever recorded.[20] The number of chartered librarians also rose to reach, by the end of 1949, 1163 Fellows and 1848

Associates, the pre-war trend towards more Fellows than Associates having been completely reversed.[21] Reference has been made earlier to the manner in which the Association's finances readily surmounted the difficulties of wartime. But the accounts showed a small deficit at the end of 1946 and a larger one a year later. At the Brighton Conference in June 1947 the basic subscription rate was raised from two to three guineas as from 1 January 1948, the sliding scale rising from 15s annually for members not on the Register and in receipt of salaries of less than £150 per annum.[22] The membership also became more closely integrated during the present period; by the end of 1949 the Branch organisation covered, for the first time, the whole of Great Britain and Northern Ireland.[23] The old Northern Counties Association was resuscitated as the Northern Branch in 1946,[24] the Eastern Branch formed in 1947[25] and the Yorkshire and South Western Branches inaugurated in 1949.[26] Bye-law revision making United Kingdom members automatically members of their local Branches was effected and a new system of capitation payments substituted for *ad hoc* grants; this gave rather greater local financial autonomy. There was no comparable expansion in Section activity since only one completely new one, the Medical, was formed, in 1948, and the School Libraries closed down at the end of 1946, substantially with the object of uniting with the independent School Library Association, the new Youth Section taking its place.[27] But during 1949 discussions were being held which would result in the formation of the Reference and Special Section in 1951.

The main concern of the Association at the end of 1949 was still with public libraries, indeed the preparations to celebrate the centenary of the first English Act in the following year were ambitious. The high water mark would certainly be reached in 1950 but in fact the tide seemed already to be on the turn. It had been anticipated by the Council, if then a little too optimistically, some time earlier. The *Annual Report* for 1947 had included the following:

It is sometimes assumed by those outside the profession – sometimes even by those inside – that the LA is an association of Public Librarians only. . . . After a period when the proportion declined considerably, it is good to see, in the post-war period, a revival of interest in the Association on the part of those working in National, Governmental, University, Research and other Special Libraries. The real strength of the Association can only be developed, and the high ideals of the profession achieved, when workers in all these libraries meet together on a common ground in one organization.[28]

The very ambitious expansion of services to and for LA members during the period was made possible by the appointment of new senior staff. Just as the expansion of educational activities already referred to would have been impossible without the devoted services of B. I. Palmer, so the development of the Membership department correlates with the arrival of D. D. Haslam as Membership Officer; both appointments were made in 1948.[29]

Although differing developments and situations up to the World War Two period caused many local disparities, the salaries and conditions of service of Local Government staffs, including those employed in libraries, were more readily susceptible to *national* consideration and review than those of most authorities other than the central departments of government. The Association published revised recommended salary scales for Chief (Local Authority) librarians in December 1945, scales ranging from £525–£650 for those serving Authorities with populations under 25,000 to £1275 – £1425 for those between 150,000 and 250,000[30] but these, like their several predecessors had the obvious disadvantage of being non-negotiated. When in 1946 the agreements reached by the various regional salary committees which had been formed before and during the war gave place to the *Scheme of conditions of service* prepared by the National Joint Council for Local Authorities administrative, professional, technical and clerical services,[31] the Association lost no time in formulating and publishing recommendations for applying the new national salary scales to public library staffs locally, and covering posts up to deputy librarians and for all population groups.[32] Now came conflict. The National Joint Council not only advised local authorities to ignore recommendations from professional associations such as the LA but also steadfastly refused to receive deputations from the associations themselves. The National Joint Council was likely to be the more influential: the Association was able to remind both it and the local authorities that its Royal Charter of 1898 – nearly half a century older than the NJC – gave it the duties of 'promoting the better administration of libraries' and 'the improvement of the position and qualifications of librarians'. The Association, in effect, invited local authorities to stand firm and to take its recommendations into full consideration.[33] The conflict doubtless seemed regrettable to some but undeniably amusing to others; the Association's stand on its Charter seemed legally impeccable. The LA's recommendations were obviously taken into account by the chief librarians whose suggestions to their own local authorities were likely to be more or less influential. But the temporary impasse was still most unfortunate. At the Annual General Meeting at Scarborough in 1948 a resolution was passed asking the NJC to formulate public library staff grading recommendations;[34] it met with no success during the period under review. The situation overall became still more unsatisfactory following the NJC's temporary refusal to accept the Association's new Registration examination and ALA qualification as alternatives to the new Promotion examination of the Local Government Examinations Board which had also begun a not entirely unchequered career.[35] The Association persisted and had some limited success in protesting to individual Local Authorities advertising posts at salaries considered very inadequate.[36] During 1947, in addition, the attention of County Councils was drawn to discrepancies between the salaries of most County librarians and their staffs and those of urban librarians serving areas of comparable population.[37]

Progress was also made during the period in the negotiation of salaries in other fields of librarianship. One notable example was the success in persuading HM Treasury to authorise Government departments to introduce or retain professional librarians on grades corresponding with the various categories of Executive officer in the Civil Service. In view of the unsatisfactory library situation applying previously in the Departments of State this was an important step forward and to the credit, jointly, of the LA and the Institution of Professional Civil Servants.[38] Progress was also being made, but more slowly, with the salaries and conditions of service of the librarians and staffs of university libraries, initiated by a recommended salary scale drawn up for the Association by its University and Research Section in 1946.[39] At the end of the period, and at the invitation of the Royal Army Education Corps, the Association even began to discuss Army library service with Lt Col D. E. Coult, FLA, and other Officers. Regular or Short Service commissions in the RAEC were introduced a year later.[40]

The LA's own library service to its members was greatly improved and expanded during the period. Important contributory factors were the appointment, in 1947, of two additional staff assistants[41] and, two years later, by the absorption, on mutually acceptable terms, of the AAL library, itself of more than 1300 volumes.[42] By the end of 1949 the total stock of the LA Library had risen to 11,000 volumes plus periodicals, of which by now more than 100 from all parts of the world were taken and filed, photographs, plans etc. Annual book issues had risen to more than 4000 and a monthly average of 600 enquiries dealt with in the Information Bureau.[43]

Association publishing regathered momentum slowly. The *Subject index* and *Year book* continued to appear for each year although the latter did not resume publication of the full list of members – discontinued in 1940 – until the issue for 1947 and then only at the cost of unprecedented delay.[44] W. B. Stevenson took over the editorship of the *LAR* from McColvin and J. H. P. Pafford that of the *Year's work* from Esdaile. Pafford's immediate task seemed the more intimidating since continuity had been broken and the war years remained to be covered. The decision to publish a volume of approximately twice normal size for 1939–1945 was obviously sensible as was also that to publish it together with an orthodox volume for 1946. Editors of books consisting of essays by many hands seldom find easy tasks unless the time factor is of little or no account. These *Year's work* volumes proved unexceptional and, although in page proof during 1949, did not in fact appear until the early weeks of 1950.[45]

Much of the Association's publishing effort up to and including

1949 was devoted to a new series of attractively produced short select subject lists, generally edited by F. M. Gardner and W. B. Stevenson, intended for cheap bulk sale to public libraries which would then normally distribute individual copies free to readers. Sixteen of these lists were issued during the period, their subjects ranging from *Mountain adventure* to *The Child in the home* and from *The Country scene* to *Georgian England*. More than 400,000 copies of the lists were sold between November, 1947 and December, 1949;[46] if the effort devoted to them now seems a little disproportionate to their value, they were considered to serve a very useful purpose at the time of publication.

The critical approach of the new schools of librarianship to some LA activities, to which passing reference has already been made, did not overlook publications. During the last year of the present period R. Stokes, Head of the Loughborough School, faulted the professional literature available to students and cited in particular incomplete coverage, the inadequacy and obsolescence of much of the material available and a wrong approach. The latter aspect was related, he thought, to a tendency which:

seems to be to regard education as the assimilation of a series of dull and frequently irrelevant facts. Some of the LA Manuals are examples of this attitude.[47]

Fortunately neither of the two new *Manuals*, Esdaile's *British Museum library* (1946) and Savage's *Manual of book classification and display* (1947) could be justifiably criticised on these grounds. The latter, indeed, seemed to the *LAR*'s own reviewer to be 'not a Manual in the accepted sense of the term', and to be concerned much more with display than with classification.[48] But then F. M. Gardner, when reviewing another book by Savage also published by the Association in 1947, *A Librarian looks at readers*, put his finger on much when he concluded:

One must take Dr Savage as one finds him. If one is outraged by one sentence, in the next there is a comment born of a lifetime of accumulated knowledge. This is not a textbook. It is a book to be read and reflected on, one that will be not only read but re-read, by all true librarians.[49]

The new titles noted above were all most useful additions to the literature of librarianship. From the point of view of the library school student preparing for the Registration examination, however, more immediately important was A. D. Roberts' *Introduction to reference books*. Its initial popularity may be judged by the fact that, after first publication in June 1949 it was reprinted in both the September and November following.[50] Yet, seen in retrospect, none of these books or serials made the Association's greatest contribution to its publishing achievement between 1945 and 1949. Its masterpiece was, instead, a serial which it was not to publish itself, *The British national bibliography*, the basic idea for which may be traced back, far beyond the McColvin Report, at least to Edward Edwards. Preparations for publication may be initially linked with a discussion on central cataloguing in the *LAR* in 1946.[51] As *BNB* itself only began publication, however, in January, 1950, further consideration will be deferred to the next chapter.

Representation on other organisations which, indeed, had not entirely lapsed even during the War years, became influential during the period under review. One of the important connections was with the British Records Association where H. M. Cashmore's outspoken claims for library interest, and public library interest in particular, were untiring; support for the librarian's approach came when a new diploma course in archives was introduced at the UCL School in 1947.[52] Other continuing associations of great value were with the National Central Library and with the *British union catalogue of periodicals* (BUCOP).[53] But some of the specially interesting developments were in the international field.

In a paper read at the American Library Association's congress of 1947 Edward Sydney had rightly asserted that:

Men and women who have to wait until they are in the late fifties or early sixties before visiting another country on a professional mission are really not qualified to make the best ambassadors nor the fullest use of their opportunities.

He went on to stress the need for scholarships to library schools in other countries; periodic exchanges of their tutors and of members of library staffs; travelling scholarships, exhibitions, etc.[54] Five of the pioneer post-war travellers were the members of the Council who visited Denmark in that same year at the invitation of the Danish Library Association; the welcome accorded them remains a vivid memory thirty years later.[55] Appreciable numbers of young librarians subsequently took up British Council library posts overseas[56] and at the end of the present period the Association's advice was sought by the American authorities administering the Fulbright scheme; a memorandum outlining projects appropriate to both British and American participants, including direct exchanges and study and research tours was duly prepared.[57] Important contributions to international cooperation were also made by the LA representatives on the national cooperating body for libraries of the United Nations Educational, Scientific and Cultural Organisation (Unesco), matters dealt with including abstracting, copyright, bibliographical services, libraries of deposit and public library services.[58] The Unesco *Public library manifesto,* distributed in 1949 in countries where English, French, Spanish, Polish, Italian or Arabic is spoken was one outstanding result.[59] If one event can be singled out as symbolising the Association's concern for activities transcending national boundaries it was the visit of the Prime Minister (Mr C. R. Attlee) to Chaucer House in December 1946 to mark the end of the work of the Inter-Allied Book Centre. The President (H. M. Cashmore) was in the Chair on this occasion and the Diplomatic Corps was exceptionally well represented. The sentiments of those attending were appropriately expressed by the French Ambassador when he said:

Each of us is very grateful to the nation, to your nation, to whose unconquerable spirit he owes the fact that he still is a free man. The most generous gift with which the Inter-Allied Book Centre is today presenting the Allied countries, is the fitting expression of this spirit.[60]

This was an occasion when spectators were surely delighted to agree that:

The prestige of the LA and the Library profession is mounting. Justification of this statement lies to some extent in the fact that today

when matters affecting libraries and librarianship are under
consideration by other bodies and organizations, such as Ministries of
the Government, the BBC, the Central Office of Information, the
Press, as well as a host of other institutions, it is to the LA that they
first turn for advice, comment and information. [61]

References

1. *AR* (1945), p 3R.
2. *LAR*, 48, p 102.
3. *LAR*, 49, p 114.
4. *LAR*, 47, p 242.
5. Executive committee, 5.12.1945.
6. *LAR*, 48, pp 139–40. A pamphlet
was reprinted in *LAR*, 48, pp 175–8.
7. *LAR*, 46, pp 188–90; 226.
8. *LAR*, 49, p 213.
9. *AR* (1945), pp 4R–5R.
10. *LAR*, 48, p 244.
11. *AR* (1949), p 6R.
12. *AR* (1945), p 5R.
13. *AR* (1947), p 6R.
14. *AR* (1949), p 5R.
15. *AR* (1947), p 7R.
16. eg *AR* (1949), p 6R.
17. *See* eg his introduction to and
sturdy defence of the new Schools in
LR, 10, pp 218–21. The story of how
the Schools came into existence, the
meetings and discussions between LA
representatives and the Directors of
Technical colleges, etc, is told in
considerable detail in an unpublished
LA thesis, *The Development of full-time
education for librarianship in Great
Britain since the War*. 1967, by
C. Bradley.
18. *AR* (1945), p 5R.
19. *AR* (1947), p 12R.
20. *AR* (1949), p 10R.
21. *Ibid*.
22. *LAR*, 49, p 162.
23. *AR* (1949), p 10R.
24. *LAR*, 48, p 21.
25. *LAR*, 49, p 161.

26. *AR* (1949), p 10R.
27. *AR* (1947), p 19R.
28. *Ibid*, p 3R.
29. *LAR*, 50, p 172.
30. *LAR*, 47, p 244.
31. *LAR*, 48, pp 54–6.
32. *Ibid*.
33. *LAR*, 48, pp 89–91.
34. *LAR*, 50, p 156.
35. *Ibid*, pp 155–6.
36. *See* eg *AR* (1949), p 11R.
37. *AR* (1947), p 13R.
38. *AR* (1949), p 11R.
39. *LAR*, 48, p 196.
40. *LAR*, 53, p 53.
41. *AR* (1947), p 11R.
42. *AR* (1949), p 8R.
43. *LAR*, 52, p 143.
44. *AR* (1947), p 14R.
45. *AR* (1949), p 14R.
46. *Ibid*.
47. *LAR*, 51, pp 282–3.
48. *LAR*, 49, pp 67–8.
49. *Ibid*, p 310.
50. *AR* (1949), p 13R.
51. *LAR*, 48, pp 217–9.
52. *AR* (1947), pp 7R–8R.
53. *AR* (1949), pp 27R–28R;
30R–31R.
54. *LAR*, 50, p 1.
55. *LAR*, 49, pp 226–7.
56. *LAR*, 51, p 171.
57. *AR* (1949), p 12R.
58. *Ibid*, p 39R.
59. *LAR*, 51, p 267.
60. Full report in *LAR*, 49, pp 1–5.
61. *AR* (1947), pp 4R–5R.

Chapter Ten

1950

Seen in retrospect 1950 in Britain was a disappointing year; only
to the Roman Catholic Church can it have seemed unusually
Holy. It was also a 'facing both ways' year. War memories were
already receding but shortages persisted. Indeed, following the
General Election in February, the Labour Party, which had
governed the country since 1945, found itself all-but-short of a
Commons majority. New wars seemed possible as the Great
Powers jockeyed for position, hostilities began in Korea and the
Attlee Government resisted the early strivings for European
federation. The literary view *back* was symbolised by the death
of George Bernard Shaw, by the award of the Nobel prize to
Bertrand Russell and even more by the first publication of the
first instalment of the Boswell papers, the *London journal*, which,
for many eager readers, added a new dimension to life in the
eighteenth-century capital. Contrasted with these the literary
view *forward*, as typified by, say, T. S. Eliot's *Cocktail party*,
Evelyn Waugh's *Helena* and Angus Wilson's *Such darling dodos*
appeared decidedly circumscribed. As for the arresting new
Festival of Britain buildings rising on the South Bank of the
Thames, these seemed to many to be tolerable only as a
contemporary reminder of the glories of the Great Exhibition of
1851 and certainly not as a foretaste of the architecture of the
future. Television too – now slowly but inexorably gaining
ground at the expense of the generally accepted, generally
respected and already twenty-five-year-old sound radio – did
television point the way to an acceptable hereafter? It is surely

ironic that, despite all which could be written to its prejudice generally, 1950 has many claims to be considered the Association's 'Annus mirabilis'.

The year began full of promise. It was already known that 'HM the King has been graciously pleased to grant his Patronage to the LA in commemoration of the centenary next year of the first Public Libraries Act', and that there was to be, for the first time, a Royal President, Prince Philip, Duke of Edinburgh. There were other indications of official approval, an OBE for the Secretary (P. S. J. Welsford)[1] at the beginning of the year, and a CBE for the Honorary Secretary (L. R. McColvin)[2] at the end of it. Further signs were to be a Government reception in the impressive new suite at the Victoria and Albert Museum and another, by the Lord Mayor of London, at the Guildhall. The annual dinner too, a banquet at the Dorchester Hotel, was to be an occasion to be remembered, thanks substantially to the generosity of the CUKT and to a most impressive list of distinguished guests, welcomed by the Past President, General Sir Ronald Adam, chairman of the British Council, in the absence overseas of Prince Philip.[3]

All library roads in 1950 obviously led to the September Conference at the Central Hall, Westminster which was also to be attended by a quite exceptional number of overseas delegates and visitors.[4] But before the conference began there were local celebrations of many kinds[5] and, since 1950 was to be forward- as well as backward-looking, every possible effort was made to improve public library services locally, aided by a new and well-illustrated thirty-two page Association pamphlet, *A century of public library service: where do we stand today?*, containing many suggestions and practical tests for assessing and expanding services. It was intended primarily for librarians and their committees and was sent to all local library authorities; an alternative edition was also produced for the general public.[6] Visual aids for local use included also publicity leaflets and posters and photographs available for hire.[7]

The Conference was heralded by a special (September) issue of the *LAR* which included a lengthy contribution, 'Public libraries 1850–1950', by W. A. Munford – anticipating his short centenary history *Penny rate: aspects of British public library history*, of 1951; a characteristic and also lengthy article, 'Movements and men of the past in the Association', by E. A. Savage, 'Public libraries today' by L. R. McColvin, and 'The last twenty years and the Association', by J. D. Stewart. The key pioneer also was not forgotten. On 14 August 1950, the exact centenary of the Royal Assent to the 1850 Act, a party of LA officers, councillors and members travelled to the Isle of Wight when, following a service of commemoration in Niton Parish Church, a wreath was laid on the grave of Edward Edwards, the maintenance of which had also been assumed by the Association.[8]

Prince Philip's naval duties prevented him from attending the 1950 Conference; he subsequently visited Chaucer House to receive his Past-President's medal.[9] His place was taken and the Presidential address delivered by his uncle, Earl Mountbatten.[10] Messages of greeting to the Association from the associations of many European, Commonwealth and foreign countries were received and a representative collection of papers read. Outstanding among them was the Annual Lecture.

The Association's Annual Lecture, dealing 'with the broadest aspects of the spirit and policy of library work', had been inaugurated in 1948 by David Hardman, then Parliamentary Secretary to the Board of Education.[11] The 1949 lecture had been delivered by R. W. Moore, Head Master of Harrow School.[12] In 1950 the lecturer was Sir Arnold Plant, Cassel Professor of Commerce in the University of London, himself the son of William Plant (1858–1929), Librarian of Shoreditch public libraries from 1892 to 1924, and who had been born and lived the first twenty-five years of his life above the Central Library in that metropolitan borough. His lecture, 'Are libraries business-like?', not only displayed quite unusual lay insight into public library problems, past and present. It paid tribute to the numerous methods and gadgets – including open access – which business firms had taken over from libraries, and posed an intriguing array of interesting questions and speculations, some of them at least of perennial interest.[13]

The scanty reporting of the annual conferences during the twentieth century has often been the subject of complaints by librarians. No complaint could reasonably be made in 1950; the newspaper and periodical coverage was most comprehensive.

1950 was, understandably, a year in which LA expenditure was heavy; at £47,500 it exceeded income by nearly £4000. Unless other sources of income – particularly publications, which showed a promising surplus of £5000 – could be augmented, then it was obvious that a substantial increase in subscriptions would have to be piloted through an annual general meeting.[14] But this was a problem for a future year. Membership certainly continued to grow steadily and, passing the 10,000 figure for the first time, reached 10,433 by the end of December.[15] The number of chartered librarians also increased to 3192 (1963 ALA's and 1229 FLA's) to the extent that some misgivings were felt as to the capacity of the profession to absorb so many new registrations. But again, for the time being at least, the relationship of the increase to the number of appropriate posts advertised seemed reasonably satisfactory.[16]

The publications of 1950 were of considerable interest. In addition to the regular serials and the centenary material already referred to, they included *The libraries of London*, edited by Raymond Irwin; more booklists; the first three of a new series of LA Pamphlets – *Books and reading for the blind,* the *Regional library systems,* and *Library binderies* – P. D. Record's *Survey of thesis literature in British libraries*; a new textbook – *County library practice*, by Osborne and Sharr; and a new edition, with additional chapters, of Savage's *Librarian looks at readers*. There were also the first four quarterly issues of a new serial, *Library science abstracts,* edited by R. N. and Muriel Lock, the relationship of which to the then well-established *Year's work*, will be commented on later. Nevertheless, as emphasised earlier, the new *British national bibliography* must be recognised as the major publishing achievement.

The Council had set up a Library research committee in 1947 and its members quickly concerned themselves with the problems of a national bibliography.[17] It was soon clear to all that a major step forward and a regular publication could only be achieved if a considerable number of other organisations could be persuaded to cooperate. In March 1949 the Council of the British national bibliography was formed, of representatives from in addition to the LA, the British Museum, Publishers' Association, Associated Booksellers, National Book League, British Council, Royal Society, Aslib, National Central Library and the Unesco cooperating body. The LA guaranteed initial expenses, the Secretary (P. S. J. Welsford) acted as honorary secretary *pro tem*, and the British Museum offered both accommodation for the staff and access to its Copyright Office deposits. A. J. Wells was appointed editor and his nucleus of assistants recruited during 1949, and the *BNB* began to appear, with itself as publisher, at the beginning of 1950. Librarians are critical folk and faults were soon found, *inter alia*, with its layout, coverage and up-to-dateness. But, although since 1950 *BNB* has gone from strength to strength, it would still be difficult to better the tribute paid by an early reviewer (J. T. Gillett):

There has surely never been a happier or more fruitful example of co-operation between librarians and others connected with the book trade than this. It reflects very great credit on all concerned.[18]

A substantial revision of the examination syllabus was brought into operation in 1950, the most significant changes being made in the new Final examination which, with its special organisation papers on public library *or* university and college *or* special library practice, and its wide variety of papers on the subject approach to the various arts and sciences as alternatives to English literary history,[19] made it possible at last to argue convincingly that the old public library bias had been substantially eliminated. To coincide with the new syllabus the Association began publishing its *Student's handbook*, to replace the *Syllabus of examinations,* the first edition in February 1950. During a new controversy, this time on the aims and activities of the new library schools, Dr Savage asserted, in typical Carlylean manner, in the original article[20] which began it all, that 'Only everlasting struggle keeps us out of tradition's devilish shackle'. Assuming the truth of his assertion, then the LA Council and education department had fully justified themselves.

Metaphorically speaking, there were indeed many roses to pick during 1950. But those who pick roses must also beware of thorns. The thorns seemed to the Council to be represented by the committee of the University and Research Section.

For many years it had been the Council's practice to entrust the University and Research Section with virtually all matters affecting its own kind of library; the *Proposals for the post-war development of university and research libraries,* of 1946, briefly referred to earlier in the salaries context, had accordingly been adopted as representing Association policy. Section representatives had subsequently taken part in the discussions leading to the revision of the examination syllabus with a view to making it 'for the first time really applicable to work in non-public libraries'.[21] During 1949 the Section committees had had discussions with the Association of University Teachers on the salaries and conditions of university library staffs and it came to the knowledge of the Council that 'no reference was made to LA qualifications for the posts under consideration'. It accordingly resolved, on the recommendation of its Membership committee,

That the Section be requested to insist, in its negotiations with the AUT, upon the possession of LA qualifications at appropriate points, in addition to any academic qualifications required.[22]

Council representatives felt it desirable to attend a meeting of the Section at Jesus College, Cambridge, in March 1950 when, following animated debate, they were successful in persuading members, despite the near-unanimous advice of their own committee, to resolve that 'it is desirable that graduate and non graduate members of university library staffs should hold LA or equivalent qualifications'. The Council's success was followed by the resignation of the Section committee but academic anti-climax was reached when the same members resumed office after a contested election. There was a lively correspondence in the *LAR*, contributions varying from:

I should refrain from taking the advice of a medical man, a lawyer, an architect or accountant who happened to be a Bachelor of Arts but who had no professional qualifications. Why should the Section committee assume that librarianship is different?

to:

I, for one, have been extremely offended by the tactics employed (by the Council) which have made it difficult for me to take up any other attitude than one of whole-hearted support of the Section committee in spite of some doubt as to the details of their policy.

and to the perhaps more realistic:

Just as a university degree apparently stamps the scholar, so should the LA's qualifications stamp the librarian.[23]

It would obviously have been difficult for the Council to have been satisfied with less than the very mild compromise achieved at Cambridge. In view of the history and development of the University and Research Section and occasionally, be it admitted, of the narcissistic approach of some university librarians who, in 1950, may well have considered LA qualifications unworthy of their attention, the attitude of the Section is also understandable, in the context. The basic differences of opinion had obviously to be reconciled and they were, but not in 1950.

The domestic triumphs of the Association during 1950 undoubtedly exceeded the frustrations. The extra-domestic scene was also quite bright, one of the outstanding events being the Bibliographical Services Conference with Aslib, the BNB, the Royal Society, BUCOP, and the NCL, held at Chaucer House in July when resolutions of importance were passed on comprehensive, selective, national and international bibliography, to be passed to Unesco in connection with its joint survey with the Library of Congress.[24] The conference derived at least partly from the Royal Society's scientific information conference of 1948, in which the Association had taken part, and the setting up then of working parties 'to consider points affecting libraries'.[25]

References

1. *LAR*, 52, p 7.
2. *LAR*, 53, p 16.
3. *AR* (1950), p 2R.
4. *Proceedings of the annual conference.* 1950, pp 96–9.
5. eg *LAR*, 52, p 125.
6. *Ibid*, p 11.
7. *Ibid*, pp 12, 140.
8. *Proceedings* . . . 1950, pp 9–11.
9. *LAR*, 53, p 406.
10. *LAR*, 52, pp 365–9.
11. *AR* (1947), p 10R.
12. *LAR*, 51, p 106.
13. *Proceedings* . . . 1950, pp 60–70.
14. *LAR*, 52, p 429.
15. *AR* (1950), p 9R.
16. *Ibid*, pp 14R–15R.
17. *AR* (1947), p 11R.
18. *LAR*, 52, pp 121–2.
19. *LAR*, 50, p 311.
20. *LR*, 12, pp 276–80.
21. Letter from R. J. Hoy in *LAR*, 52, p 204.
22. Minutes of Membership committee, 24.11.1949.
23. *LAR*, 52, pp 202–7, 244–8.
24. *Ibid*, pp 462–3.
25. *AR* (1949), p 12R.

Chapter Eleven

1951-1959

Organisations and associations, like ambitious human beings, need periods of meditation when the achievements of past years can be reflected upon and consolidated, and the way prepared for further development and progress. Although, as viewed from some angles, the LA period from 1951 to 1959 is one such, from others the progress seemed continuous and unimpeded. These years of mixed development also reflect personnel changes, L. R. McColvin resigning the Honorary Secretaryship at the end of 1951 in anticipation of his Presidential year[1] – to be succeeded immediately by W. A. Munford and in 1955 by W. B. Paton – and P. S. J. Welsford retiring from the Secretaryship in 1959.

The LA owes quite exceptional debts to five of its Honorary Secretaries. MacAlister, for all that he behaved too frequently in ways traditionally associated with the spoilt prima donna, formulated much higher standards than the Association was then capable of reaching but, nevertheless, drove it on to achieve much more than seemed possible. Jast coruscated with ideas and piloted the professional register. Pacy, with debonair self-assurance, carried the Association through a long period of trial and tribulation when, but for him, it might easily have disintegrated. Savage, for all his dogmatism and impatience, rebuilt the Association and gave it enduring habitation. McColvin effectively used the rebuilt Association to transform public librarianship, not only in this country but throughout the world. His conception of one type of librarianship – the municipal – as much more than *primus inter pares* was comparable

with that of Edward Edwards nearly a century earlier.
Nevertheless the new British 'tools' with which he helped
to equip it – the library schools in particular – proved infinitely
useful also to all the other types. Although it is not easy
to visualise McColvin as Honorary Secretary during the more
ecumenical period of the 1960s and 1970s, his contribution
towards making that ecumenicalism possible was very great.
Welsford helped to make *all* possible by providing the LA with
the kind of staff and office organisation which is most taken for
granted when it is most efficient. Percy Welsford was made an
Honorary Fellow in 1960; few men can ever have deserved the
honour more.

The library background throughout the country during the
1950s was one of expansion. Total public library expenditure
rose from £9m in 1950 to £16m in 1957–8,[2] and total circulation
from 314m to 432m[3] but Government restrictions on Local
Authority capital projects – which were specially severe during
the first half of the period – ensured that most of the larger
buildings completed and opened – apart from war-damage
renovations, as at Shoreditch and Plymouth – were of other
kinds of library. These were as varied as the National Libraries
of Wales and Scotland, the Scottish Central Library, the
university libraries of Leicester and Sheffield and the Northern
branch of the National Library for the Blind in Manchester.
Public library building, while still important, was mostly in the
field of inexpensive conversions and smaller branches. By the
end of the period, however, some larger public library
buildings, eg Holborn and Kensington, were nearly ready
for use.

The possibility of much greater future expansion in Scotland
was facilitated by the passing of the Public Libraries (Scotland)
Act in 1955 which at last removed the anomalous rate limits
which had persisted there despite their removal in England and
Wales in 1919, and extended powers to inter-lend and to
cooperate. The private member's bill had a hazardous and
chequered passage through the House of Commons and might
well have foundered had it not been for intensive 'lobbying' by
individual members of the LA Council and of the Scottish LA.[4]

An unusual tribute to the Association's growing maturity was the gift of £100 in 1956 from an anonymous member who

> has always been proud of his Membership and is likewise proud of the position the Association has now attained as representing British librarianship the world over.
> The intention is that the money shall be invested and the interest produced used annually for the purchase of a suitable beverage in which the Council can toast the incoming President at the first meeting of the Council over which he presides, the toast being – "To the health of the President, and to the harmony and progress of the LA."
> It is suggested that in appreciation of his services as Secretary, the toast shall include the name of Mr P. S. J. Welsford for as long as he remains in that office.[5]

It may be argued that the introduction of the new toast was apposite since some of the Association's progress, at least quantitatively, was unremarkable and its harmony incomplete. The total membership rose, during the period, only from 11,217 in 1951[6] to 12,536 in 1959[7] and the total examination entries settled down to an annual average of 6000, plus or minus a few. That membership became, nevertheless, a much more professional one; the number of chartered librarians rose from 3402 to 5202.[8] The financial situation fluctuated between indifferent and difficult. Annual income rose from £43,000 to £79,000 and expenditure from £45,000 to £75,000, the latter figure admittedly including provision, from 1954 onwards, for an average annual transfer to capital reserve of £3400. There was also the unwelcome legal obligation, from 1956 onwards, to pay local rates; up to then total exemption had been obtained by virtue of the now repealed Scientific Societies Act of 1843. The account for examination and registration activity showed only a small annual credit by the end of the present period, admittedly by intent, and the publications account a substantial deficit, granted that this was substantially due to the cost of producing and posting the *LAR* to members.[9]

Seen in retrospect the Council's embarrassed self-consciousness – as displayed in its annual reports during the 1950s – on the subject of the annual deficit on the Chaucer House kitchen account is pleasantly funny. The provision of lunches and teas for visiting members and permanent staff involved, during the nine years, a total expenditure of £18,414 and an income of £16,048, ie an annual charge on the LA's funds of £270. It was assuredly felt that provincial members might be aggrieved that income was being spent on an amenity of which they were normally deprived, although welcome to enjoy, when visiting London; insufficient attention was often paid to the alternative expenditure which would have been incurred had the facilities been withdrawn, notably at the time of Council and committee meetings and throughout the year in respect of staff teas and coffees.*

The Council enforced economy 'drives' in 1953 and 1957 and the basic annual subscription was raised from 4 to 5 guineas in 1954, with corresponding increases in the lower rates. The increases proved exceptionally controversial since the Council's proposals were only accepted as modified by an amendment moved from the floor of the 1953 Annual General Meeting, reducing the impact of the increases on those paying lower subscriptions, and causing the resignation of the Honorary Treasurer, Raymond Irwin.[10]

Two peculiarities of the Association's constitution had led to occasional differences at General Meetings. Since federation the AAL had, from time to time, mustered its voting power to defeat or amend Council proposals. Naturally enough its emphasis was likely to be strongest when the interests, or assumed or apparent interests, of the younger members were thought to be at risk. The General Meeting of June 1945 and the Annual General Meeting just referred to had been such occasions. But this cause of controversy, or at least lack of harmony, had existed only since 1929; there was another as old as the Association and inherent in the existence of institutional membership.

* Tradition had also grown up over the years. It was considered no small honour to be invited to join the 'top table' for lunch where, although the food was no different, the genial presidency of the Association's secretary, P. S. J. Welsford, and the frequent companionship of senior librarians and visitors from overseas, made such occasions pleasures to be savoured and long remembered.

Local public library authorities accepting invitations to the Association's annual conferences normally sent their librarians and chairmen or other members of library committees to represent them. All would also probably attend the annual general meetings which, although not part of the conferences, were usually, for convenience, integrated with them. Local votes would normally be cast in unison but there might, occasionally, be differences of opinion. The librarians attending could then feel, quite understandably, that since they had been sent at the expense of their local authorities and to represent them, their own voting freedoms were in jeopardy. Over the years the problem had proved much greater in potential than in reality. It was easy to exaggerate and E. A. Savage and others duly exaggerated it from time to time. But the matter came to a head at the Annual General Meeting at Southport in 1955, at a time of public debate on local government reorganisation – when a Council motion entitled 'The public library service and local government reorganisation' was tabled. This derived essentially from the McColvin Report of 1942 and the *Proposals* of 1943 and recommended, *inter alia*, the surrender of library powers to county councils by non-county authorities whose 1953–4 rateable values were less than £300,000, and the introduction of grants-in-aid, administered by a suitable government department. It was moved by McColvin and rejected by 539 votes to 311, following lively debate. Most of the minority thereupon rose to their feet and demanded a postal ballot. This was held as soon as possible thereafter and resulted in the Council's original motion being approved by 2344 votes to 1194.[11] But at the Annual General Meeting at Folkestone in the following year, not only was the resolution again revoked, on a motion from the floor; a further motion was passed, providing

That the Council . . . before making any statement or submitting any proposal to the body of its members which may directly affect the powers, constitution and boundaries of Local Authorities shall first take all reasonable steps to obtain the opinion of its Institutional Members.[12]

Two developments were now virtually inevitable – a growing determination by the Council that institutional membership, at

least in its then existing form, should be ended; and an
agitation by the authorities and libraries serving the smaller
municipal areas in favour of their continued existence.
Institutional voting rights would be ended although not during
the present period; preparations for the change were soon made,
if indirectly, by the newly displayed and increasing interest of the
local authority associations in public library matters.[13]
The propaganda activities of the newly formed Smaller Libraries
Group in England and in Wales and Monmouth were not
unsuccessful. When the second of three Government White
Papers published in 1956 and 1957 covered the redistribution of
functions as between county councils and other authorities,
public libraries were specifically excluded and a Committee
appointed by the Minister of Education

To consider the structure of the public library service in England and
Wales, and to advise what changes, if any, should be made in the
administrative arrangements, regard being had to the relation of
public libraries to other libraries.[14]

The Chairman was S. C. (later Sir Sydney) Roberts who had
been Secretary of the Cambridge University Press, Master of
Pembroke College, Cambridge and University Vice-Chancellor,
but also chairman of both the Cambridge University
and Cambridge City libraries. The other fifteen members were
broadly representative of the various types and sizes of local
authorities but also included three librarians, F. C. (later Sir
Frank) Francis of the British Museum and, nicely reminiscent of
the *Report* of 1942 and of the *Proposals* of 1943, McColvin and
Sydney. If the wheel had not yet come full circle, it was
certainly turning.

Written evidence, and some oral evidence, was submitted to the
Roberts Committee by a wide variety of local government,
educational and voluntary bodies, including groups of librarians,
and by a few individuals. In view of the many contrasted points
of view held by members of the Association and of the Council,
the compilation of the LA's own *Memorandum of evidence* (1958)
was a long and difficult task, made no easier, on the one hand, by
the uncompromising opposition of county-librarian members to

17. *Arundell Estaile* (*1880–1956*)
Editor, Library Association Record, 1923–1935

18. *L. R. McColvin (1896–1976)*
Hon. Secretary 1934–1951
President 1952

19. *P. S. J. Welsford(1893–1968)*
Secretary 1931–1959

20. *Miss L. V. Paulin*
First woman President, 1966

21. H. D. Barry
Secretary 1959–1974

22. *R. P. Hilliard*
Secretary since 1974

23. *D. D. Haslam*
Membership Officer 1948–1962
Deputy Secretary 1960–1976

24. *B. I. Palmer*
Education Officer 1948–1974

the continued existence, *inter alia*, of public library authorities
serving populations of less than 100,000 and with book-funds of
less than £28,000[15] and, on the other, by the attempt by small
library authorities, repeated up to and during the Annual
General Meeting at Brighton in September 1958, to omit all
references to minimum book-funds.[16] The resulting document,
which was therefore unexpectedly long – twenty-three pages –
was criticised soon after publication as

A manifestation of compromise rather than of leadership. Few if any
are proud of it, and it is interesting much less for its own
inconsiderable merits than because its compromises can hardly fail to
run parallel with those which the Roberts Committee must itself
inevitably consider. Faced by strong opposition to the delimiting of
minimal areas by the Local Authorities in its institutional
membership, and by some of the librarians who at present administer
the smaller units, the LA has had to argue its case obliquely. Its
Memorandum refers, *inter alia*, to the possibility of some small library
units being assimilated by some county libraries; to the possible
extension of some urban units by the inclusion of their "fringes" (ie
by taking them over from county libraries); and to possible
amalgamations and joint services. Among the firmest of other
medusal recommendations are those favouring a "supra-local source
of support and guidance" (perhaps the Ministry of Education).
It is the librarians who are in search of the support and the Local
Authorities who are least keen on the guidance.[17]

But this implied no criticism of the work of the sub-committee
responsible for drafting the *Memorandum* nor of the outstanding
achievement of its Chairman, F. M. Gardner. Their reward
came when it was evident that the Roberts Committee
recommendations were much closer to those of the LA than to
those of any other body. This applied in particular to the basic
questions of Ministerial oversight of public libraries; to the
minimum size of book-fund which, at 1958 prices, was set at
£5000 or 2*s* per head of population, whichever was the greater;
and to the need for improving staffing and buildings.[18]

Like the LA's *Memorandum*, the *Roberts Report* had an extremely
mixed reception, among both librarians and library authorities.
Criticisms were many, some of the more extreme being
pleasantly exaggerated by Sir Sydney himself when he said:

My wonder is tinged with a certain apprehension when I read that, from Lancashire in the north to Cornwall in the south, the barricades are going up, the tumbrils are rolling, and I begin to speculate whether my ultimate destiny may not be suspension from a Falmouth lamp post. . . .[19]

The repercussions of the Report were of great importance; consideration of these must stand referred to the next chapter.

The preparations of the representations to the Roberts Committee were certainly the most laborious and time-consuming of all the evidence submitted to other bodies during the present period. But they formed merely one of a considerable number. Others made included those to the Committee on Copyright (1951) with later submissions during consideration of the resulting Parliamentary Bill which became the Copyright Act of 1956 – particularly on the thorny subject of 'fair copying'; to Unesco on the organisation of international exchanges of publications (1956); to the Central Advisory Committee on education (on young people's reading) (1958); to the Ministry of Housing and Local Government on the rating of charities (1958); to the Royal Commission on local government in Greater London, and to the Consultative Committee for the National Lending Library of Science and Technology (1959), the last named being of exceptional importance as the Association was understandably highly critical of the policy proposal to give professional qualifications low priority in staff recruitment. There were also statements and reports on subjects as varied as the distribution of records of local interest and a number – reflecting long-continued interest – on the libraries and library staffs of technical colleges (1953, 1954, 1956, 1957, 1959).[20] Friendly cooperation also facilitated such matters as the continuance of funds from the Colonial Office for the Eastern Caribbean regional library,[21] and the decision, jointly with the English Association, to devote the funds collected in memory of Arundell Esdaile, to finance a public lecture on a literary or bibliographical theme.[22] The Association also continued to be represented on a wide variety of other bodies, as different from each other as the British Institute of Recorded Sound, the

Educational Puppetry Association, the Seafarers' Education
Service and the British Standards Institution as well as its now
time-honoured representation on the National Book League,
National Central Library and University College London's
school of librarianship committee.[23] The appointment of the
Association's first public relations adviser at the end of the
period was also a concession to the view that the scope for active
policy was still great.[24]

The syllabuses of the professional examinations were under
virtually continuous review during the whole of the present
period, not only because of the obvious need for regular
scrutiny, modification and updating but also because of
developing relationships with the rapidly expanding library
schools and with three other bodies with a lively interest in
Association qualifications. A substantial syllabus revision
became effective from 1956 when the Entrance examination
gave place to the First Professional examination – based on an
introductory approach to the purpose and methods of
librarianship and to the description, arrangement and use of
library stock – which was intended to set a higher standard and
to be a more searching test of ability to proceed to the
Registration examination.[25] A more important long-term,
change, began however with the introduction and establishment
of Moderating committees in 1952 and 1953. By satisfactorily
arranging, for the first time, for *regular* meetings of teachers and
examiners, not only were syllabus interpretation difficulties more
easily and quickly resolved; the cross-fertilisation of ideas was
encouraged.[26] Further opportunities of cooperation and
integration came as the Heads of the Schools began to fill
Council vacancies and to sit on the Register and Examinations
executive committee which had taken the place of the education
committee. It is reasonable to suppose that, from the point of
view of the schools, the worst effects of the system of 'external'
examining were being mitigated; their Heads were, however,
already beginning to look forward to a time when the
Association would admit to its Register graduates of a possibly
smaller number of larger library schools which had devised their
own syllabuses. This was a subject which in the 1950s, however,
was still regarded as controversial.[27]

The three other bodies interested in Association qualifications were the School Library Association, Aslib and the Local Authorities National Joint Council and its Examinations Board. In 1956 the Association and the School LA agreed to sponsor a certificate in school librarianship to be granted to teachers with a minimum of three years teaching experience and who satisfied the examiners in a written examination based on a syllabus covering a limited field of study deemed suitable for a part-time two-year course. The first examination was held in 1958.[28] The conflict with the Local Authorities Council and Board over their decision to equate only the Final examination with their own Promotion examination – referred to earlier – was resolved when, in 1951, the Registration examination was accepted as qualifying for appointments to posts graded APT I–IV.[29] Discussions with Aslib over the training of special librarians and information officers continued over a longer period and may be regarded as less conclusive.[30] An Aslib proposal in 1956 to establish a Register of Information Officers was strenuously opposed by the Association as it considered the profession too small to justify two registers which would inevitably tend to become competitive; the proposal was withdrawn in 1957.[31] The subject was, of course, closely allied to the perennial question of the university graduate in librarianship.

University graduates on municipal library staffs were still quite rare if no longer as unusual as during the pre-war period. Discussion of the subject was renewed from time to time[32] and took on a new dimension in 1954 when a decision by the NJC for local authorities staffs provided for the appointment of graduate entrants at grades APT I and II ie the lowest rungs of the professional ladder. The LA Council, while displaying sympathy,[33] was uneasy since only three years earlier it had at last, through Nalgo, been successful in persuading the NJC to provide for a minimum grading of APT III for posts held by chartered librarians supervising three other whole-time officers or the equivalent (salary then £500–£545). Although the APT III 'award' had quickly led to the up-grading of hundreds of public library posts,[34] it was soon popularly regarded as unsatisfactory and inadequate. The proximity of the grading now provided for 'raw' graduates seemed to many to depreciate dangerously the value of practical library experience and of the LA qualifications and register. Worse came when the salaries structure was revised and a new APT I applied both to the library 'award' and to graduates. Worse still came when an additional award in 1959 provided that 'the post occupied by a chartered librarian in charge of a branch or district library, or in charge of a department of a library, and supervising a staff of six other whole-time officers or the equivalent' was to be only the new APT II (ie £765–£880).

The Council was furious and protested strongly to Nalgo and to the Ministries of Education and Housing and Local Government.[35] There was, however, at least one partial, if domestic, success on the graduate front. The Council and the committee of the University and Research Section agreed in 1951 to resolve the conflict of views described in the previous chapter; this was achieved by the Committee modestly affirming

That save in appropriate circumstances it is desirable that members of University library staffs should have examination qualifications in librarianship, in addition to such academic or specialist qualifications as are necessary, and that it desires to encourage the employment in University libraries, whenever practicable, of Chartered Librarians, and the provision of facilities to enable members of University library staffs to add professional qualifications to their academic or specialist qualifications.[36]

Whatever its shortcomings the NJC award at least provided, and for the first time, a standard by which the grading of other and more senior posts could be assessed. The Association now became much more active in taking up relevant matters with Authorities advertising vacant posts at salaries considered inadequate judged by responsibilities to be carried. Local authorities were obviously mostly affected but it was possible for the Association to concern itself also with posts other than those in public libraries eg in technical college libraries. The pages of the new supplement to the *LAR*, *Liaison*, from its inception in January 1957, presented innumerable reports of protests, successes, part-successes and temporary failures. Individual examples can obviously not be dealt with here. It may be of interest, nevertheless, to tell the story of one municipal case in some detail. This Cambridge story of 1956–7 is, in some respects, reasonably representative. It has, however, one unusual feature in that the opposition to the Association's case was expressed primarily by a councillor who was a professionally unqualified, non-graduate, non-municipal library assistant, better known in local operatic circles than in the LA.

The Cambridge story began when the librarian-in-charge of the central lending library resigned his post following his appointment to the chief librarianship of another authority. The vacancy was advertised on the existing grade of APT II and applicants, including professionally unqualified local staff, were interviewed by the chairman of the library committee and the city librarian; no appointment was made as no applicant was considered suitable. Meantime the LA had written to the Local Authority suggesting a higher grading for the vacant post. The library committee then recommended up-grading to APT III to the general purposes committee and also the consequential up-grading of one comparable and another more senior post, the dissenting councillor voting against. The up-grading was then recommended to the council by the general purposes committee. At the council meeting following, the dissenting councillor moved the rejection of the recommendations, arguing that 'the present wages set-up' should not be disturbed and that local applicants should not be discouraged 'just because they lacked the necessary paper qualifications for the job'. Contributions were now made by two senior aldermen of the controlling, majority, party. The first was of the opinion that 'in a university city the library service to the public should be first class'. The second, by contrast, argued that 'it was time the council put its foot down and told outside bodies that they – the council – had a responsibility to the ratepayers . . . he could not see how any library assistant needed more than a good pair of feet and courtesy towards the public. . . .' After forty-five minutes of moving debate of unequal quality the library committee's recommendations were rejected by twenty-seven votes to nineteen.

The still-vacant post was re-advertised, applications no longer being restricted to chartered librarians. The chairman and city librarian again interviewed and still found no one suitable. This was, perhaps, hardly surprising as, following contact with the Association, four applicants had withdrawn and the only ones left were two local and professionally unqualified staff and 'one outside person at present unemployed'. The library committee again recommended the up-grading and the same male councillor again dissented, gaining the support this time of a female colleague. The general purposes committee again confirmed but now only by a bare majority. The matter came again before the council when the dissenting councillor claimed that it was being dictated to by the LA: 'a solution to the whole problem would be to reward experience and long service'. Not to be outdone, his female colleague claimed that 'the purpose of a public library was to satisfy the public and not to amass a staff with a great number of paper qualifications – it is horrifying to think that the Library Association should interfere'. The argument was now tossed this way and that, the Association's involvement being praised by some and resented by others. Zest was added when the dissenting councillor's attitude was described by another as that of 'a dog in the manger'. But at the end of another forty-five minutes' debate and an unsuccessful appeal by the chairman of the library committee, the reaffirmed recommendation was again rejected, this time by twenty-four votes to twenty-one. One of the local, professionally unqualified, applicants was subsequently appointed; some few years later the post *was* re-graded and a chartered librarian appointed to it. The dogs bark; the caravan goes on.[37]

The attempts of the Association to obtain negotiated salary scales for chief (municipal and county) librarians were completely unsuccessful and, for lack of a standard other than the original APT III award, approaches to local authorities necessarily lacked precision, bearing in mind always that the Association could discipline neither the Authorities nor its own members; both had to be persuaded. The responsibility for protest action was transferred in 1959 to the Society of Municipal and County Chief Librarians[38], which had been formed in 1948 at a time when it was felt that a body other than the LA, and a certificated trade union at that, might be better able to conduct negotiations with representatives of the local authorities if and when these became possible.

The Association's publishing services to members were as important as ever. The *LAR* continued to appear monthly; careful examination of the files for the years now under review may remind older librarians and reveal to their younger colleagues that this was a journal whose contents reached high standards at the time of publication and which remains an indispensable record of things past. Individual members of the Association grumble, of course, at their professional journal and fault such of its articles and regular features as have little appeal for *them*, just as their predecessors have criticised it since it began to appear in 1899. But in truth each editor from Esdaile onwards has been able to modify the *LAR*, to reshape it nearer to his desire, and to improve it. W. B. Stevenson and his successor from 1953, A. J. Walford (Librarian, Ministry of Defence), had no reasons to be dissatisfied with their respective achievements and when J. D. Reynolds (Librarian, Finchley Public Libraries) took over from Walford at the end of the present period, he inherited a post of which any occupant had good reason to be proud. Walford, too, was responsible for the successful suggestion that the Association inaugurate an annual prize essay competition.[39] But it is not – and never has been – easy, in one monthly magazine, to satisfy the needs and wishes of all kinds of librarian since these range from Association members who enjoy most a journal comparable with those published by eminently and entirely learned societies to others seeking much lighter fare. A tolerably successful compromise began in 1957 when each monthly issue was published with a supplement, *Liaison*, going to press later and compiled on more popular and 'newsy' lines and with different editors from the main journal.

The other serials also continued. The delay in publishing the annual volumes of the *Subject index to periodicals* was not only very substantially reduced but from 1954 onwards it appeared as a quarterly, with annual cumulations. Some regional lists were also introduced a year later. The situation when T. Rowland Powel retired from the editor's chair in 1959 was indeed better than it had ever been. The quarterly issues of *Library science abstracts* also proceeded satisfactorily but, as has been normal experience with Association serials over the years, the subscription list of libraries for whom it was primarily intended was built up extremely slowly; if more interest had been practically displayed earlier, it would have been unnecessary to control the size of the quarterly issues quite so strictly. The volumes of the *Year's work in librarianship* for 1947 to 1950 were also published between 1951 and 1954, being now edited by W. A. Munford, but *Library science abstracts* now existing, it was felt by 1952 that there was a strong case for a substitute which would review the work of a substantially longer period. The *Year's work* was discontinued after the volume for 1950 had appeared and the first volume of *Five years' work in librarianship,* covering the years 1951 to 1955, and edited by P. H. Sewell, was published in 1958.

The successive editions of the *Student's handbook* appeared with admirable regularity each January. The *Year book,* by contrast, was never published earlier than April and was frequently delayed until May. This was doubtless regrettable, bearing in mind that the Association's year, like the western calendar, runs from January to December but, remembering always the near-incredible number of detailed changes in each year's list of members, it was hardly reprehensible.

Some of the other major publications of the present period, in addition to J. L. Thornton's *Classics of librarianship* – short biographies of outstanding librarians, with selected extracts from their writings – had close links with earlier ones. There were new editions of Esdaile's *National libraries of the world,* completely revised by F. J. Hill (First edition, Grafton, 1934) and of his LA Manual of 1931, *A Student's handbook of bibliography*; R. Stokes' revision of 1954 retained the greater part of the original test with rearrangement and updating. There was one entirely new Manual, J. P. Lamb's *Commercial and technical libraries* (1955). There were also the second (1951) and third (1956) editions of A. D. Roberts' exceptionally successful *Introduction to reference books* of which the first has already been noted; the far too early death of the gifted author

regrettably precluded further revisions by the same hand.
A. J. Walford's *Guide to reference material* (1959) may be regarded
as effective successor to Minto's *Reference books* of thirty years
earlier just as the three volumes of *Books for young people*
(1952–1957), edited by H. M. McGill, E. Osborne and others
succeeded Nowell's *Books to read* (1931) and Sayers' *Books for
youth* (1936). Other new publications of importance were
Cataloguing principles and practice, edited by M. Piggott, and
J. L. Thornton's and R. Tully's *Scientific books, libraries and
collectors,* a bibliographical approach to the history of science.

The Association awarded its Carnegie Medal each year from 1951
to 1959, winners including Mary Norton's *The Borrowers* (1952),
Eleanor Farjeon's *Little bookroom* (1955) and Philippa Pearce's
Tom's midnight garden (1958). The new Kate Greenaway Medal
was introduced in 1955 for the artist considered to have
produced the most distinguished work in the illustration of
children's books during the preceding year. No awards were
made in 1955 and 1958 as no books were considered suitable.
Edward Ardizzone (*Tim all alone*) was honoured in 1956,
V. H. Drummond (*Mrs Easter and the storks*) in 1957 and
W. Stobbs (*Kashtanka* and *A Bundle of ballads*) in 1959. The
practice of making tape-recordings of the voices, not only of
the medallists, but also of senior members of the profession, was
a notable innovation of the period.[40]

One of the largest publications of the 1950s was the 519-page
Catalogue of the library (1958), recording the stock on 1 March
1956. This was timely for not only did it indicate that the stock
had risen to nearly 20,000 books, pamphlets and volumes of
periodicals; it was also an indirect reminder that, since October
1954, following the termination of the lease of the third floor
rooms at Chaucer House held by the Society of Genealogists,
the library had been situated there and no longer in its cramped
accommodation on the floor above. Provision was now made,
not merely for much better facilities for users, but also for
expansion of an indispensable service to members which had
been growing and developing steadily since the original
move into Chaucer House.[41] During 1959, when the Librarian,
D. C. Henrik Jones, retired,[42] three thousand readers,

including many from overseas, made use of the improved facilities. By then, too, the stock had reached nearly 25,000 and was spilling over on to every other floor of the building and into the basement. It had become in fact a reminder to the Council and to members visiting headquarters that their own library, like others, was outgrowing its accommodation. But then the Association was outgrowing Chaucer House.

By the middle 1950s Chaucer House, after twenty years of heavy wear and tear, accentuated by war strain and damage, was not only being outgrown; it was beginning to show its age. This was hardly surprising since the use of it for Association meetings of every description had been extremely heavy. By good fortune its situation, like that of the National Central Library, within the expanding campus of University College, made it inevitable that the University of London would, sooner or later, seek to acquire the buildings for college purposes. After protracted discussions, spread over years rather than months, an offer was made by the University in March 1958[43] and, a year later, the Association, the National Central Library and the University signed an agreement for the exchange of the buildings for new properties to be erected on a site in nearby Store Street – Ridgmount Street.[44]

It is difficult, in an historical survey such as this, to study in detail both the central and also the local and more specialised activities of the Association. Most attention has been, and must continue to be, devoted to the central organisation; the work of the already complete Branch system and of the growing Sectional network must, however, also be referred to. Some Branches were, as always, more active than others, some more cooperative with the local AAL Divisions. The arrival of a few enthusiastic and forward-looking young librarians in any given parts of the country has more than once revitalised Branches. All continued to provide opportunities for professional meetings and conferences in various parts of their areas and some issued news-letters and/or specialised bibliographies.

The old established Sections were also notably active during the period. The County Libraries Section arranged conferences and week-end schools, published statistical surveys, a valuable new series of *Readers' guides* and a *Report on county library transport* (1954) issued by the Association as one of its *Pamphlets*. The University and Research Section cooperated notably with the new Standing Conference of National and University libraries (SCONUL) and acquired a Colleges of Technical and Further Education Sub-section which soon began to add sub-groups unto itself. The Medical Section encouraged the formation of the London medical libraries cooperation scheme and was largely responsible for the very successful First International Congress on Medical Librarianship in 1953.

The most spectacular sectional development came, however, with the rapid growth of the Reference and Special (subsequently the Reference, Special and Information) Section which had been formed at the very end of the previous period. During its first ten years of most vigorous life it not only arranged meetings, conferences and annual lectures; it began to work effectively through various groups to attempt to solve some of the problems experienced by the special library, eg by issuing union lists of periodicals and directories and by stimulating cooperation, not only between special libraries but also between them and public libraries. The successful experiments in and growth of regional information services in particular owe much to the enthusiasm of members of this new Section. In this and other ways the Section made its own very substantial contribution towards the more ecumenical Association of the 1960s and 1970s.[45]

References

1. *AR* (1951), p 2R.
2. *Roberts report*, p 36.
3. *AR* (1958), p 2R.
4. *See* eg W. B. Paton, 'The Public Libraries (Scotland) Act, 1955', *LAR*, 57, pp 269–270.
5. *LAR*, 58, pp 434, 436.
6. *AR* (1951), p 8R.
7. *AR* (1959), p 8.
8. *Ibid*, p 11.
9. eg *AR* (1958), pp 32R–33R.
10. Statement by R. Irwin in *LAR*, 55 pp 190–1.
11. *LAR*, 57, pp 314–5, 440–1.
12. *LAR*, 58, p 435.
13. eg *Liaison*, March, 1958, p 119.
14. S. C. Roberts, 'Some reflections on the Roberts report', *Proceedings of the Annual conference, 1959*, pp 30–37.
15. *Liaison*, March 1958, pp 117–8.
16. *Liaison*, October 1958, pp 182–3.

17. W. A. Munford, 'Library administration in Great Britain', *Library Trends* 7, p 372.
18. *Roberts report,* pp 28–90.
19. *Ibid,* pp 30–7.
20. Full list in 'Policy statements: standards of service and memoranda of evidence produced by the LA from 1942 to 1972; an annotated bibliography', LA *Library and information bulletin,* no 19, pp 2–18.
21. AR (1953), p 3R.
22. AR (1959), p 3.
23. eg *Ibid,* pp 13–20.
24. *Ibid,* p 3.
25. L*A*R, 57, p 28; AR (1955), p 9R.
26. L*A*R, 55, p 71; AR (1953), p 7R.
27. *See* eg R. Stokes, 'The future of British Library Schools', L*A*R, 56, pp 7–10; and correspondence resulting, pp 98–103, 138–9.
28. L*A*R, 58, pp 273–4.
29. AR (1951), pp 11R–12R.
30. L*A*R, 58, pp 314–5.

31. AR (1957), p 9R.
32. Notably by D. J. Foskett, 'The Graduate in librarianship', L*A*R, 57, pp 213–8.
33. eg L*A*R, 56, p 91.
34. AR (1951), p 9R.
35. *Liaison,* February 1959, pp 9–10.
36. Minutes of Membership committee, 24.5.1951 (Minute 16).
37. *Liaison,* April 1957, pp 28–9; *Cambridge Daily News* 1.12.1956, p 11; 18.1.1957 *p* 6.
38. *Liaison,* February 1959.
39. L*A*R, 56, p 5.
40. AR (1958), p 8R.
41. AR (1954), p 4R.
42. AR (1959), p 3.
43. AR (1958), p 2R.
44. AR (1959), p 4.
45. References to the various activities of the Branches and Sections will be found in the 2 vols of *Five years' work in librarianship* (ie 1951–5 and 1956–60), both edited by P. H. Sewell.

Chapter Twelve

1960-1969

The present period, from 1960 to 1969, reflected, in miniature, a steadily accelerating and inflationary national expansion. It was for the Association, as for the nation, a time of spectacular growth and ever-increasing expectation, and throughout the country as well as at headquarters. That expansion, too, still seems immense when it is remembered that in one general activity – professional education – and in another and more specialised one – public library development – the LA began to 'hive off' substantial and quite unprecedented quantities of its erstwhile responsibilities. They were 'hived off', in addition, to other bodies over which the Association might exercise significant influence but over which it had no overall control.

It fell to the new Secretary, H. D. Barry, who succeeded P. S. J. Welsford following the latter's retirement in 1959, to design the essential framework for the expansion. His design was set out in detail in two reorganisation reports submitted, at its request, to the Council.[1]

Seen in retrospect the Barry reports were political in the sense that 'politics is the art of the possible'. He first argued the case for the LA to become a wholly professional association. This inevitably brought under review the established voting rights and the representation on the Council of two categories of member – the Authorities or institutional members, and the unqualified or only partly qualified junior members whose status had been underwritten by the 1929 agreement with the AAL to which reference has been made earlier.

The second Barry report was concerned much more with the internal structure of the Association and with the need to eliminate the remaining public library bias while still maintaining a unitary in preference to a federal constitution. This, he felt, could be facilitated by restructuring the Council's committees and in particular by setting up three new ones ie Public Libraries, Special Libraries, and National and University Libraries. These were, however, not to be seen merely as net additions to the committee list since three of the existing ones, ie Membership, Finance and House and Library, were to disappear although immediately to be resurrected as a sub-committee of the Executive committee. The committees controlling education, publications, and library research were to continue on familiar lines. The creation of the three new committees also provided the opportunity to discontinue most of the existing Sectional representation on the Council, the Sections themselves to be renamed Groups. Provision was also made for the abolition of the office of Honorary Secretary; the view was expressed that the Chairman of the Executive Committee could act more satisfactorily as the Association's 'Prime Minister' since he could call more readily and directly on the support of his committee for confirmation of his actions. The Council also decided to abolish the office of Honorary Legal Adviser.

Members of the Association were given reasonable opportunity to discuss the Barry proposals after they had been substantially approved in principle by the Council. The views of Branches, Sections and of individual members were taken fully into account as also were those of other bodies directly or indirectly concerned, the local authority associations in particular.* The reorganisation programme was then formulated into a complicated series of bye-law revisions which passed the

* One interesting result of the changes was the ending of the Association's rôle as third party in the Joint advisory committee with the Publishers and Booksellers to authorise the issue of library licenses under the Net Book Agreement. That rôle had now to be assumed by the local authority, etc, associations.

Annual General Meeting at Hastings in 1961, not without
controversy, the quantity of which was not unreasonable in the
light of the magnitude of the changes. Barry himself initiated a
morning discussion prior to the formal consideration of the
bye-law revision on the afternoon of 20 September.[2] Privy
Council approval followed.

1962 was, then, the Association's first year as a wholly
professional association, aiming more than ever to attract
members from all types of library and with ultimate control
vested now in the chartered librarians, due provision being made
for established voting rights. It heralded substantial growth.
Total membership rose from 14,585 in 1962 to 17,331 by the end
of the period, chartered librarians increasing in numbers from
6066 to 9766.[3] It must be admitted, however, that, while
significant numbers of members of the staffs of academic
libraries joined the Association, the reaction of workers in the
industrial and commercial fields was still extremely
disappointing. The attractions of Aslib and of the new
Institute of Information Scientists proved much stronger.[4] The
increase in individual memberships was, however, in some
respects, less significant than the proliferation of new Groups.
The full list of new foundations is of special interest:

1962 Hospital Libraries and Handicapped Readers
1963 Library History
1964 Sound Recordings (Renamed Audio-Visual Group from
      1973)
1965 Branch and Mobile Libraries
1965 Cataloguing and Indexing
1966 Rare Books
1968 International and Comparative Librarianship
1969 Two sub-sections of the old established University and
      Research Section (founded in 1929), which itself became
      the University, College and Research Section in 1966,
      'hived off' as the Colleges, Institutes and Schools of
      Education, and the Colleges of Technical and Further
      Education.[5]

One further change may be noted. As from 1963 the Council

arranged a short Annual Conference at which the Annual
Lecture was delivered and the Annual General Meeting held. A
quite separate Public Libraries Conference, very much on the
lines of the old conferences, was also arranged, but later in the
year.[6]

The steady expansion in the country was reflected by a
considerable expansion of the headquarters staff, notably by the
appointment of a Deputy and two Assistant secretaries.[7] Staff
expansion was greatly facilitated by the move from Chaucer
House to 7 Ridgmount Street in 1965.

The agreement with the University of London had provided
that the new building, to be erected at the cost of the University,
was to be 'in reasonable substitution' for the old.
Arrangements were also made, however, for it to be
considerably larger, the cost difference, estimated at £80,000 to
£100,000, to be met by the Association from its accumulated
reserves.[8]

When 7 Ridgmount Street was inspected it was found to provide
much better and more spacious accommodation than at Chaucer
House.[9] As a building it proved reasonably successful in
providing offices for an expanding staff, committee rooms and
council chamber, members' room, enormously improved library
accommodation, together with some upper floor space available,
at least temporarily, to let to the University.*

The new building was considered to 'work' satisfactorily, with
the exception of the very disappointing Council chamber. It
must be admitted, however, that the building as a whole has
been considered ponderous. Indeed, had its architect been Sir
John Vanbrugh, then the mock epitaph on the latter might
surely have been justified anew:

Lie heavy on him earth for he
Laid many heavy loads on thee.

* Is it possible that, at some future date, the University – intent on the expansion of its 'campus', may seek to provide the Association with yet another building, 'in reasonable substitution'?

Association expansion was particularly noteworthy in the field of publishing, an average of ten new books and seven reprints or new editions being issued each year. But averages conceal many individual variations – five new and three reprint titles were in fact published in 1960, ten new and nine reprints in 1963, twenty-one new and nine reprints in 1966, the peak year, and thirteen new and fourteen reprints in 1969. Even granted a stabilised annual output, then the progress of inflation – assuming that publication prices did no more than reflect increased production costs – would have led to a substantially higher sales figure in 1969 than in 1960. Yet the total sales of 1969 – £127,000 – still contrasts remarkably with that for 1960 – £27,000.

It was a remarkable achievement to have so successfully built up production and sales that, by 1969, not only was the cost of the *LAR* being borne by the publications account; there was still a surplus of nearly £9,000.[10] The credit may be shared by the Association's Publications committee and by their officer, F. J. Cornell, and his staff. In order to exploit the market potential still further the new post of Manager of Publications was created in 1968, Mr Ian Wilkes being the first holder.[11]

A few of the outstanding new titles published during the period were M. F. Thwaite *From primer to pleasure: an introduction to the history of children's books: Hospital libraries and work with the disabled,* edited by Mona Going, and W. A. Munford *Edward Edwards: portrait of a librarian,* all in 1963; A. J. Walford *Guide to foreign language grammars and dictionaries* in 1964 (second edition 1969), T. Kelly *Early public libraries: a history of public libraries in Great Britain before 1850* in 1966 and Alison Shaw *Print for partial sight* in 1969. There were also two Festschriften – *The Sayers memorial volume,* edited by D. J. Foskett and B. I. Palmer, in 1961, the royalties on which were used partly to endow a memorial prize for classification, and *Libraries for the people: international studies in librarianship in honour of LR McColvin,* edited by R. F. Vollans in 1968. Another title which was specially welcome was published in 1967. This was the British text of the *Anglo-American cataloguing rules,* prepared jointly by the Association and by the American Library Association, the

Canadian Library Association and the Library of Congress. This
was a revised and expanded edition of the 1908 Code referred to
earlier and was the crowning achievement of committees which,
apart from the years of World War Two, had been steadily at
work since 1936. Many individual librarians contributed, led as
chairman until 1961 by J. D. Stewart and subsequently by
N. F. Sharp.[12] There were also two volumes of *Library buildings*,
the 1966 (1968) volume edited by J. D. Reynolds and that for
1967–8 (1969) by S. G. Berriman. The second and greatly
enlarged edition of A. J. Walford *Guide to reference material*
began with Volume One 'Science and technology' in 1966 and
continued with Volume Two 'Social and historical sciences,
philosophy and religion' in 1969.

The serial publications developed in promising fashion. As
noted earlier, the *Year's work* was not issued after the volume for
1950 had appeared in 1954; the second and third volumes of
Five years' work in librarianship, both edited by P. H. Sewell, were
published during the present period, that covering 1956–1960 in
1963 and the successor for 1961–1965 in 1968. The *Subject index
to periodicals*, which had had so chequered a history during
earlier years, was now well established. From 1962 onwards it
excluded technical journals and was renamed *British humanities
index*. A new serial, *British technology index,* began publication in
the same year and was favourably received from the outset. This
was specially satisfying, bearing in mind the failure of earlier
technical indexes issued by other organisations and the
scepticism of DSIR on the need for this one.[13] Although initial
costs exceeded the estimates and its financial situation was not
satisfactory until 1966, by the end of the period the production
and sales account of *British technology index*, thanks largely to the
editor E. J. Coates, was in satisfactory surplus. The *British
education index*, compiled by the librarians of the British institutes
of education and published on their behalf by the Association,
began to appear in 1962. *Library science abstracts* became *Library
and information science abstracts* in 1969 being now produced in
cooperation with Aslib. One final inflationary note may be
introduced. The Association's own *Year book*, which continued
annual publication throughout the period, although without the
usual list of members in 1965, was sold to members in 1969 at

30*s* (£1 · 50). This was indeed a far cry from the 2*s* 6*d* (12½p) of twenty years earlier.

The editorship of the *Record* was taken over from J. D. Reynolds by Edward Dudley in 1967. As noted earlier, some librarians – like practioners in other professions – may criticise and belittle their official journal and assume airily that most of the copies distributed to members quickly find their way into the nearest waste paper baskets. But in hard fact the *Record* continued to maintain very high standards, and published a wide variety of useful and original material, much of it, admittedly and understandably, of interest primarily only to *some* librarians. In view of the ever broadening and widening profession this was surely inevitable. But the *Library Association Record* also continued to be an indispensable *journal of record*, a role which Esdaile never succeeded in imparting to it, despite his many other successes as editor from 1923 to 1935, but to which all his successors from R. D. Hilton Smith onwards have notably contributed. Dudley also acted as Chairman of the Editorial board of a new quarterly, *Journal of librarianship* which, aiming to print articles and reviews which were sometimes too long and sometimes too specialised for the *Record*, began its life in 1969 and quickly achieved a circulation of more than 1000.[14]

All these publications, those noted and the others – books, pamphlets, periodicals and miscellaneous items – made their special contributions towards equipping librarians with appropriate tools of their trade and the wider public with essential bibliographic and other information. Further contributions were made by the Branches and Groups, the issue twice yearly since 1967, by the Library History group, of *Library History* being an outstanding example. In the editorial hands of P. A. Hoare this magazine enjoyed a world reputation by the end of the period. The contribution made by the London and Home Counties Branch was more unusual. In a new kind of collaborative enterprise with the old established library firm of Cedric Chivers Ltd, the Branch began to sponsor in 1963 a series of 'Portway' reprints of out-of-print books,[15] mostly, at least initially, of popular titles likely to appeal to public library buyers; the venture proved useful to the libraries and remunerative for the projectors.

The Association's secretariat – for staff expansion now justified the new nomenclature – was responsible for a wide variety of statements, memoranda and recommendations, designed, *inter alia*, to establish standards and to persuade other bodies to improve or facilitate the improvement of library services. Bodies memorialised were as different as the House of Commons,[16] the Parry Committee on Libraries,[17] the Reviewing Committee on the Export of Works of Art,[18] and the Open University.[19] Not least important were two brief paragraphs set out in the *Annual Report* for 1963:

The function of the library service is to provide, so far as resources allow, all books, periodicals etc, other than the trivial, in which its readers claim legitimate interest. In determining what is a legitimate interest the librarian can safely rely upon one guide only – the law of the land. If the publication of such matter has not incurred penalties under the law it should not be excluded from libraries on any moral, political, religious or racial ground alone, or to satisfy any sectional interest. The public are entitled to rely upon libraries for access to information and enlightenment upon every field of human experience and activity. Those who provide library services should not restrict this access except by standards which are endorsed by the law.[20]

The consistent opposition of the Association over its first century to the thorny subject of censorship is something of which it has every reason to be proud.

Continuing and unrelenting pressure by the secretariat was also brought to bear on the employing authorities to improve the salaries and conditions of service of members of their library staffs. In the local government field it was still not possible to achieve nationally approved salary scales for chief librarians although substantial improvements for those in Northern Ireland were obtained in 1967.[21] It must be admitted, overall, that the major improvements for staffs were obtained, *via* Nalgo, and as part of improved salaries and conditions for all local governments staffs. Special concessions were gained in 1968 when provision was made for enhanced payments for those working outside normal office hours; these were obviously of special benefit to public library staffs.[22] But the introduction of a new Trainee grade in 1966, dividing the professions into two groups and placing librarians in the lower grade, caused grave dissatisfaction.[23] As to individual approaches, the LA's Annual reports show that requests for salary and other improvements were made to a yearly average of fifteen Authorities, including local authorities, and that nearly half of them could ultimately be reported as successful or part-successful. It had become clearly noticeable also that the Association was now operating with confidence, and with considerable success, in the fields of university and college and special libraries as well as in the public library one.

The Association continued to award its Carnegie and Kate Greenaway Medals, examples of the winners of the former being Lucy Boston *Stranger at Green Knowe* (1961), Hester Burton *Time of trial* (1963) and Kathleen Peyton *Edge of the cloud* (1969) and, of the latter, Brian Wildsmith *ABC* (1962), Raymond Briggs *Mother Goose treasury* (1966) and Pauline Baynes' illustrations to *Dictionary of chivalry* (1968).[24] These awards were by now very highly regarded, certainly by the publishers concerned, to judge by no more than their subsequent press advertising.

Two further medals were introduced during the period. The most aptly named Wheatley Medal was awarded from 1962 onwards for an outstanding index first published in the United Kingdom during the preceding three years. This new award could obviously claim a catchment area infinitely wider than those for the earlier medals; the awards were sufficiently varied to include J. M. Dickie *How to catch trout*, 3rd edition (1963), Alison Quinn *Hakluyt's principal navigations* (1965), and Doreen Blake and Ruth Bowden *Index to the Journal of anatomy 1866–1966* (1968).[25] The Robinson Medal, on the other hand, was to be awarded every other year, following its inauguration in 1968

to reward the originality and inventive ability of librarians and other interested persons or firms in connection with devising new and improved methods in library technology and any aspect of library administration.

In 1968 it went to Mansell Information/Publishing Ltd for their development of an automatic abstracting camera for use in producing book catalogues from library cards etc.[26] The Robinson Medal is of unusual interest as it was funded with a bequest of £1225 from Fred Robinson, sometime Deputy Librarian of Colchester Public Library.[27] Benefactions of this kind, indeed benefactions of any kind, have been rare and unusual events in the LA's history. Two others were, however, made during the present period. In 1966 the Association received the residue, amounting to more than £2000, of the estate of Miss K. E. Pierce (1873–1966), Librarian of Kettering Public Library from 1896 to 1939 who, as noted in an earlier chapter, had been, in 1915, the first woman member of the Council.[28] In 1963 Mr A. J. Cawthorne bequeathed the dividends on shares in his bookbinding firm in memory of his father, Albert Cawthorne (1871–1958), Librarian of Stepney Public Libraries from 1901 to 1936, to provide an annual prize for the student gaining the highest marks in Part 1 of the professional examinations.[29]

Although the Association's own library should, ideally, always have provided the quantity and quality of service which it sought to encourage in other authorities, financial stringency and acute lack of space had, during past years, made exemplary activity of this kind extremely difficult. Indeed, although the will was certainly not lacking, at the beginning of the present period the hopelessly overcrowded accommodation at Chaucer House was a chronic handicap. The move to Ridgmount Street made infinitely more possible. The new accommodation on the ground floor and in the basement was much more attractive, commodious and comfortable for readers and more convenient for the staff and stock. By 1968 the staff had been increased to ten; 12,000 books and 1750 periodicals were being borrowed annually and – a token of growth – the number of periodicals currently received had risen to 830.

The total annual cost of maintaining the Association's library and information service rose from £8433 in 1959 to £36,000 in 1969, the increase reflecting not only the progress of inflation, but, even more, the growing significance of the service and particularly of the information bureau as an indispensable part of the national information centre on librarianship which the Association was providing from its own funds. The publication since 1967 of the LA's *Library and information bulletin* underlined the course of development. By the end of the period the success of that development was open to so little doubt that the Council inevitably found itself forced to consider seeking a Government grant-in-aid.[30] Such aid was to come in due course but not in the form originally envisaged and not during this period.

The value of a good library for purposes of research needs no emphasis. But there is a great deal more to it than this. The growing maturity of a profession may be assessed by various criteria, not the least significant being its attitude to research into its own past, present and future. Reference has already been made to the establishment of the Association's Library Research committee in 1946. A new and much more positive approach became apparent from 1960 onwards when, at the suggestion of D. J. Foskett, the Council began to make money available and in support of suitable projects; it also began to approach the fund-granting foundations. The appointment of a Research Officer (M. Yelland) in 1964 may be regarded as underwriting the success of a new departure[31] just as the formation of the Advisory board on research in 1969 consolidated it. Some of the early grants, such as those for Mrs M. Toase's compilation of a detailed guide to British periodicals,[32] and the survey of existing charging systems,[33] were naturally modest but by 1964 it had proved possible, for example, to attract a grant of £10,000 from the Viscount Nuffield Auxiliary Fund to study the problems of reading matter for those with defective sight. With the aid of this grant Miss Alison Shaw was employed for two years to produce – for publication in 1969 – the important, indeed epoch-making, report already referred to, *Print for partial sight*. Miss Shaw was subsequently appointed to study future needs in the field of writing and reading aids for the disabled, the Association now receiving a grant from a committee of the National Fund for research into crippling diseases.[34]

From 1968 onwards the *Year book* included a feature 'Research in progress'. The first list gave details of more than one hundred

projects then in progress by organisations and individuals.
Many of them were admittedly being sponsored by organisations
other than the Association, notably, of course, by universities;
some of the specially interesting entries were in description of
projects sponsored jointly by the Association and other
important bodies such as F. M. Gardner's 'Study and
comparison of international library law' with Unesco, and
Mrs R. J. Roth's 'Survey of collections of economic statistics in
United Kingdom libraries and other institutions', with the
Royal Statistical Society.[35] Examination of the complete list
suggests inevitably to the reader not only that the profession of
librarianship was indeed coming of age but also that research
was enhancing professional education.[36] And professional
education was itself undergoing changes of considerable interest.

The substantially revised syllabus of 1956 was soon again under
review. It was still felt by some to reflect excessively the
part-time needs of the past. It was also considered insufficiently
in touch with current needs – a not uncommon criticism of
syllabi; was regarded as still too public-library biased and hence
narrow and inflexible; and paid insufficient attention to
knowledge of books. The further argument that it provided for
examining in the same subjects but at different levels was
perhaps the least convincing.

The unsuccessful Aslib proposal in 1953 to initiate a quite
separate qualification for industrial and technical librarians led to
a committee of the two associations in 1955 to attempt a suitable
revision of the 1950 syllabus. The LA then set up its own
Syllabus sub-committee in 1957 – fully representative of the
schools of librarianship as well as of practising librarians –
which began a thorough overhaul. The discussions, and the
opportunities given for expressions of opinion by Branches,
Groups and individual members were more far-reaching than on
any earlier occasions and the new syllabus was introduced, not
without controversy, in 1964.[37] In fairness, however, to those
who had passed or been exempted from parts of the 1950
Final examination, those members could still sit this
examination until 1968.[38]

In 1969, at the end of the present period, admission to the Register of Chartered Librarians could be obtained by LA members of two years' standing who had passed the professional examination, and who had completed three years' full-time service, one of which could have been spent on a full-time librarianship course at a school, and at least one of which must have elapsed after passing the examinations. The additional need for a GCE pass at O level in a language other than English or in a science was dropped in 1969. The Entrance examination had also been discontinued and there were now three examinations, two of these being the revised versions of the Registration and Final of 1950 renamed – following contemporary trends – Parts I and II. The third examination provided an alternative for those who had already graduated – this was the Postgraduate Professional examination, introduced in 1966. English and Welsh candidates for the Part I examination had to produce evidence of success in the General Certificate of Education in five subjects, of which one was in English language and two at Advanced level; comparable qualifications were required from those whose school education had taken place in Scotland or Northern Ireland.

The Part I examination consisted of four papers of three hours each, all to be taken at one and the same sitting, in:

i   The library and the community (ie the kinds of library and their history; cooperation; professional and other associations, etc)
ii   Government and control of libraries (including management, finance, staffing, stock control, reader access)
iii   The organisation of knowledge (ie classification, cataloguing and indexing)
iv   Bibliographical control and service (including the selection of library materials)

Part II consisted of a minimum of six papers of three hours each, to be sat together or separately and in any order, one paper being selected from List A and one or more papers from each of lists B and C:

List A
1. Academic and legal deposit libraries
2. Special libraries and information bureaux
3. Public (municipal and county) libraries

List B
11. Theory of classification
12. Theory of cataloguing
13. Practical classification and cataloguing
21. Bibliography
22. History of libraries and librarianship
31. Handling and dissemination of information
32. Library service for young people in schools and public libraries
33. Hospital libraries
91. Archive administration and records management
92. Palaeography and archives

List C
Consisting of an approved list of alternatives covering a very wide field from the bibliography and librarianship of a wide range of subjects from Old and Middle English to Archaeology and Ancient history, and from Electrical engineering to the Caribbean region.

It was clear that the new syllabus was not only grounded on the accumulated practice and experience of the past; better provision than ever before was now being made for the non-public and specialist librarian.

The Postgraduate Professional Examination was essentially a condensed version of Parts I and II, consisting of five compulsory and two optional papers, two of the compulsory ones being assessed on the results of examined course work; the whole examination was available only to those attending Schools of librarianship, normally on one-year courses. But, in fact, although it was still not compulsory for those sitting Parts I and II to have attended a full-time course, most examinees by 1969 would have done so.[39]

The professional examinations now led to the Associateship

(ALA). Progress to the FLA was now normally possible only through the submission of a thesis, the second and up to date the most successful reintroduction of which was an outstanding feature of the new syllabus. As, however, the full effects of this change were not felt until the later part of the present period, consideration of the thesis may be conveniently deferred to the next chapter.

The most revolutionary changes came now, however, not through syllabus revision but through the gradual introduction of internal examining – seen in retrospect as an eventually unavoidable consequence of the establishment of schools of librarianship. But in view of the Association's past insistence, before and after World War Two, on complete responsibility for the system of professional examining, this meant a completely new approach. It began gradually.

During 1966, following reports by visitors appointed by the Association and the satisfactory establishment of minimum standards of school staffing, accommodation and service, permission to conduct the Part I examination, *on behalf of the Association*, was granted to the Schools at Leeds, at the North Western Polytechnic, and at the College of Librarianship Wales, at Aberystwyth.[40] The Birmingham School followed suit in 1968 and Manchester in 1969. The North Western Polytechnic then pioneered the extension to Part II also, in 1968, and Aberystwyth quickly followed.[41] If such an analogy is permissible then these changes reflected one revolution within another. The substantial expansion of the Schools coincided with another major educational development resulting in the creation of the new Polytechnics and the establishment of the Council for National Academic Awards with responsibility for the first non-university degrees. By the end of the present period CNAA degrees in librarianship were being offered by the Leeds, Birmingham, Manchester and Newcastle Schools. The postgraduate diplomas of Strathclyde, Sheffield and Belfast (Queen's) Universities were also granted the same recognition as those of the pioneer School at University College, London. A further elaboration of the now ever increasingly complicated pattern was caused by the introduction of university degrees in librarianship. From 1967 those holding the new degree of BA of the University of Strathclyde, with librarianship as first principal study, were exempted from the Association's professional examinations. Similar treatment was given to the First and Master's degrees in librarianship to be offered by Loughborough University of Technology, in collaboration with the School at Loughborough Technical College.[42] Yet another permutation was provided by Aberystwyth which arranged, with the University of Wales, to introduce a joint honours degree in librarianship.[43]

Another change during the period – at the other end of the academic scale, so to speak – must also be noted. Although the view was not infrequently expressed that a sub-professional examination and certificate for service staff might undermine the status of chartered librarian, a majority of the Council felt that the advantages of having a service test of this kind were greater than the possible drawbacks, provided always that the qualification was awarded by a body other than the Association. Discussions with the City and Guilds of London Institute resulted in a syllabus and examination scheme which received Council support in July 1966; the qualification was accordingly introduced.[44]

Within the space of a few short years the scope for professional qualification in librarianship had become – judged by the standards of the past – almost unbelievably variegated. There seemed, in fact, to be a new and very real danger that the Association's own responsibilities might be seriously undermined. But thanks to the close and cordial relationships between the Association and the schools and, overall, to the effective influence of the LA's Education officer, B. I. Palmer, the risks were probably smaller than might otherwise have been the case. A pessimist might argue, nevertheless, that the trends in professional education meant that the Association was risking school developments comparable with those experienced in the United States two generations earlier. But the risks have at least been taken in the knowledge – if not necessarily in the full knowledge – of the potential dangers. A danger of a different, but closely related kind manifested itself when, following the retirement of Professor R. Irwin from the directorship of the School at University College, London, in 1963, another

Professor who was not and had not been a librarian was appointed to succeed him. The College's regrettable eighteenth century-type decision was the subject of negotiations between the College and the Association at the end of the period.[45] Irrespective of the merits of this individual appointment, it was clear that another library wheel had come full circle. Before librarianship had become a profession, appointing authorities were liable – for good or bad reason – to fill vacancies by appointing applicants whose experience and suitability – as viewed by established practitioners in other places – must have been gravely in doubt. The risks diminished as librarianship became a profession but still an exceptionally ill-paid one. As its financial relativities improved so returned the danger of outside and unsuitable appointments.

The Association's success in shedding its public library bias was underwritten in due course by the Ministry of Education, later the Department of Education and Science, which gradually assumed responsibilities which the LA had previously borne alone. But success in shedding bias had not thereby diminished interest or concern; this was important since Government action following publication of the Roberts Report in 1959 came quickly.

Early in 1961 the Minister of Education appointed two Working Parties – most of the members of each being practising librarians – the first:

To study the technical implications in the Roberts Report about the basic requirements for an efficient service, with particular reference to non-county borough and urban district authorities with populations under 40,000.

and the second:

To study the technical implications of the recommendations of the Roberts Report about inter-library cooperation.[46]

The Working Parties' reports, published in December 1962, confirmed, *inter alia*, the Roberts recommendations that primary standards should be based on annual book purchase and that there should be statutory responsibility on Local Authorities to provide an efficient system of cooperation.[47]

Once again, there was little delay. The Government's Public Libraries and Museums Bill, its provisions formulated following discussions with the Association and with other interested bodies, had its formal First Reading in the House of Commons in January 1964; passed Second Reading and the usual later stages during the following February and April; passed through the Lords in June and July and received the Royal Assent at the end of the latter month.[48]

As soon as the Bill was published a committee of the Council met to consider its contents and the various points to be raised during the Parliamentary Debates. Members of Parliament were lobbied untiringly and a deputation was received by the Parliamentary Secretary to the Ministry of Education. The reception of the Association's representatives and of their points of view was exceptionally friendly and each topic which the Association sought to raise was publicised by one or more of the Members approached.

The Public Libraries and Museums Act, 1964 (Chapter 75), which repealed the Public Libraries Acts 1892–1919, was a legislative landmark for England and Wales because it:

i   Laid on local library authorities the *duty* of providing comprehensive and efficient services (neither term being, however, defined) and gave the Minister overall responsibility for supervision (thus necessitating the appointment of professional librarians, as 'Library advisers', to his staff)

ii   Dealt with the old problem of the small authority by abolishing parish authorities and by making it possible – subject to safeguards – for the Minister to abolish borough and urban district authorities with populations of less than 40,000 at the date of review

iii Provided for the establishment of a Library advisory councils b Regional councils for inter-library cooperation

It seemed indeed as if the 'Proposals' of 1943 had officially come of age. But it must be admitted that the Association did not succeed in making it legally obligatory – merely discretionary – for a local library authority to appoint a library committee and a chief librarian; both government and county authority representatives were too strongly opposed. It could not obtain any promise of general or specific grants-in-aid of the service, nor in making National Central Library financing a matter wholly for the Treasury. It was unable to prevent the authorisation of charges for the loan of pictures and records. But the Parliamentary Debates made it abundantly clear that the LA and its opinions were now officially considered always to deserve close and sympathetic attention.[49] Another matter appropriately but incidentally publicised was the still unsatisfactory state of librarians' salaries and of chief librarians' negotiating machinery. But then there had been an earlier example of evasive action by the Ministry of Education when, in a Commons Debate in 1961, the Parliamentary Secretary had said:

It was true that there was still a considerable shortage. This fact seemed to stem mainly from the wastage which took place rather than from a failure to recruit . . . library work attracted a nice type of girl who attracted a nice type of boy and neither bribery nor blandishments could prevail against this.[50]

A Library advisory council for England and another for Wales were appointed in January 1966, their members including practising librarians, together with members and representatives of local authorities and of adult education organisations. Their deliberations were important not only because of their intrinsic merits but, much more, because they began to assume duties which, previously, had had to be undertaken by the Association itself. Their report *On the supply and training of librarians* (1968) was useful because it expressed views which could be regarded as more specifically official than the Association's own, on the need to avoid the creation of further schools of librarianship by expanding those already in existence and particularly those in universities. Bearing in mind that in January 1968 there were nearly 2500 students attending the schools and that the numbers of full-time teachers had risen to 246, the relevance is obvious. Bearing also in mind that the first school, other than the pioneer one at University College London, had opened its doors only twenty-one years earlier, the achievement was already remarkable.[51]

Much had grown from one Act of Parliament. There was, however, during the period, a continuous series of attempts to secure amending legislation for purposes other than the improvement of the library service. Publishing changes, not excluding changes in author – publisher relationships, encouraged both to seek sources of revenue in addition to royalties and trading profits. The enormous annual circulations of books from public libraries and particularly from their lending departments, seemed to offer promising scope for modifying the free service initiated in 1850.[52] One consequence was the growth of the idea of a 'public lending right', presented as analogous to that of the 'performing right' for music, substantial contributions to the thinking being made, initially, by Mr John Brophy and later by Sir Alan Herbert. It was not necessarily easy to accept fully the reasoning of those who produced statistics to demonstrate just how low were the rewards of authorship when it seemed clear that many of them were outstanding part-timers. Neither was it obvious that a *public* lending right was clearly compatible with the act of reading which is performed so often by consenting adults in *private*. But there have been earlier events in our island history which have satisfactorily demonstrated that myths and folk-lore are not always less influential than logical reasoning. The Association's attitude throughout the public debate was critical, indeed the Member of Parliament moving the Second Reading of the unsuccessful 'Herbert' Bill of 1960 went so far as to describe it as 'intransigent'.[53]

The Arts Council published new proposals for a scheme early in 1968, now recommending that the free public library service should continue and that a fund from which authors and publishers were to be rewarded should be provided solely by Government grant. The Association's resulting memorandum to the Department of Education and Science argued that, far

from library lending reducing the sale of books as the
accumulated folk-lore now contended, it ultimately increased it.
It also criticised the proposal to bring publishers as well as
authors within the scope of the subsidies proposed which, in
any case, should not be based on library circulations.[54] No
public lending right was created during the period under
review.

The LA continued to be represented on a wide range of other
bodies. With some, such as the British Records Association,
the National Committee on Regional Library Cooperation, and
the National Book League, there were long established
connections. The association now with others, such as the
Microfilm Association of Great Britain, and the National
Reprographic Centre for documentation meant, not merely new
ties; it was a natural consequence of the LA seeking, as always, to
keep abreast of current developments and not only in its own
but also in peripheral fields of activity.[55] Representation on the
International Federation of Library Associations – still not yet
one of the most satisfactory or creative international
organisations – continued. At the Copenhagen conference in
August 1969 the restructuring of that body was discussed and
the retiring President, Sir Frank Francis, of the British Museum,
expressed the widely held view that major tasks for the
Federation were the improvement of techniques, professional
education, and work in developing countries.[56] But then the LA
was itself already playing no mean rôle. It helped to arrange
staff exchanges throughout the period, notably with the New
York Library Association,[57] and to place Commonwealth
librarians temporarily in British public libraries.[58] In
cooperation with the British Council, representatives visited and
reported on libraries in the developing countries of the
Commonwealth, and, in connection with official cultural
exchanges, others visited other European countries, notably
Russia[59] and West Germany[60] – with appropriate reciprocity.
LA participation in the successful Anglo-Scandinavian
conferences was also noteworthy.[61] One of the more
unusual events was the appointment, in May 1963, of
Mr F. G. B. Hutchings, retired City Librarian of Leeds, to the
staff of the Association as a lecturer on librarianship on loan to

the University of Malaya for two years, the cost being borne by the Gulbenkian Foundation. [62] A more flamboyant example of projecting the image of British librarianship occurred in Britain itself. The first National Library Week, arranged in association with the Publishers Association, Associated Booksellers and the National Book League, was held in 1966. Mr K. C. Harrison, City Librarian of Westminster, became joint chairman of the function and the festival arranged then, and its successors in 1967 and 1969, may have done something to promote the reading habit. Their success in attracting the attention of the press, radio and television made unprecedented impact on the public. Some feared that the impact was as short-lived as the fruit-fly; others were more optimistic. [63]

Notwithstanding the economic success of the Association's own publishing activities, already referred to, some increased or new income, eg from rents received at Ridgmount Street during the second half of the period, and some savings, eg registration as a charity in 1964 [64] – resulting in the annual local rate burden being halved – despite all these ameliorations the financial implications of exceptional expansion during burgeoning national inflation were serious. There were overall deficits in the Association's accounts in 1962, 1964 and 1965 [65] and the usual careful reviews of income and expenditure. Subscriptions had, in consequence, to be raised twice, in 1963 and 1967. On the second occasion there was little, if any, serious opposition from members, on the first a great deal. The sliding scales of payment according to salary were retained; these were equated now with 'top' annual subscriptions of £8 in 1963 for those receiving more than £2000 per annum, [66] and of £15 in 1967 for those receiving more than £3000. [67] Consequent on the additional income, the income and expenditure accounts for the last two years of the present period, 1968 and 1969, each showed surpluses of nearly £30,000. These seemed tolerably satisfactory but were obviously not excessive when viewed against total annual expenditures during the same two years of £109,000 and £117,000. [68] Short of unexpected and unlikely windfalls, the progress of inflation made it obvious that further subscription increases would be needed during the early 1970s.

There were many changes in the membership of the Council during the period as younger librarians took the places of those who had served since World War Two and, in some cases, since pre-war days. The outstanding and happiest event was surely the election for 1966 of Miss Lorna Paulin, County librarian of Hertfordshire, as the Association's first woman President. Women have played a significant, if always minority part in Council affairs since Miss Pierce's election to it in 1915. Miss Paulin's Presidency may certainly be regarded as symbolic of that contribution. It was much more important, nevertheless, as overdue recognition of the service to the profession of one of the outstanding librarians of the twentieth century.

References

1. 3/1047, 1.3.1960; 3/1063/2. *See also* *LAR*, 62, pp 208–18; 63, pp 83–4.
2. 'Reorganisation of the LA', *Proceedings of the Annual conference*. 1961, pp 29–34.
3. *AR* (1962), pp 8, 11; (1969), p 10.
4. H. D. Barry, 'The membership of the Association', *LAR*, 70, pp 142–3.
5. Letter to present author from Miss A. Turner, LA Registrar, 17.4.1975.
6. *AR* (1963), p 9.
7. *Year book*, 1970, pp xii–xiii.
8. *LAR*, 64, pp 56–7.
9. 'Housewarming', *LAR*, 68, pp 241–5.
10. *AR*s (1960–9).
11. *AR* (1968), p 25.
12. *Preface*.
13. *Liaison*, May 1961, p 33.
14. *AR* (1969), p 29.
15. *LAR*, 65, p 74.
16. *Memorandum . . . to the Select Committee on Estimates*. 1960–1.
17. *Memorandum . . . to be laid before the Committee on libraries*. 1964.
18. *LAR*, 70, pp 20–1.
19. 'Book provision for the Open University' (Executive committee papers Ex 697, 1968).
20. pp 6–7.
21. *AR* (1967), pp 13–14.
22. *AR* (1968), p 15.
23. *AR* (1966), p 10.
24. *Year book*, 1975, pp 66–7.
25. *Ibid*, p 67.
26. *Ibid*, p 68.
27. *AR* (1963), p 7.
28. *AR* (1966), p 6.
29. *AR* (1963), p 7.
30. *AR* (1968), pp 12–14.
31. *AR* (1964), p 6.
32. *AR* (1960), p 5.
33. *AR* (1961), p 10.
34. *AR* (1968), p 10.
35. *Year book*, 1968, pp 84–97.
36. For a mid-term study of progress and development *see* K. A. Mallaber, 'Research in librarianship', *LAR*, 67, pp 222–7.
37. L. V. Paulin 'Revision of syllabus: a statement', *LAR*, 62, pp 219–225; and P. G. New, 'The new syllabus and the library schools', *LAR*, 65, pp 187–91.
38. *Year book*, 1968, p 29.
39. *Ibid*.
40. *AR* (1966), p 16.
41. *AR* (1968), p 22; (1969), p 25.
42. *AR* (1967), pp 17–18.
43. *AR* (1968), p 22. *See also* two important articles by the LA Education Officer (B. I. Palmer) ie 'Degrees in librarianship', *LAR*, 67, pp 305–310; and 'Degrees in librarianship II', *LAR*, 70, pp 205–6.
44. *AR* (1966), pp 15–16.

45. *AR* (1969), p 5.
46. *Liaison*, April 1961, p 25.
47. *Liaison*, January 1963, pp 1–3.
48. Draft Bill and report of the Debates in *LAR*, 66, pp 66–7, 104–9, 264–7, 312–3, 326, 350–5.
49. *LAR*, 66, pp 375–6.
50. *LAR*, 63, pp 133–4.
51. L. V. Paulin, 'The Work of the Library Advisory Councils', *JL*, 7, pp 132–140.
52. For an earlier discussion of the subject *see* N. Birkett and others. *Books are essential*. 1951; and particularly 'The Author's predicament', by J. L. Hodson pp 23–38).
53. *Liaison*, January 1961, p 1.

54. *AR* (1968), pp 3–4.
55. *See* eg *AR* (1969), pp 31–42.
56. *Ibid*, pp 36–7.
57. eg *AR* (1960), p 8; (1962), p 4.
58. eg *AR* (1962), p 4.
59. *AR* (1964), p 7.
60. *AR* (1966), p 5.
61. eg *AR* (1967), pp 6–7.
62. *AR* (1963), p 8.
63. For National Library Week *see* eg *AR* (1966), p 3; (1967), p 4; (1969), pp 6–7, also *LAR*, 68, pp 284–8.
64. *AR* (1964), p 6.
65. *LAR*, 65, p 165; 67, p 91; 68, p 91.
66. *LAR*, 64, pp 426–7.
67. *LAR*, 68, pp 227–8.
68. *LAR*, 72, pp 110, 114.

Chapter Thirteen

The *1970*

The most recent years of the Association's history again mirror
the national experience. The 1960s may be viewed as a period of
expansion and of ever-increasing expectation. During the
1970s, by contrast, came the realisation that the environmental
horizons – far from being infinitely distant – were
now disturbingly close. Stability began to seem much more
important than expansion and much harder to secure. It was
uncomfortably difficult to come to terms with an experience
which – for the post-World War Two generations at least – was
new. By the middle 1970s the financial economies imposed upon
libraries – as upon other services – by national and local bodies
responsible for them were beginning to have marked effect. It
seemed as if the profession, like the nation, was starting to climb
an escalator programmed only for descent.

Inflation followed, on the whole, the pattern outlined in
innumerable text-books of elementary economics. After
stimulating growth and expansion in the 1960s, it became a drag
on all activity in the 1970s. British citizens might well
sympathise fully with their mid-sixteenth-century ancestors, one
of whom had effectively exemplified his own problem in *The
Commonwealth of this realm of England* (*c* 1549):

I have seen a cap for 14*d*, as good as I can get now for 2*s* 5*d*, of cloth
ye have heard how the price is risen. Then a pair of shoes costeth me
12*d*, that I have in my days bought better for 6*d*. Then I can never get

a horse shod under 10*d* or 12*d*, where I have seen the common price was 6*d*.[1]

Librarians' salaries tended, overall, to keep pace with inflation, an achievement substantially to the credit of the Association, if often indirectly:

The LA has been responsible for initiating negotiations with and providing information for all the trade unions concerned in salary agreements made over the past 25 years with Civil Service and Local Government and University Authorities and with recommendations for those employed in colleges of further education and in special libraries and information services.[2]

It is often still surprisingly difficult, however, for individuals to remember that the organisations to which they owe loyalty are likely to be affected by inflation at least as severely as themselves. LA experience conformed to rule. Membership continued to increase during the period, exceeded 20,000 before the end of 1972,[3] and had reached 23,138 by the end of 1975.[4] The number of chartered librarians, too, which had exceeded 10,000 for the first time during 1970,[5] reached the astonishing total of 15,716 by the end of 1975.[6] These remarkable increases brought, however, little, if any, financial benefit to the Association; since the publications account was also in deficit for the first time since 1965[7] it became necessary – to achieve a new budget equilibrium – not only to increase the prices of publications but also to raise subscriptions. A Council proposal to increase the basic rate of subscription to £20 – with the usual lower gradations according to salary received – was passed by a majority at the 1972 AGM but decisively rejected in a postal ballot recommended by the President since fewer than 100 members were present.[8] Revised proposals, with a basic subscription of £19 instead of the £20 rejected, passed the 1973 AGM and became effective from January 1974.[9] Subscriptions for affiliated institutional members were also subsequently increased substantially.[10] Further increases, granted existing services and the continuance of inflation, are inevitable.

Inflationary trends suggest, however, not only increased subscriptions but also possibly smaller expenditures. Speculations of this sort suggest, in their turn, simplified or at least rationalised procedures. Future Association policy was, in any case, coming under review – for professional and educational reasons.[11] Working Party investigations were undertaken between 1971 and 1974[12] and resulted in reports which were submitted, not only to the Council but also to the Branches and Groups. The staff and establishment review, following another report – of the kind currently fashionable, by a firm of management consultants – proposed changes which were, in fact, facilitated by staff retirements. The most important of these was that of the Secretary, H. D. Barry, quite unexpectedly early for health reasons. Mr Barry, who had been the Association's chief officer since the retirement of P. S. J. Welsford in 1959, was succeeded by R. P. Hilliard, who had been the Association's Finance Officer for nearly four years. Mr Barry, who had been made an Honorary Fellow in 1973,[13] received the award of the CBE in 1975.[14]

The Barry Reports of 1960–1, referred to in the previous chapter, had led the Council to make special provision, in a revised committee structure, for the exceptional representation of the interests of librarians other than those of local authorities. The final draft (sixth report) of the Working Party on Association Services, of February 1975, suggested that the important objective aimed at had now been achieved: 'It is probable that the concept of a single unified profession of librarianship is no longer in question'. Yet, 'We are aware that there is no easy answer to the problems of balancing the specific and general concerns within a professional association'. And, 'We also consider it important that the Council becomes increasingly concerned with the broad lines of policy'. Due consideration of these principles led to proposals for committee restructuring, as follows:

i   General purposes: House, staff, membership, finance (including publishing control), relations with Branches and Groups, public relations and international relations, legislation, Government policy etc. (The Boards for *Library Association Record* and *Journal of Librarianship* to report to this Committee)

ii   Professional development and education: Education,

research and development, services to members,
consultancy services. (The Boards of Advanced studies and
of the Assessors to report to this Committee)
iii   Library services: Methods, promotion, salaries and
      conditions
iv   Executive Coordinating: Executive, Presidential
      nomination, selection
v   Disciplinary[15]

It is, perhaps, almost too easy to view this development as a
substantial reversion to the pre-Barry situation, with, of course,
new names for the old and regrouped committees on lines made
fashionable in Local Government and elsewhere by the *Bains
Report* of 1972.[16] The associated proposal to have a leader of the
council (ie the chairman of the Executive Coordinating
committee) may also be presented as a thinly disguised return to
the appointment of an Honorary Secretary, discontinued since
the implementation of the Barry reports. Be these things as they
may, time and experience alone will show whether the new
structure proves satisfactory for the needs of the early years of
the Association's second century.

The appointment for the first time of a Disciplinary committee –
expected, surely, to meet only infrequently – is an effective
reminder of an all-but-unprecedented situation which arose in
1971, when the Council had to sit as a quasi-judicial body to
consider a complaint against a member, and, subsequently, to
reprimand him.[17] New bye-laws to cover any future occurrences
and procedures were approved at the AGM in 1973.[18]

The continuance of the highly important changes in professional
education manifested throughout the 1960s, and referred to in
the previous chapter, ensured that by the middle 1970s most
of the assessment and examining, as well as the teaching of
librarianship students – although not the assessment of
examinations – was being undertaken by bodies other than the
LA itself. In fact:

It is possible now to attain a liberal education through library science
studies ranging from a two-year course for non-graduate students,

via pass degrees, honours degrees, masters degrees – of library
science, of arts, of science, of philosophy, and, of course, you can get
a PH D at any of the university schools, if you can think of a subject
sufficiently erudite . . . The national registration of librarians has made
a contribution to the standards of the profession, and I think it is now
making a contribution to its unity, for qualifications of the
Association or of university or of the Council for National Academic
Awards, which lead, with appropriate experience, to the award of
Associate of the LA, are now expected by a majority of employing
authorities.[19]

The students taking the Association's own examinations have,
indeed, shrunk in numbers and have even been described, by a
pleasant paradox, as 'external'.[20] But there will be a continuing
need for some part-time facilities during the later 1970s at least,
particularly for students in non-public libraries for whom library
school leave may be impracticable. A review of the Association's
1964 syllabus – resulting in limited changes introduced in 1971 –
provided the examination framework for them.[21] The
fundamental change in educational approach was, nevertheless,
effectively symbolised by the appointment of a Registrar
(Miss A. Turner) to succeed the Association's Education Officer
(B. I. Palmer) when he retired in 1974.[22]

Librarianship in the middle 1970s is indeed becoming a graduate
profession and we may well look forward to the not very distant
time when – in common with other professions – a university
degree will be the normal pre-entry qualification. But the
concept is still highly controversial; during recent years few
subjects have aroused more controversy in the correspondence
columns of the *Record*.[23] Much of the criticism has been of the
kind consistently expressed whenever pre-entry standards have
been raised; the critics, as in other professions, will have to come
to terms with trends and tendencies. A much greater danger for
the Association may arise if and when any considerable number
of library school graduates may be in a position to decide that it
is unnecessary to seek chartered status. The designation is,
however, now so important and so universally recognised that
the risk may, perhaps, be regarded at present as small. But it
would certainly be the greatest irony of all if the Association's
continuing and extremely successful efforts over the century

past to improve educational and professional standards were to result in the better educated librarian considering it unnecessary to become a member or to continue membership.

The Association's Fellowship (FLA), once sought by all aspiring members, now attracts much smaller numbers, partly at least because it can normally be obtained only *via* an approved thesis. In a history of our Association – indeed of any comparable association – a good deal of attention must be given, necessarily, to the problems of 'domestic housekeeping' as they have arisen during the period covered. But if librarianship is anything it is essentially a learned profession; an immense contribution to its scholastic achievement since the middle 1960s has been made by the librarians who have submitted Fellowship theses and had them accepted.

The number of theses accepted has already mounted well into the hundreds. The variety of subjects chosen is, of course, wide but, naturally enough, many have been bibliographcial: for example, *Bibliography of English ballet* (F. S. Forrester), *Kenya coffee: a bibliographical survey 1900–1966* (J. L. Abukutsa), *The Edinburgh Stage 1715–1820: a bibliography* (N. Armstrong), *Bibliography of the history and organisation of horse racing and thoroughbred breeding in Great Britain and Ireland 1565–1973* (E. P. Loder), *Guide to the despatches from and to the Gold Coast of the British Administration 1850–1902* (D. O. Bampoe), *Chronological synopsis and index to Oxfordshire items in Jackson's 'Oxford Journal' 1753–1780* (E. C. Davies). There have also been histories of libraries nationally, eg *Carnegie library buildings in Great Britain: an account, evaluation and survey* (A. J. Smith), and locally, eg *Libraries in Bath 1618–1964* (V. J. Kite) and *History of the King's Lynn libraries 1797–1905* (R. Wilson), together with biographies of some of the notables whose activities have been outlined in earlier pages of the present work, eg *Henry Richard Tedder* (R. J. Busby) and *Sir John Y. W. MacAlister* (S. Spanner). A few of the theses have been published either by the Association itself or by other publishers, among them *Cryogenics and refrigeration: a bibliographical guide* (E. M. Codlin), *Bibliography of British railway history* (G. Ottley), *London theatres and music halls 1850–1950* (D. Howard), *The literature of jazz*

(D. Kennington), *History of the Association of Assistant Librarians 1895–1945* (M. J. Ramsden) and *Bibliography of the dog* (E. G. Jones). If any member of the Association ever views the future of librarianship with despondency, few better cures are perhaps obtainable than a visit to the room at Association headquarters where bound copies of successful theses are shelved.[24]

The 'hiving off' process practised by the Association so thoroughly in respect of professional education has also been effectively applied to another important service – the Library.

The financial strains imposed upon the Association by the growth of the library and information bureau into a national information centre, referred to in the previous chapter, continued during the early 1970s. Increasing support expenditure was obviously necessary but it was equally obvious that the funds necessary must come from sources other than the Association.[25] The Government grant-in-aid envisaged during the 1960s was not in fact forthcoming; in its place came assistance on a much more comprehensive scale.

The Dainton Committee on the national libraries appointed late in 1967 was influenced to considerable degree by the representations made to it by the Association.[26] The resulting Government scheme for the creation of the new British Library from the existing British Museum Library, National Central Library, National Reference Library of Science and Invention, National Lending Library of Science and Technology, and British National Bibliography, announced in 1971,[27] made it desirable for the new organisation to itself acquire a satisfactory working and reference library. Arrangements were made for it to accept the Association's library on deposit as from 1 April 1974 and to undertake to maintain services to LA members at not less than existing levels. The British Library purchases book-stock, pays staff taken over, and rents the existing library accommodation from the LA to ensure uninterrupted service. Until such time as the British Library acquires a new building, the library will remain at Association headquarters.[28] The first important consequential change was the administrative separation of the Information Bureau – which will remain the

Association's responsibility – from the Library and the appointment by the LA of an Information Officer.[29]

The continued expansion of the LA's research and development during the early 1970s won recognition when the 'Research in progress' feature appearing in the *Year book* from 1968 to 1973 gave place to the separately published *RADIALS Bulletin* (ie research and development – information and library science), to be published three times annually and aiming to be a comprehensive national register of research; the first issue appeared in August, 1974.[30] The Association's own research activities have included continuing work on the revision of the 1967 Anglo-American Cataloguing Rules[31] and on the Dewey Classification[32] and, via sub-committees, on reading for the visually handicapped[33] and on the illiteracy problem; the latter resulting in the publication of 'Trigger Books' by the Ulverscroft Foundation in conjunction with the Association. By the end of 1974 the Association had also published a total of fourteen titles in its own series of Research Publications, subjects ranging from *Music in British libraries*[34] to *Select biographical sources*,[35] and from *Objectives and administration of library research*[36] to *United Kingdom catalogue use study*.[37] Research grants were also made for a variety of investigations including hospital library services,[38] cooperation between public and academic libraries,[39] and insurance in libraries.[40]

Two new medals introduced during the present period may also be regarded as awards in recognition of outstanding contributions to research and development; both were awarded for the first time in 1970. The McColvin Medal, splendidly named to honour also the Association's great Honorary Secretary, is awarded annually for an outstanding reference book first published in the United Kingdom during the preceding year. The first books honoured were I. G. Anderson, ed, *Councils, committees and boards: a handbook of advisory, consultative, executive and similar bodies in British public life* (1970), W. Shepherd *Shepherd's glossary of graphic signs and symbols* (1971), A. Jacobs, ed, *Music yearbook 1972–3* (1972).[41]

The Besterman Medal, named after Theodore Besterman, the

international bibliographer, is now awarded annually for an outstanding bibliography or guide to the literature first published in the United Kingdom during the preceding year. The first awards were to J. F. Arnott and J. W. Robinson *English theatrical literature 1559–1900* (1970), B. White *Sourcebook of planning information* (1971) and G. H. Martin *and* S. McIntyre *Bibliography of British and Irish municipal history*, vol 1 (1972).[42]

Awards of the longer established medals during the same period have included Richard Adams *Watership Down* and Penelope Lively *Ghost of Thomas Kempe* (Carnegie, 1972 and 1973); John Burningham *Mr Gumpy's outing* and Raymond Briggs *Father Christmas* (Kate Greenaway, 1970 and 1973);[43] and C. C. Banwell *Encyclopaedia of forms and precedents* (Wheatley, 1974).[44] New developments in games and computers were appropriately acknowledged by the Robinson awards which went, in 1970, to Mr F. Gurney, of Automated Library Charging Systems Ltd, for computer book charging; and, in 1972, to the University of Lancaster Library Research Unit for the development of simulation games in education for library management.[45]

The Association's own regular publications continued to appear and a new series of short, select *Fiction bibliographies*, primarily for public library use, was introduced in 1970 and may be regarded as successors to the subject lists of the late 1940s. The list of new publications included titles as contrasted as D. F. Keeling, ed, *British library history bibliography*, the first two volumes in 1972 and 1975; T. Kelly *History of public libraries in Great Britain 1845–1965* (1973); A. Thompson *Bibliography of nursing literature 1961–1970* (1974); and A. C. Montgomery *Acronyms and abbreviations in library and information work* (1975). New editions have included A. J. Walford *Guide to reference material*, vol 2 (1975), vol 3 (1970); J. L. Thornton *Scientific books, libraries and collectors* (1971); M. Thwaite *From primer to pleasure in reading* (1972); M. Going, ed, *Hospital libraries and work with the disabled* (1973); and J. Burkett *Government and related library and information services in the United Kingdom* (1974). A new drive to increase overseas sales was initiated with the appointment of an American agent in 1970 and the taking of stands at American and Canadian LA exhibitions during the same year.[46]

The greatest publications change of the 1970s may well prove to be the new style *Record*, beginning in January 1976, no longer with an honorary editor but with a full-time professional (Mr R. Walter).[47] Historians may regret the break in an annual sequence, complete since 1899, of what had become, at least during the post-Esdaile period, an invaluable journal of record. Cynics may anticipate changes comparable with those experienced in the United States when, in 1970, *American libraries* succeeded the *ALA Bulletin*. Optimists will hope that a new and valuable development will have taken place. As we pass the threshold of another century, let us all be optimists.

The Association's publishing programme now ensures impact on a world much wider than that of librarianship. More directly positive influence has continued to be exercised on bodies as different as Unesco,[48] Aslib,[49] the Open University,[50] the Layfield Committee on the financing of local government,[51] the Whitford Committee on the law of copyright and designs,[52] the Russell Committee on adult education,[53] and on the Government in connection with the indeed comprehensively titled Cinematograph and Indecent Displays Bill, the last named in an attempt to ensure that librarians ran no risk of prosecution following displays of book jackets in their libraries.[54] The hazards of a paternalistic welfare state are indeed great but this Bill eventually lapsed. The continuing influence of the Association on many other organizations, to the governing bodies of which it continues to appoint representatives, should also not be overlooked.[55]

The continuance of the Public Lending Right controversy called for Association attention and vigilance throughout the period. An extract from a 1975 contribution by Mr E. Clough, a past-President of the LA, usefully summarises current official attitudes:

The Association is not in favour of PLR but it is strongly in favour of helping and encouraging authors, and particularly concerned to ensure that authors of significant works of creative imagination and of scholarship should have their works published and be adequately remunerated for them. . . . the administration of any such (PLR) scheme is going to be expensive [and] . . . must bristle with anomalies and contradictions. . . [56]

The advent of the European Economic Community has made important the harmonization of library qualifications throughout the Community's area; draft directives have been discussed with the Department of Education and Science, and the Association's services have been proffered for use in future negotiations.[57] Its own active international relations policy has also continued.[58] One of the most completely satisfactory developments of the 1970s with which the LA has been most intimately concerned has been the formation of the Commonwealth Library Association (COMLA) at Lagos in November 1972, Mr K. C. Harrison, City Librarian of Westminster, being its first President. The new Association should have a vital part to play when:

As every year goes by, more and more governments are appreciating the place of libraries in the development of their culture, realising that they are irreplaceable investments, and gradually, though not yet quickly enough, they are allocating improving fiscal grants to them. If this situation goes on, and indeed gathers momentum, there can be no doubts for the future. We await with confidence the just harvest.[59]

The most important event for public libraries during the present period has been, unquestionably, the rearrangement of local government areas – outside Greater London – consequent on the implementation of the Local Government Act of 1972 and the allocation of library powers in England to only seventy-five of the new Authorities (thirty-nine non-metropolitan counties and thirty-six metropolitan districts in place of the 308 Authorities previously administratively responsible).[60] This radical change to much larger administrative areas, following closely the pattern of official LA thinking from the days of the *McColvin Report* of 1942 and of the *Proposals* of 1943, was achieved despite heavy opposition from the smaller, new District Authorities. The new pattern will certainly have disadvantages as well as merits; some years of the Association's second century will need to elapse before its success or partial failure can be placed beyond doubt. If it may be viewed, from some angles, as 'the triumph of the counties', it is ironic that one of the inevitable first results, Association-wise, should have to be the winding up of the County Libraries Group, founded in 1929, in favour of the new Public Libraries Group as from 1 January 1975.[61] Less significant changes in the areas of Branches have also been agreed. It will fall to the new Group to arrange its own conferences; as from 1976 the Association itself will organise only one national conference.[62]

The new administrative groupings in local government have also been adopted, with some modifications, in Wales. In Scotland, however, the new situation has proved less satisfactory from the professional point of view as the new District Councils assume library powers. The Association had previously appointed an Executive Secretary for Scotland (Professor W. B. Paton, previously the Association's last Honorary Secretary);[63] in conjunction with the Scottish LA, he was active in endeavouring to secure the most satisfactory administrative structures for library services.[64] These administrative variations may seem eccentric – at least to the logician. But Celtic fringe alternatives have again become fashionable in western Europe and it would be surprising if British librarianship were so favoured as to be permitted completely to contract out of them. A solution more attractive to the Association has, however, been achieved in Northern Ireland where, from 1973, the public library service became the responsibility of the Ministry of Education, its powers being exercised through five Education and Library Boards.[65]

Any ending to an historical survey of this kind must seem – and indeed ought to seem – open rather than closed; the foundations of the second century have assuredly been laid before the termination of the first. If the Association's greatest achievement during the century has been – as may well be thought – the creation of the chartered librarian, then the extension of the influence of the graduate chartered librarian – aided to the maximum extent possible by the LA – should be the most important event of the second. There is immense scope and in all kinds of librarianship, if most now in special and school libraries. The recent reorganisation of local government had one serious disadvantage, the effects of which will be felt for some years to come; far too many chartered librarians, previously in senior posts, chose, quite understandably, to retire at abnormally low ages. The profession lost thereby a great deal of talent, a great deal of experience and a great deal of still fully unrealised potential. It may also be argued, of course, that, at a time of financial stringency, national and local, their removal from the active scene solved, in advance, a problem of excessive staffing which did not therefore in fact arise. Be that as it may, their chartered successors will certainly be offered considerably more scope than might otherwise have been the case; it is now to them – since public librarianship accounts for so great a proportion of the total library service – that the nation, the Association and the profession must look for much of the library future. It is presupposed, of course, that the nation and the world succeed in overcoming or – to put it no higher – coming to terms with inflation as least as successfully as did our Tudor and Stuart forebears.

References

1. Reprinted in A. E. Bland and others. eds. *English economic history: select documents.* 1914. p 405.
2. D. D. Haslam, 'Salaries of professional librarians 1965–1975; a ten year review', *LAR*, 77, pp 264–5.
3. *AR* (1972), p 10.
4. *AR* (1975), p 6.
5. *AR* (1970), pp 9–10.
6. *AR* (1975), p 6.
7. *LAR*, 73, p 51.
8. *LAR*, 74, pp 103–4, 125; also *Liaison*, June 1972, pp 42–3.
9. *LAR*, 75, p 114.
10. *LAR*, 77, p 140.
11. *AR* (1970), pp 4–5.
12. *AR* (1972), p 6; (1973), pp 6–7; (1974), p 6.
13. *AR* (1973), p 4.
14. *AR* (1974), p 7.
15. Ex 681.
16. *The New local authorities: management structure.* 1972, particularly Ch 4.
17. C. W. J. Harris, *Fifty years of progress: the London and Home Counties Branch of the L.A., 1923–1973.* (1975), pp 26–7.
18. *LAR*, 75, p 113.
19. P. Havard-Williams, 'The Role of a professional association', *LAR*, 74, pp 187–90.
20. *LAR*, 77, p 185.
21. *LAR*, 70, pp 81–7.
22. *Liaison*, April 1974, p 22.
23. eg *LAR*, 76, pp 105–110, 134–5, 157, 174–6, 228–9.
24. Lists compiled from author's personal examination of LA file copies.
25. *AR* (1972), p 13.
26. Havard-Williams *op cit.*
27. *AR* (1971), p 1.
28. *AR* (1973), p 12.
29. *AR* (1974), p 13.
30. *Ibid*, pp 11–12.
31. eg *AR* (1970), p 11.
32. eg *AR* (1971), pp 7–8.
33. *Ibid.*

34. AR (1974), p 10.
35. AR (1971), p 9.
36. AR (1972), p 13.
37. AR (1973), p 9.
38. AR (1972), p 12.
39. AR (1971), p 9.
40. AR (1973), p 9.
41. *Year book*, 1975, p 68.
42. *Ibid*, p 69.
43. *Ibid*, pp 66–7.
44. LAR, 77, p 135.
45. *Year book*, 1975, p 68.
46. AR (1970), p 28.
47. LAR, 77, p 42.
48. eg AR (1971), p 3.
49. eg AR (1970), pp 6–7.
50. *Ibid*, pp 5–6.
51. AR (1974), p 6.
52. *Ibid*.

53. LAR, 70, pp 61–2.
54. AR (1974), p 5.
55. For list *see* eg AR (1974), pp 29–36.
56. 'How best to help the authors',
LAR, 77, pp 34–5.
57. AR (1973), pp 5–6.
58. eg LAR, 77, pp 54, 65.
59. K. C. Harrison, *The Importance and relevance of librarianship for developing countries*. (The Commonwealth Foundation, Occasional papers, no 33) 1975, p 26.
60. AR (1974), p 17.
61. *Ibid*, p 7.
62. LAR, 76, p 42.
63. AR (1972), pp 8–9.
64. AR (1974), p 18.
65. AR (1973), p 17.

Appendices

Appendix a

Royal Charter 1898: Purposes and Powers of the Library Association

1. To unite all persons engaged or interested in library work, by holding conferences and meetings for the discussion of bibliographical questions and matters affecting libraries or their regulation or management or otherwise.

2. To promote the better administration of libraries.

3. To promote whatever may tend to the improvement of the position and the qualifications of Librarians.

4. To promote the adoption of the Public Libraries Acts in any City, Borough or other district within the United Kingdom of Great Britain and Ireland.

5. To promote the establishment of reference and lending libraries for use by the public.

6. To watch any legislation affecting public libraries, and to assist in the promotion of such further legislation as may be considered necessary for the regulation and management or extension of public libraries.

7. To promote and encourage bibliographical study and research.

8. To collect, collate, and publish (in the form of Transactions, Journals, or otherwise) information of service or interest to the Fellows and Members of the Association, or for the promotion of the objects of the Corporation.

9. To form, collect, and maintain a library and museum.

10. To hold examinations in librarianship and to issue certificates of efficiency.

11. To do all such lawful things as are incidental or conducive to the attainment of the above objects.

Presidents of the Library Association

1877 J. Winter Jones (Director and Principal Librarian of the British Museum).
1878 J. Winter Jones.
1879 H. O. Coxe (Bodley's Librarian).
1880 H. O. Coxe.
1881 His Honour Judge Russell (Master of Gray's Inn).
1882 Henry Bradshaw (Librarian of Cambridge University).
1883 Sir James Picton (Chairman, Liverpool Public Libraries Committee).
1884 J. K. Ingram (Librarian of Trinity College Library, Dublin).
1885 Edward James (Mayor of Plymouth).
1886 E. A. Bond, CB (Principal Librarian of the British Museum).
1887 G. J. Johnson (Chairman, Birmingham Public Libraries Committee).
1888 W. P. Dickson (Curator of Glasgow University Library).
1889 Richard Copley Christie (Chancellor of the Diocese of Manchester).
1890 E. Maunde Thompson (Principal Librarian of the British Museum).
1891 Robert Harrison (Librarian of the London Library).
1892 Alexandre Beljame (Professor of English Literature, Sorbonne, Paris).
1893 Richard Garnett (Keeper of the Printed Books, British Museum.)

1894   The Most Honourable The Marquess of Dufferin and Ava, KP, GCB.
1895   Lord Windsor.
1896   Alderman H. Rawson (Chairman, Manchester Public Libraries Committee).
1897   Henry R. Tedder (Librarian of the Athenaeum).
1898   The Rt Hon The Earl of Crawford, KT.
1899   Alderman James W. Southern JP (Chairman, Manchester Public Libraries Committee).
1900   The Rt Hon Sir Edward Fry, PC.
1901   G. K. Fortescue (Keeper of the Printed Books, British Museum).
1902   W. Macneile Dixon (Birmingham University).
1903   W. Macneile Dixon.
1904   Thomas Hodgkin (Member, Newcastle Public Libraries Committee).
1905   Francis Jenkinson (Librarian, Cambridge University).
1906   Sir William H. Bailey (Governor of the John Rylands Library, Manchester).
1907   Francis T. Barrett (Librarian, Glasgow Public Libraries).
1908   Charles Thomas-Stanford (Member, Library Sub-Committee, Brighton).
1909   Alderman W. H. Brittain, JP (Chairman, Sheffield Public Libraries Committee).
1910   Frederic G. Kenyon (Director and Principal Librarian of the British Museum).
1911   Sir John A. Dewar, Bt MP.
1912   Frank J. Leslie, CC (Chairman, Liverpool Public Libraries Committee).
1913   The Rt Hon The Earl of Malmesbury.
1914   Falconer Madan (Bodley's Librarian).
1915   J. Y. W. MacAlister (Secretary, Royal Society of Medicine).
1916   J. Y. W. MacAlister.
1917   J. Y. W. MacAlister.
1918   J. Y. W. MacAlister.
1919   G. F. Barwick (Keeper of the Printed Books, British Museum).
1920   The Rt Hon J. Herbert Lewis, PC, MP (Parliamentary Secretary, Board of Education).

1921   Alderman T. C. Abbott, JP (Chairman, Manchester Public Libraries Committee).

1922   John Ballinger, CBE (Librarian, National Library of Wales).

1923   The Most Honourable The Marquis of Hartington, MP.

1924   R. S. Rait, CBE (Historiographer Royal of Scotland).

1925   C. Grant Robertson, CVO (Birmingham University).

1926   H. Guppy (Librarian, The John Rylands Library, Manchester).

1927   The Rt Hon The Earl of Elgin and Kincardine, CMG.

1928   A. D. Lindsay, CBE (Master of Balliol College, Oxford).

1929   Lord Balniel, MP.

1930   L. Stanley Jast (Chief Librarian, Manchester).

1931   Lt Col J. M. Mitchell, OBE, MC.

1932   Sir Henry A. Miers.

1933   Sir Henry A. Miers.

1934   S. A. Pitt (City Librarian, Glasgow).

1935   E. Salter Davies, CBE (Director of Education, Kent).

1936   Ernest A. Savage (Chief Librarian, Edinburgh).

1937   William Temple, Archbishop of York.

1938   W. C. Berwick Sayers (Chief Librarian, Croydon).

1939   Arundell Esdaile (Secretary of the British Museum).

1940   Arundell Esdaile.

1941   Arundell Esdaile.

1942   Arundell Esdaile.

1943   Arundell Esdaile.

1944   Arundell Esdaile.

1945   Arundell Esdaile.

1946   H. M. Cashmore (City Librarian, Birmingham).

1947   R. J. Gordon (formerly City Librarian, Leeds).

1948   Charles Nowell (City Librarian, Manchester).

1949   Sir Ronald Forbes Adam, Bt, GCB, DSO, OBE

1950   His Royal Highness The Duke of Edinburgh.

1951   James Wilkie (Secretary, Carnegie United Kingdom Trust).

1952   Lionel R. McColvin, CBE (City Librarian, Westminster).

1953   S. C. Roberts (Master of Pembroke College, Cambridge).

1954   C. B. Oldman, CB (Principal Keeper of the Printed Books, British Museum).

1955 Sir Philip Morris, CBE (Vice-Chancellor, University of Bristol).

1956 E. Sydney, MC (Borough Librarian, Leyton).

1957 Jacob Bronowski (Director, Coal Research Establishment, National Coal Board).

1958 R. Irwin (Director of School of Librarianship & Archives, University College, London).

1959 The Rt Hon Earl Attlee, KG, PC, OM, CH.

1960 B. S. Page (Librarian of the Brotherton Library, University of Leeds).

1961 Sir Charles Snow, CBE.

1962 W. B. Paton (County Librarian, Lanarkshire).

1963 J. N. L. Myres (Bodley's Librarian).

1964 F. M. Gardner (Borough Librarian, Luton).

1965 Sir Frank Francis, KCB (Director and Principal Librarian of the British Museum).

1966 Miss L. V. Paulin (County Librarian, Hertfordshire).

1967 F. G. B. Hutchings, OBE (formerly City Librarian, Leeds).

1968 Thomas E. Callander (Borough Librarian, Croydon).

1969 Wilfred Ashworth (Librarian and Information Officer, ICI Fibres, Pontypool).

1970 D. T. Richnell (Director and Goldsmiths' Librarian, University of London Library).

1971 Dr George Chandler (City Librarian, Liverpool).

1972 Dr D. J. Urquhart, CBE (National Lending Library for Science and Technology).

1973 K. C. Harrison, MBE (City Librarian, Westminster).

1974 E. A. Clough (City Librarian, Southampton).

1975 E. V. Corbett (Borough Librarian, Wandsworth).

1976 D. J. Foskett (Librarian, University of London Institute of Education).

Honorary Officers of the Library Association

Honorary Secretaries

1877–78	E. B. Nicholson and Henry R. Tedder.
1878–80	Henry R. Tedder and Ernest C. Thomas.
1880–82	Ernest C. Thomas and Charles Welch.
1882–87	Ernest C. Thomas.
1887–90	Ernest C. Thomas and J. Y. W. MacAlister.
1890–92	J. Y. W. MacAlister and Thomas Mason.
1892–98	J. Y. W. MacAlister.
1898–1901	Frank Pacy.
1902	Basil Soulsby.
1902–5	Lawrence Inkster (L. S. Jast, Acting Secretary 1904–5).
1905–15	L. Stanley Jast.
1915–18	Frank Pacy (Acting Secretary).
1918–19	Frank Pacy and G. F. Barwick.
1919–28	Frank Pacy (G. W. Keeling appointed full-time Secretary, 1928).
1928–33	Ernest A. Savage (P. J. S. Welsford appointed Assistant Secretary 1930; Secretary 1932).
1933–34	Ernest A. Savage and Lionel R. McColvin.
1934–51	Lionel R. McColvin.
1952–55	W. A. Munford.
1955–61	W. B. Paton (H. D. Barry appointed Secretary, 1959; R. P. Hilliard appointed Secretary, 1975).

Honorary Treasurers
1877–89   Robert Harrison.
1889–97   Henry R. Tedder.
1897–98   T. J. Agar, FCA.
1898–1924   Henry R. Tedder.
1925–28   Bernard Kettle.
1928–29   J. Henry Quinn.
1929–35   H. Tapley-Soper.
1936–45   H. M. Cashmore.
1946–53   R. Irwin.
1953–66   F. G. B. Hutchings.
1967–70   W. Tynemouth.
1971–73   E. A. Clough.
1974–   G. Thompson.

Honorary Legal Advisers
1893–1927   H. W. Fovargue (Hon Solicitor).
1927–30   The Rt Hon H. P. (Later Lord) Macmillan, KC, MP
            (Hon Legal Adviser on Scottish Library Law, 1927;
            Hon Legal Adviser, 1928).
1930–40   Alderman J. S. Pritchett, JP, BCL, MA (Hon Legal
            Adviser).
1941–42   (Vacant.)
1942–47   Sir Parker Morris.
1947–56   J. Waring Sainsbury, MA, LL B.
1957–61   Sir Charles Norton, MBE, MC.

Appendix d

Honorary Fellows of the
Library Association

James Bain (1896)
Conte Ugo Balzani (1896)
Prof Alexander Beljame (1896)
J. S. Billings, LLD (1896)
R. R. Bowker (1896)
C. W. Bruun (1896)
Andrew Carnegie (1896)
C. A. Cutter (1896)
Leopold Delisle (1896)
Melvil Dewey (1896)
Sir George Grey (1896)
Justin Winsor (1896)
C. Dziatzko (1896)
J. Passmore Edwards (1896)
S. S. Green (1896)
P. G. Horsen (1896)
Rt Hon Sir John Lubbock (1896)
Sir Henry Tate (1896)
Baron O. de Watteville (1896)
J. Y. W. MacAlister (1898)
Marquess of Dufferin and Ava, KP, GCB (1899)
Rt Hon Lord Windsor (1899)
Rt Hon Lord Avebury (1899)
Samuel Timmins (1899)
Thomas Greenwood (1901)
Frank Pacy (1902)

339

W. Macneile Dixon (1902)
Henry Guppy, MA (1903)
Lawrence Inkster (1905)
Henry D. Roberts (1906)
Rt Hon Earl of Plymouth (1907)
J. J. Ogle (1908)
James Duff Brown (1913)
T. C. Abbott (1909)
H. W. Fovargue (1909)
J. Potter Briscoe (1914)
R. K. Dent (1914)
W. E. Doubleday (1918)
L. S. Jast (1915)
A. W. Pollard, CB (1924)
Sir John Ballinger, MA (1929)
W. W. Bishop, LITT D, LL D (1931)
Rt Hon Earl of Elgin and Kincardine, CMG (1932)
George H. Locke, MA, LL D, (1931)
J. M. Mitchell, CBE, MA, LL D (1932)
Rt Hon Stanley Baldwin (1933)
Ernest A. Savage (1933)
H. Tapley-Soper, FSA, FR HIST S (1935)
William Benson Thorne (1938)
Arundell Esdaile, MA, LITT D, (1946)
Albert Mansbridge, CH, MA, LL D (1946)
H. M. Cashmore (1947)
W. C. Berwick Sayers (1947)
R. J. Gordon, HON MA (1948)
J. D. Stewart, MBE (1959)
P. S. J. Welsford, OBE, FCIS (1959)
L. R. McColvin, CBE (1961)
B. S. Page, MA (1961)
E. J. Carter, BA (1962)
Sir Frank Francis, KCB, MA, FSA (1962)
R. Irwin, MA (1963)
C. B. Oldman, CB, CVO, LITT D, MA, FSA (1963)
Sir Sydney Roberts, MA (1964)
E. Sydney, MC (1964)
Miss E. J. A. Evans, CBE (1965)
W. J. Harris, BA, FNZLA (1965)

Miss F. E. Cook, MA   (1966)
F. M. Gardner, CBE   (1966)
E. Austin Hinton   (1966)
S. W. Martin   (1968)
E. F. Patterson, MA   (1968)
N. F. Sharp, BA (1968)
T. Besterman, DLITT, LLD, D-ES-L   (1969)
F. N. Withers, OBE, BSC(ECON)   (1969)
R. D. Macleod   (1970)
W. Tynemouth   (1970)
A. H. Chaplin, CB, MA   (1970)
Miss A. S. Cooke   (1970)
W. R. Lefanu, MA   (1970)
Miss E. H. Colwell, MBE   (1971)
W. S. Haugh, BA, DPA   (1971)
S. H. Horrocks   (1971)
H. Coblans   (1972)
A. J. Walford   (1972)
A. J. Wells   (1972)
H. D. Barry   (1973)
A. D. Jones, CBE, FSA   (1973)
W. B. Paton, OBE, MA   (1973)
D. J. Foskett, MA   (1974)
F. W. Jessup, CBE, MA, LLB, FSA   (1974)
T. Kelly, MA, PHD,, FRHISTS   (1974)
B. I. Palmer, MSL   (1974)
E. A. Clough   (1975)
S. W. Hockey   (1975)

Select Bibliography

Library Association Records and Publications

Minutes of the Council, Committees, Monthly and Annual
Meetings. 1877–. (Referred to by simple dates or, for earlier
years, as *LAM 877*, *LAMC 878*, *LACOM 881*, and for
Metropolitan Free Libraries Committee (later Association)
as *MFLC*.)
Transactions and proceedings of the Conferences. 1877–.
Annual Reports of the Council. 1877–. (*AR*)
(The earlier ones are numbered.)
Year Books. 1895–.
(Not published regularly and annually until 1932).
The Year's work in librarianship. 1928–1950. (*YW*)
Five years' work in librarianship, 3 vols: 1951–5; 1956–60; 1961–5.
British librarianship and information science 1966–70. 1972.
Monthly notes of the Library Association. 1880–1883. (*MN*)
The Library Chronicle. 1884–8. (*LC*)
The Library. 1889–1898. (*L*)
The Library Association Record. 1899–. (*LAR*)
(From 1923 to 1930 published as 'New Series'; from 1931 to
1933 as 'Third Series', and from 1934 to 1939 as 'Fourth
Series'. Now numbered continuously.)
Liaison. 1957–1975.
Journal of librarianship. 1969–. (*JL*)

Other periodicals

The Library Journal. 1876–. (*LJ*)
The Library (New Series). 1899–. (*L*) (NS)
The Library Assistant (subsequently *The Assistant librarian*).
1898–. (*L Asst*)
The Library World subsequently *New Library World.* 1898–. (*LW*)
The Library Review. 1927–. (LR)

Books and Articles

Aitken, W. R. *A History of the public library movement in Scotland to 1955.* 1971.
Fry, W. G. *and* W. A. Munford. *Louis Stanley Jast: a biographical sketch.* 1966.
Haslam, D. D. 'A Short history of the Library Association' in *JL*, 6, pp 137–64.
Kelly, T. *A History of public libraries in Great Britain 1845–1965.* 1973.
Munford, W. A. *James Duff Brown 1862–1914: portrait of a library pioneer.* 1968.
       "   *Edward Edwards 1812–1886: portrait of a librarian.* 1963.
       "   *Penny rate: aspects of British public library history 1850–1950.* 1951.
       "   (Ed) *Annals of the Library Association 1877–1960.* 1965.
Ramsden, M. J. *A History of the Association of Assistant Librarians 1895–1945.* 1973.
Robertson, W. *Welfare in trust: a history of the Carnegie United Kingdom Trust.* 1964.
Savage, E. A. *A Librarian's memories: portraits and reflections.* 1952.
Thornton, J. L. *Selected readings in the history of librarianship.* 1966.

Index

(Entries in bold indicate the more important references)

Index